AMERICAN POLITICAL, ECONOMIC, AND SECURITY ISSUES

THE FEDERAL PRISON POPULATION

GROWTH AND COST ISSUES

AMERICAN POLITICAL, ECONOMIC, AND SECURITY ISSUES

AMERICAN POLITICAL, ECONOMIC, AND SECURITY ISSUES

THE FEDERAL PRISON POPULATION

GROWTH AND COST ISSUES

MASON C. DARWIN
EDITOR

nova publishers
New York

For permission to use material from this book please contact us:
Telephone 631-231-7269; Fax 631-231-8175
Web Site: http://www.novapublishers.com

Library of Congress Cataloging-in-Publication Data

ISBN: 978-1-63463-902-6

Published by Nova Science Publishers, Inc. † New York

CONTENTS

PREFACE

Correctional services is the Department of Justice's (DOJ) Bureau of Prisons' (BOP) largest operational cost, and BOP has undertaken a number of initiatives to reduce costs. This book describes BOP's major costs and actions to achieve savings; assesses the extent to which BOP has mechanisms to identify additional efficiencies; and describes potential changes within and outside of BOP's authority that might reduce costs. This book also provides an overview of the federal prison population buildup, policy changes, issues and options of the BOP.

Chapter 1 – The Department of Justice's (DOJ) Bureau of Prisons (BOP) is responsible for the custody and care of 216,000 federal inmates—an almost 9-fold increase since 1980. At the same time, BOP appropriations increased more than 20-fold. DOJ states that the costs of the growing population are BOP's greatest challenge. BOP's population size is driven by several factors, such as law enforcement policies and sentencing laws.

GAO was asked to review BOP's opportunities to save costs. This report (1) describes BOP's major costs and actions to achieve savings, (2) assesses the extent to which BOP has mechanisms to identify additional efficiencies, and (3) describes potential changes within and outside of BOP's authority that might reduce costs.

GAO analyzed BOP financial data for fiscal years 2009 through 2013, reviewed but did not test its internal control system and processes for achieving efficiencies, and interviewed BOP officials. On the basis of sentencing reform options identified by experts and actions by the Attorney General, GAO developed a list of policy options that could reduce BOP's population. GAO gathered views on their potential effects from entities and 4 states selected for their criminal justice expertise. The views are not generalizable, but provide insights.

Chapter 2 – Since the early 1980s, there has been a historically unprecedented increase in the federal prison population. Some of the growth is attributable to changes in federal criminal justice policy during the previous three decades. An issue before Congress is whether policy makers consider the rate of growth in the federal prison population sustainable, and if not, what changes could be made to federal criminal justice policy to reduce the prison population while maintaining public safety. This report explores the issues related to the growing federal prison population.

The number of inmates under the Bureau of Prisons' (BOP's) jurisdiction has increased from approximately 25,000 in FY1980 to over 219,000 in FY2013. Since FY1980, the federal prison population has increased, on average, by approximately 5,900 inmates each year. Data show that a growing proportion of inmates are being incarcerated for immigration- and weapons-related offenses, but the largest portion of newly admitted inmates are being incarcerated for drug offenses. Data also show that approximately 7 in 10 inmates are sentenced for five years or less.

Changes in federal sentencing and correctional policy since the early 1980s have contributed to the rapid growth in the federal prison population. These changes include increasing the number of federal offenses subject to mandatory minimum sentences; changes to the federal criminal code that have made more crimes federal offenses; and eliminating parole.

There are several issues related to the growing federal prison population that might be of interest to policy makers:

- The increasing number of federal inmates, combined with the rising per capita cost of incarceration, has made it increasingly more expensive to operate and maintain the federal prison system. The per capita cost of incarceration for all inmates increased from $21,603 in FY2000 to $29,291 in FY2013. During this same period of time, appropriations for the BOP increased from $3.668 billion to $6.445 billion.
- The federal prison system is increasingly overcrowded. Overall, the federal prison system was 36% over its rated capacity in FY2013, but high- and medium-security male facilities were operating at 52% and 45%, respectively, over rated capacity. At issue is whether overcrowding might lead to more inmate misconduct. The results of research on this topic have been mixed. One study found that overcrowding does not affect inmate misconduct; but the BOP, based on its own research, concluded that there is a significant positive relationship between the two.
- The inmate-to-staff ratio has increased from 4.1 inmates per staff member in FY2000 to 4.8 inmates per staff member in FY2013. The inmate to correctional officer ratio was the same in FY2013 as it was in FY2000 (9.9 inmates for each correctional officer), and the current inmate to correctional officer ratio is down from a high of 10.9 inmates per correctional officer in FY2005.
- The growing prison population is taking a toll on the infrastructure of the federal prison system. The BOP reports that it has a backlog of 159 modernization and repair projects with an approximate cost of $342 million. Past appropriations left the BOP in a position where it could expand bedspace to manage overcrowding but not reduce it. However, reductions in funding since FY2010 mean that the BOP will lack the funding to begin new prison construction in the near future. At the same time, it has become more expensive to expand the BOP's capacity.

Should Congress choose to consider policy options to address the issues resulting from the growth in the federal prison population, policy makers could choose options such as increasing the capacity of the federal prison system by building more prisons; investing in rehabilitative programming (e.g., substance abuse treatment or educational programs) as a way of keeping inmates constructively occupied and potentially reducing recidivism after inmates are released; or placing more inmates in private prisons.

Policy makers might also consider whether they want to revise some of the policy changes that have been made over the past three decades that have contributed to the steadily increasing number of offenders being incarcerated. For example, Congress could consider options such as (1) modifying mandatory minimum penalties, (2) expanding the use of Residential Reentry Centers, (3) placing more offenders on probation, (4) reinstating parole for federal inmates, (5) expanding the amount of good time credit an inmate can earn, and (6) repealing federal criminal statutes for some offenses.

Chapter 3 – The Bureau of Prisons (BOP) was established in 1930 to house federal inmates, professionalize the prison service, and ensure consistent and centralized administration of the federal prison system. The BOP is the largest correctional agency in the country, in terms of the number of prisoners under its jurisdiction. The BOP must confine any offender convicted and sentenced to a term of imprisonment in a federal court.

All BOP correctional facilities are classified according to one of five different security levels: minimum, low, medium, high, or administrative. An inmate's designation to a particular institution is based primarily on the level of security and supervision the inmate requires; the level of security and staff supervision the institution is able to provide; and the inmate's program needs. All inmates undergo a comprehensive intake screening when they are admitted to a BOP facility. The BOP provides health care for all inmates either through each prison's ambulatory care clinics or by contracting for services through local hospitals. The BOP also provides mental health treatment to inmates who demonstrate a need for it through staff psychologists. The BOP has an established inmate disciplinary system, whereby sanctions are imposed on inmates for committing prohibited acts. An inmate is allowed to request a review of his or her conditions of confinement through the BOP's Administrative Remedy Program. Inmates have access to a variety of rehabilitational programs including education programs, substance abuse treatment, vocational education, and work opportunities. In order to help aid an inmate's transition back into the community, inmates can be placed in a Residential Reentry Center (i.e., a halfway house) for a period of time before their sentence expires.

Changes in federal criminal justice policy since the early 1980s have resulted in a continued increase in the federal prison population. The number of inmates under the BOP's jurisdiction has increased nearly eight-fold (790%) from approximately 24,600 inmates in FY1980 to nearly 219,300 inmates in FY2013. Since FY1980, the federal prison population has increased, on average, by approximately 5,900 inmates each year.

The burgeoning federal prison population has led Congress to increase appropriations for the BOP's operations and infrastructure. In FY1980, Congress appropriated $330.0 *million* for the BOP. By FY2014, the total appropriation for the BOP reached $6.859 *billion*. The additional funding for the BOP was necessary to cover the costs of providing services to a growing prison population, expanding prison capacity, and hiring additional staff to manage the expanding federal prison system.

The annual growth in the federal prison population has outstripped the BOP's prison capacity, resulting in overcrowding in the federal prison system. Congress could choose to mitigate some of the issues related to federal prison population growth by appropriating more funding so the BOP could hire additional staff and expand prison capacity to alleviate overcrowding. On the other hand, Congress could also consider ways to reduce the number of inmates held in federal prison by considering alternatives to incarceration, such as increasing good time credit for inmates who participate in certain rehabilitative programs, placing more low-level offenders on community supervision in lieu of incarceration, or reducing mandatory minimum penalties for some offenses.

In: The Federal Prison Population
Editor: Mason C. Darwin

ISBN: 978-1-63463-902-6

Chapter 1

Bureau of Prisons: Information on Efforts and Potential Options to Save Costs*

United States Government Accountability Office

Why GAO Did This Study

The Department of Justice's (DOJ) Bureau of Prisons (BOP) is responsible for the custody and care of 216,000 federal inmates—an almost 9-fold increase since 1980. At the same time, BOP appropriations increased more than 20-fold. DOJ states that the costs of the growing population are BOP's greatest challenge. BOP's population size is driven by several factors, such as law enforcement policies and sentencing laws.

GAO was asked to review BOP's opportunities to save costs. This report (1) describes BOP's major costs and actions to achieve savings, (2) assesses the extent to which BOP has mechanisms to identify additional efficiencies, and (3) describes potential changes within and outside of BOP's authority that might reduce costs.

GAO analyzed BOP financial data for fiscal years 2009 through 2013, reviewed but did not test its internal control system and processes for achieving efficiencies, and interviewed BOP officials. On the basis of sentencing reform options identified by experts and actions by the Attorney General, GAO developed a list of policy options that could reduce BOP's population. GAO gathered views on their potential effects from entities and 4 states selected for their criminal justice expertise. The views are not generalizable, but provide insights.

What GAO Recommends

GAO recommends that BOP establish a mechanism to consistently monitor if bureau-wide corrective actions address repeated deficiencies and findings. DOJ concurred.

* This is an edited, reformatted and augmented version of the United States Government Accountability Office publication, GAO-14-821, dated September 2014.

WHAT GAO FOUND

Correctional services—which includes salaries and benefits for correctional officers—is the Department of Justice's (DOJ) Bureau of Prisons' (BOP) largest operational cost, and BOP has undertaken a number of initiatives to reduce costs. Specifically, on the basis of GAO's analysis of BOP's fiscal year 2013 obligations of approximately $6.6 billion, BOP obligated the largest share—about $3.9 billion, or 59 percent—for personnel compensation and benefits. Further, BOP has undertaken a number of initiatives, such as renegotiated contracts, to achieve cost savings of about $61 million over the last 3 years.

BOP has designed internal processes to identify opportunities for additional cost efficiencies, but could improve the monitoring of corrective actions to achieve them. For example, BOP focuses on cost efficiency and innovation in its strategic plan and has developed mechanisms for staff to share information on best practices and cost savings efforts. BOP also employs an internal control system with processes, such as program reviews, that allows it to identify opportunities for cost efficiencies. However, when program reviews repeatedly cited frequent deficiencies or significant findings that could increase costs—such as insufficient contract monitoring—responsible BOP Central Office divisions did not provide specifics or documentation for how they always monitor the effectiveness of corrective actions to prevent the same deficiency or issue from reoccurring. Establishing a mechanism for relevant Central Office divisions to consistently monitor the progress of bureau-wide corrective actions in the presence of repeated frequent deficiencies or significant findings could help BOP better ensure that it is resolving such deficiencies or issues promptly and, ultimately, operating more efficiently.

BOP's current authorities to reduce inmate sentence length result in limited cost savings, but potential actions outside of its authority could have a greater impact on costs. GAO has reported previously on BOP authorities to reduce inmate sentences, and thus its costs, in detail, and found that inmate eligibility for certain programs and lack of capacity affect BOP's use of them. For example, greater use of programs such as Compassionate Release for terminally ill inmates could reduce sentences, but cost savings relative to BOP's budget would be small— about $651,000 in 2013. Additional opportunities outside of BOP's authority, including those requiring legislative or executive action, such as options to reduce sentence length, could reduce BOP's population, and thus potentially significantly reduce its costs. For example, an option to reduce sentences of incarcerated drug offenders by an average of 44 percent could save about $4.1 billion. Potential savings could be even higher if the changes sufficiently reduced the inmate population to allow BOP to reduce its staff or close facilities. Expert entities GAO consulted reported that all of the options GAO reviewed also have advantages and disadvantages unrelated to costs that should be taken into consideration, such as potential effects on public safety if released inmates reoffend. GAO is not taking a position on any of these options, but presents information on estimated cost savings and experts' views of advantages and disadvantages for such options to inform policymakers as they weigh whether and how to address rising costs at BOP.

ABBREVIATIONS

ABA	American Bar Association
BOP	Bureau of Prisons
DOJ	Department of Justice
FSA	Fair Sentencing Act GCTgood conduct time
HHS	Department of Health and Human Services
HRMD	Human Resource Management Division
HSD	Health Services Division
IG	Inspector General
IPTP	International Prisoner Transfer Program
JRI	Justice Reinvestment Initiative
OMB	Office of Management and Budget
PRD	Program Review Division
RDAP	Residential Drug Abuse Treatment Program
RRC	residential reentry center
RRM	Residential Reentry Management
RRMB	Residential Reentry Management Branch
RSD	Reentry Services Division
USSC	U.S. Sentencing Commission

* * *

September 30, 2014

Congressional Requesters:

The inmate population at the Department of Justice's (DOJ) Federal Bureau of Prisons (BOP)—the primary cost driver of BOP's budget—has increased almost 9-fold since the early 1980s—from about 25,000 in fiscal year 1980 to about 216,000 as of July 2014. Given these population increases, and inflation, BOP's appropriations have increased more than 20-fold during the same time period—from $330 million in fiscal year 1980, about 14 percent of DOJ's total budget that year, to almost $7 billion requested for fiscal year 2015, or about one-quarter of DOJ's requested fiscal year 2015 budget.[1] According to the DOJ Inspector General, the rising costs for BOP threaten the department's ability to fulfill its mission in other areas, including maintaining national security, enforcing criminal law, and defending civil rights. Moreover, DOJ projects that BOP costs will increase if the federal prison population grows through 2019 as forecast by DOJ in its Fiscal Year 2015 Performance Budget Congressional Submission for the Federal Prison System.[2]

BOP's mission is to confine federal offenders in safe and secure prisons and community-based facilities, and to provide work and other self- improvement opportunities to assist offenders in becoming law-abiding citizens. Additionally, one of BOP's strategic goals is to continually strive toward improvements in its effective use of resources and its efficient delivery of services. As of June 2014, BOP operates 120 prison institutions nationwide, as well as paying for and monitoring 14 prisons and, as of July 2014, 200 residential reentry centers (RRC) (halfway houses)—operated by private contractors. According to officials, BOP's biggest challenge is managing the increasing federal inmate population, and related responsibilities, within budgeted levels.

We have previously reported that the size of the federal prison population is a function of many factors, including the nation's crime levels, federal sentencing laws, and law enforcement policies, all of which are beyond the control of BOP.[3] In addition, the Sentencing Reform Act of 1984 abolished parole for federal offenders, and subsequent legislation established mandatory minimum sentences for many federal offenses, facts that limit the authority BOP has to affect the size of the prison population or the length of prison sentences.[4] BOP has discretionary authorities, or flexibilities, to reduce a federal prisoner's period of incarceration through programs such as the Residential Drug Abuse Treatment Program (RDAP).[5] BOP also has statutory authority to award "good conduct time" credit toward reducing an inmate's sentence up to 54 days per year of sentence served, if the inmate has displayed exemplary compliance with institutional disciplinary regulations.[6] To help alleviate costs associated with an increasing inmate population and inflation, as noted in its fiscal year 2015 Performance Budget Congressional submission, BOP continues to streamline operations and increase efficiency in order to operate as efficiently and effectively as possible.

Additionally, actions involving policy changes outside of BOP's authority could reduce BOP's inmate population and therefore its costs. These include potential legislative actions by Congress, executive orders by the President, policy changes implemented by the Attorney General, or changes in federal sentencing guidelines by the U.S. Sentencing Commission (USSC).[7]

The Attorney General's August 2013 Smart on Crime Initiative is an example of a policy change that will affect the size of the BOP population. The Attorney General issued a memorandum to the U.S. Attorneys and Assistant Attorneys for the Criminal Division instructing prosecutors to decline to charge the quantity necessary to trigger a mandatory minimum sentence for certain defendants in cases involving the applicability of drug law mandatory minimum sentences based on drug type and quantity.[8]

Growth in the federal inmate population and its effects on BOP's budget are a matter of continuing congressional interest. You asked us to review the transparency of BOP's budget justification and opportunities for BOP to realize operational efficiencies. In December 2013 we reported that by providing additional funding data to Congress in its budget justification, BOP could clarify what it proposes to spend on specific categories and subcategories.[9] We recommended that the Attorney General consult with congressional decision makers on providing additional BOP funding detail in future budget justifications, and in conjunction with BOP, take action as appropriate. DOJ concurred with this recommendation and is taking action to implement it. This report responds to the latter part of your request by further describing BOP's major costs and the actions it has taken to identify and implement cost efficiency opportunities and reduce costs. Specifically, this report addresses the following questions:

1. What are the major costs for BOP operations, and what actions has BOP taken to implement cost savings?
2. To what extent does BOP have mechanisms to identify opportunities for cost efficiencies and to take corrective actions that may improve cost efficiency?

3. What potential changes, both within and outside of BOP's authority, could lead to cost reductions or improved efficiencies in BOP operations, and what might be the potential impact of these changes?

To address the first question, we obtained historical obligation data from BOP's Financial Management Information System for fiscal years 2009-2013—a 5-year time frame to provide us with an adequate understanding of trends in BOP obligation levels—to identify the major costs incurred by BOP for its Salaries and Expenses account, which generally represents 98 percent of BOP's budget.[10] We have assessed the reliability of these data and determined them to be reliable for the purposes of this report. This assessment included performing checks on the data received and interviewing officials responsible for compiling and maintaining these data. We also collected data (e.g., cost savings estimates prepared by BOP) and documentation, such as memos and concept papers approved by executive staff from fiscal years 2009 through 2013; through review of these data and documents and interviews with relevant agency officials, we determined that these data are also reliable for the purposes of this report. In addition, we interviewed Central Office-, regional-, and institutional-level officials to identify to the extent possible all existing cost efficiency and savings initiatives adopted by BOP and their impact on its overall budget.

To address the second question, we reviewed the processes and tools at BOP during the same time period (fiscal years 2009-2013) that are used to identify, implement, and promote cost-efficiency and savings initiatives throughout its institutions, such as executive staff meetings and a catalog compiling cost-savings initiatives. With respect to identifying additional opportunities to realize cost efficiencies or reduce costs, using our financial analysis as context, we analyzed elements of BOP's internal control system related to the control objective of achieving operational efficiencies and interviewed relevant officials to assess whether BOP has designed a management structure and processes to routinely assess its administrative and operational activities for possible corrective action. Specifically, we reviewed BOP's mechanisms and processes leading to its internal review of operational and administrative functions, including its process for taking corrective action related to high-cost areas, and compared these characteristics with those called for in *Standards for Internal Control in the Federal Government.*[11]

To address the third question, on potential policy changes both within and outside BOP's authority that could lead to BOP cost savings, we collected and reviewed analysis and documentation from DOJ, BOP, the USSC, and entities that we selected for their expertise in criminal justice issues, and, in particular, potential changes to federal sentencing policies, and to ensure that a wide range of views on the advantages and disadvantages of these potential changes.[12] These entities may not be representative of the universe of expert entities in the criminal justice field and therefore may not represent all views on this topic; however, their views provide insights. We obtained data from BOP for 2013 and 2014 on the impact on BOP's population and costs resulting from changes within BOP's authority. We assessed the reliability of these data by reviewing documentation and interviewing knowledgeable officials, and determined the data to be sufficiently reliable for the purposes of this report.

Further, on the basis of our assessment of proposals put forward by several sources, including the Attorney General, expert entities, states with experience with criminal justice reform, and advocacy entities with a range of views on criminal justice reform, we identified eight options outside of BOP's authority that could reduce the size of the inmate population.

GAO is not taking a position on any of these options, but presents information on estimated cost savings and experts' views of advantages and disadvantages for such options to inform policymakers as they weigh whether and how to address rising costs at BOP.

For each of these eight options, we asked the USSC to estimate the impact on the size of the BOP inmate population and, using the USSC estimates, we then calculated cost savings or cost avoidance that could result from implementing a given option.[13] According to our audit objectives, we determined that based on the expertise of the USSC, the evidence obtained from the USSC provides a reasonable basis for our findings and conclusions.

In addition, we asked the 14 expert entities to comment on the options with regard to their view of the advantages or disadvantages of implementation of the eight options. We also asked 4 states to comment on the potential options for change. One of the 4 was Texas, which had the largest number of incarcerated offenders in the nation (as of 2012) and which was identified as a model for changes in state criminal justice systems by the Justice Reinvestment Initiative (JRI), a public-private partnership of DOJ and the Pew Charitable Trusts, to provide technical assistance and financial support for system-wide criminal justice reform efforts.[14] The other states were chosen on the basis of having had at least 1 year's experience in implementing JRI programs; of these 8, we chose the 3 that had the largest annual corrections budgets as of the year in which JRI started in those states. We received acknowledgement of receipt from 17 of the 18 entities (the 14 expert entities and 4 states) to which we sent the letter.[15]

Further details on our scope and methodology are contained in appendix I. See appendix II for the letter sent to expert entities asking for their assessment of options, which provides a list of the proposals that were used to develop the selected options.

We conducted this performance audit from July 2013 to September 2014 in accordance with generally accepted government auditing standards. Those standards require that we plan and perform the audit to obtain sufficient, appropriate evidence to provide a reasonable basis for our findings and conclusions based on our audit objectives. We believe that the evidence obtained provides a reasonable basis for our findings and conclusions based on our audit objectives.

BACKGROUND

BOP's Cost-Accounting Methods

BOP uses a network of cost centers—individual accounting units in which costs can be segregated—to obligate, account for, and manage various costs.[16] Managers of each cost center are provided with information to control and manage costs within their area of responsibility. Cost centers can be structured along different dimensions, such as organizational units, operating processes, and activities.[17] For example, BOP cost centers include Correctional Services, Inside Medical Services, and Food Services at each institution.

BOP also tracks its obligations and expenditures by budget object and subobject classification.[18] Object classes are categories used in budget preparation to classify obligations by the items or services purchased by the federal government (e.g., personnel compensation, contractual services). Within these object classes, the Department of Justice has assigned subobject class codes that further define the nature of services or articles obligated and provide DOJ with a detail of expended funds. For example, under the personnel compensation object class, BOP has defined subobject class codes for items such as compensation for full-time, permanent appointment employees; overtime; and holiday pay. Object and subobject classes are used for direct tracking of specific items on which funds are being spent (e.g., salaries, supplies, pharmaceuticals, etc.) and are used across all cost centers.

BOP Organizational Structure

To carry out its responsibility for the custody and care of federal offenders, as of June 2014, BOP houses inmates across six geographic regions in 120 federal institutions, 14 privately operated secure contract facilities, home detention, and as of July 2014, 200 residential reentry centers.[19] These federal institutions and other facilities are managed and overseen through the following offices:

- **Central Office.** The Central Office, which serves as BOP's headquarters, consists of nine divisions that provide oversight of major BOP program areas and operations, such as correctional programs and health services, as well as the National Institute of Corrections.[20] BOP's Program Review Division, which leads BOP's process for conducting internal reviews of each program or operation at each BOP institution, is among these nine divisions.
- **Grand Prairie Office Complex.** This complex, located in Grand Prairie, Texas, was created to consolidate various processes into one location. It consists of three components: human resource services, designation and sentence computation, and field acquisitions exceeding $100,000.
- **Regional offices.** BOP has six regional offices, each led by a regional director, covering the Mid-Atlantic, North Central, Northeast, South Central, Southeast, and Western regions of the United States. These offices provide oversight, technical assistance, and training to the BOP facilities located within each region.
- **Residential Reentry Management field offices.** BOP has 25 field offices that administer contracts for community-based programs and serve as liaisons with various federal, state, and local groups within their judicial districts. Staff at these offices also monitor residential reentry centers (RRCs), which provide offenders with community- based services to assist with their reentry needs.

BOP generally houses sentenced inmates in its long-term institutions. Male long-term institutions include four security level designations— minimum, low, medium, and high—and female institutions include three security designations—minimum, low, and high. The security-level designation of a facility depends on the level of security and staff supervision that the institution is able to provide, such as the presence of security towers; perimeter barriers; the type of inmate housing, including dormitory, cubicle, or cell-type housing; and inmate-to-staff ratio. Additionally, BOP designates some of its institutions as administrative institutions, which house male and female inmates and specifically serve inmates awaiting trial, or those with intensive medical or mental health conditions, regardless of the level of supervision these inmates require.

The Sentencing Reform Act of 1984 and Federal Sentencing Guidelines

Prior to passage of the Sentencing Reform Act of 1984, federal judges generally had broad discretion in sentencing.[21] Most criminal statutes provided only broad maximum terms of imprisonment. Federal law outlined the maximum sentence, federal judges imposed a sentence within a statutory range, and the federal parole official eventually determined the actual duration of incarceration. The Sentencing Reform Act of 1984 changed the federal sentencing structure. The act was effective for offenses committed on or after November 1, 1987. The act abolished parole for federal offenders sentenced after its effective date, and subsequent legislation established mandatory minimum sentences for many federal offenses.

The Sentencing Reform Act of 1984 also established the independent USSC within the judicial branch and charged it with, among other things, developing federal sentencing guidelines.[22] USSC establishes sentencing policies and practices for the federal criminal justice system that provide certainty and fairness in meeting the purposes of sentencing, avoiding unwarranted sentencing disparities among defendants with similar criminal records who have been found guilty of similar criminal conduct while maintaining sufficient flexibility to permit individualized sentences when warranted.[23] To foster this goal, the guidelines specify sentencing guideline ranges—a range of time (in months) that offenders should serve given the nature of their offense and other factors—but also permit sentences to depart upward or downward from guideline ranges because of aggravating or mitigating circumstances. In 2005, the Supreme Court found the Sentencing Guidelines, which had previously been binding for federal judges to follow in sentencing criminal defendants, to be advisory in nature.[24] Regardless of the guidelines' advisory nature, judges are still required to calculate properly and consider the Sentencing Guidelines and other sentencing goals.[25]

In applying the USSC's guidance, federal district judges are to determine the appropriate sentencing guideline range for an offender based on various factors related to (1) the offense and (2) the offender. The offense is assigned an offense level; drug offenses are based on several factors, such as the quantity and type of drug involved and whether the offense involved violence.

The offender is also assigned a criminal history category based on the number of criminal history points. USSC sentencing guidelines assign criminal history points based on a defendant's criminal record:

- A single point is assigned for every other federal or state prior sentence of conviction, subject to certain exceptions.[26]
- Two or more points are assigned for every prior sentence of imprisonment or juvenile confinement of 60 days or more or for offenses committed while the defendant was in prison; was an escaped prisoner; or was on probation, parole, or supervised release;
- Three points are assigned if an offender has been previously sentenced or is being sentenced to a prison term of 13 months or more.

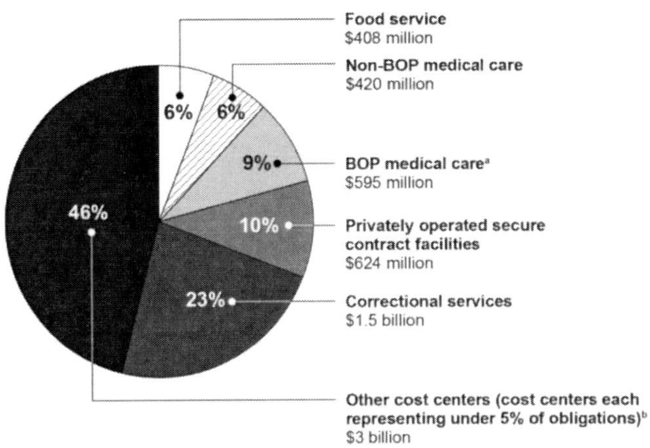

Source: GAO analysis of BOP data. | GAO-14-821

Notes: The budget data for all cost centers include all staff salaries, operational supplies, contract services, equipment, and other items related to that department. BOP organizes its cost centers based on location within the organization; thus, there are cost centers at the institution level, regional level, national training level, national program level, Central Office level, and contract confinement level. Institution-level cost centers—which represent the majority of BOP obligations—are further broken down by security level (e.g., high, medium, low, etc.). For the purposes of our review, we combined the various institution security-level cost centers into common cost centers for all institutions. This allows us to present data on, for example, correctional services, BOP medical care, and so forth, for all institutions BOP-wide.

According to BOP, it considers some funds obligated within the "Other cost centers" category to be part of the larger cost centers displayed in figure 1. Including BOP's estimates of these funds in the totals of the larger cost centers listed above would change totals approximately as follows:

- Correctional services: An additional $100 million if special projects, urinalysis surveillance, clothing allowances, and other items were included.
- Medical services (both BOP and non-BOP): An additional $47 million if referral labs, dialysis, emergency airlift, and other items were included.
- Food service: An additional $10 million if farm and special projects were included.
- Private operated secure facilities: An additional $11 million if BOP privatization staff salaries were included.
- Recategorizing these obligations would subsequently reduce the Other cost centers category to approximately $2.8 billion, or 42% of totals for fiscal year 2013.

In addition, according to BOP, staff at institutions—regardless of the cost center functions that they primarily serve—are trained as correctional officers and thus may be called upon to assist in correctional services or other functions whenever necessary.

[a] The BOP medical care cost center also contains approximately $103 million in funds transferred to pay salaries and other costs associated with Public Health Services staff. According to BOP, these are medical professionals employed by the Department of Health and Human Services (HHS) who provide medical services to BOP institutions. While these Public Health Services staff are technically paid by HHS, BOP transfers the necessary funds to HHS to pay for their services.

[b] The "other cost centers" category contains a number of cost centers that together account for 46 percent of BOP's total costs, as shown above; however, individually, each cost center included in the "other" category accounts for 5 percent or less of BOP's total costs

Figure 1. Bureau of Prisons' (BOP) Fiscal Year 2013 Obligation Levels by Cost Center.

Taken in combination, the offense level and criminal history category correlate with a sentencing guideline range, expressed in months. For certain types of offenses, including certain drug and weapons offenses, statutorily specified mandatory minimum sentences supplant the lower end of the otherwise applicable guidelines range. While federal law generally requires a sentencing judge to impose a minimum sentence of imprisonment following conviction for any of a number of federal offenses, there are two statutorily provided exceptions. One—the substantial assistance exception—is available upon motion of the government, and allows the court to impose a sentence below the level established by statute as a minimum to reflect a defendant's substantial assistance in the investigation or prosecution of another person who has committed an offense.[27] The other, commonly referred to as the safety valve, was created by the Violent Crime Control and Law Enforcement Act of 1994 and is available for certain types of defendants for certain drug offenses that carry minimum sentences.[28]

Correctional Services Is BOP's Largest Operational Cost, and BOP Has Initiated a Number of Efforts to Reduce Costs

BOP's Correctional Services, Private Prison Contracts, Medical Care, and Food Services Account for the Majority of Its Costs, with the Largest Share of Spending on Personnel

During fiscal year 2013, BOP obligated approximately $6.6 billion for all its programs and operations. According to our analysis of BOP's fiscal year 2013 obligations by cost center, correctional services, privately operated secure contract facilities, medical care, and food services represent the majority (approximately $3.56 billion, or 54 percent) of BOP's expenses, as illustrated in figure 1. See appendix III for a breakout of cost trends in these and other key cost centers over the last 5 fiscal years.

Figure 2 provides further information on the key cost centers represented above.

Within its cost centers, the majority of costs across the bureau are payment of staff salaries and benefits. Detailed data on these expenses are tracked using budget object and subobject classifications. These budget classifications are used consistently across all cost centers and represent items or services actually purchased by BOP. Figure 3 shows the budget object classifications that accounted for BOP's total fiscal year 2013 obligations.

As figure 3 shows, personnel compensation and benefits (retirement contributions, health insurance benefits, etc.) account for approximately 59 percent of BOP's overall obligations. Moreover, BOP's personnel costs are actually higher than 59 percent because compensation for other staff employed on a contractual basis is included in the "other contractual services" object class. This object class consists of privately operated prison expenses, outside medical services, and other items—as well as contract staff—and accounts for nearly 26 percent of fiscal year 2013 obligations. See appendix IV for more detailed data on object and subobject class obligations from fiscal years 2009 through 2013.

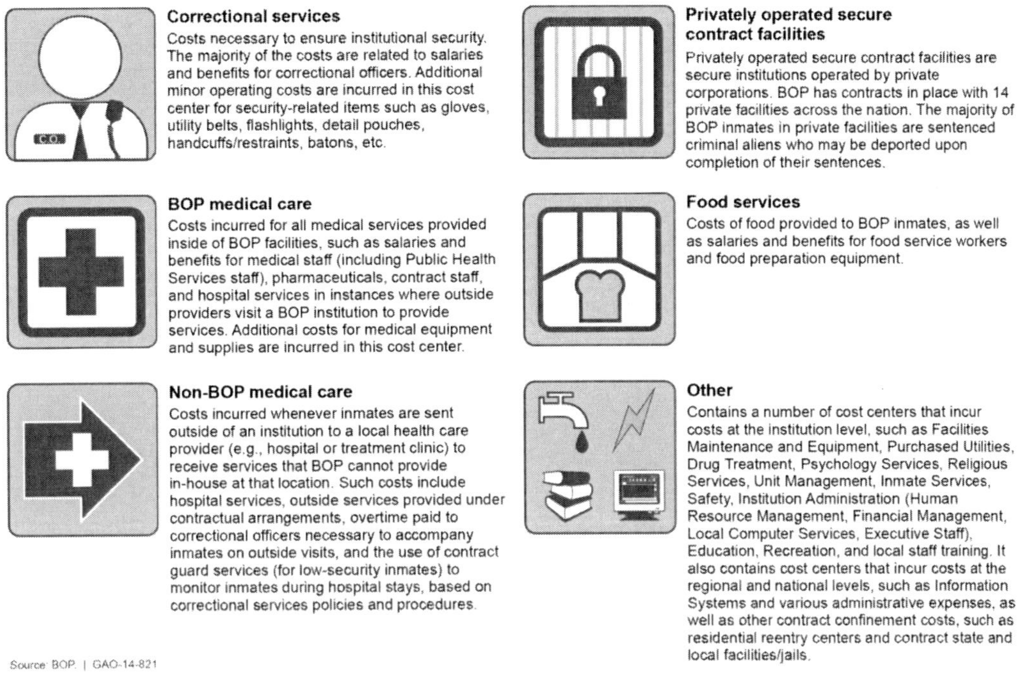

Figure 2. Descriptions of Bureau of Prisons' (BOP) Largest Cost Centers.

BOP Has Identified and Implemented Various Cost Savings Efforts

BOP's Director, in an April 2014 statement before Congress, highlighted BOP's commitment to stewardship of financial resources by seeking cost avoidance and greater efficiencies throughout the bureau.[29] In accordance with this focus, BOP has embarked on a number of initiatives in recent years that have resulted in actual or projected cost savings. Key initiatives for which BOP has estimated cost savings over the last 3 fiscal years are listed in table 1.

These efforts reflect a focus on the part of both BOP management and staff to identify and implement cost savings initiatives, on both a large and a small scale. BOP-developed estimates of savings from these efforts total about $61 million, which is just under 1 percent of total obligations for fiscal year 2013. BOP officials stated that since such a large component of BOP's costs is related to paying salaries and benefits necessary to manage its inmate population, their ability to recognize cost savings beyond those efforts presented here is fairly limited.

In addition, BOP is in varying stages of taking additional actions such as converting inmate case files from paper to electronic records that may reduce costs—for which it has not determined or provided savings estimates—that can be found in appendix V. According to BOP officials, they may undertake such initiatives in order to operate more efficiently, and these initiatives may also result in immediate cost savings. However, the officials said that they do not always develop cost savings estimates for initiatives whose primary purpose is to improve efficiency, rather than achieve cost savings.

Table 1. Examples of Cost-Savings Initiatives Adopted by the Bureau of Prisons (BOP)

Cost savings initiative	Description	Estimated cost savings[a]
Renegotiated medical contracts	BOP's institutions attempt to contract with medical service providers to set a fee structure for necessary services that BOP cannot provide in-house. These contracts typically establish a rate of payment for services at a certain premium over a benchmark, such as standard Medicare rates. Savings are generated by trying to reduce premiums paid over the Medicare rate for many BOP medical services contracts.	BOP reports that from April 2013 through April 2014, it has saved nearly $33 million through renegotiated contracts.
Industries, Education, and Vocational Training efficiency efforts	Industries, Education, and Vocational Training Division recorded cost-saving items (most of which are related to Federal Prison Industry operations) completed during fiscal year 2013. These items represent cost savings efforts identified through the use of Lean Six Sigma methodologies, such as changes to warehouse lighting or materials processing.[b] BOP reports that it recently developed a process to validate the actual cost savings achieved through these efforts, and plans to validate cost savings for fiscal year 2014 efforts.	BOP reports estimated savings of about $14 million in nonappropriated funds (i.e., the costs of operating Federal Prison Industry programs) during fiscal year 2013.
Administrative efficiencies	During fiscal year 2013, BOP conducted a reorganization of its regional offices and administrative operations, which resulted in a reduction of 60 positions.	BOP reports salary savings of approximately $7.2 million in fiscal year 2013, with additional operational savings.
National Paving Project	Minimum security inmates from one BOP institution have performed road-paving services at 30 BOP institutions over the last 2 1/2 years, in lieu of hiring contractors to perform such work.	BOP estimates that this project has saved a minimum of about $2 million versus the cost of employing a contractor, and officials believe that actual savings have been higher when taking into account factors such as markup and overhead associated with the use of a contractor.
Information technology savings	BOP is involved with a Department of Justice (DOJ)–level working group to identify areas for savings by combining the purchasing power of DOJ components. For example, BOP is using DOJ's enterprise license agreements for Microsoft, Oracle, and Adobe products.	BOP reports that through use of another DOJ component's delivery order contract, it has saved about $2.4 million in purchase and maintenance agreements. BOP does not track cost savings through the aforementioned enterprise license agreements.

Cost savings initiative	Description	Estimated cost savings[a]
Food digester	A machine that converts food waste into gray water, which is disposed of through the institution's sewer system, rather than at a landfill, saving BOP on landfill costs. BOP currently has 94 units in place at various institutions, with another 10 awaiting installation.	According to data provided by BOP, we calculate that these units may save approximately $1.8 million annually across BOP.
Telemedicine	Use of videoconferencing to provide clinical and consultative services in psychiatry and dermatology. This enables BOP to have a physician on contract at any location to perform these services, rather than contracting to bring in specialists for on-site consultations.c BOP also contracts with a company to provide remote interpretations of inmate X-rays, rather than paying for the service on-site. This approach has been in place since 2004.	BOP estimates that it saved approximately $448,000 in calendar year 2013 through videoconferencing for dermatology services. It also states that it can make more cost-effective decisions on medications and reduce referral and treatment times for inmates. BOP estimates that in fiscal year 2012 (the last year for which data are available), it was able to avoid approximately $387,000 in costs at 86 institutions through this "teleradiology" approach.

Source: GAO analysis of BOP information. | GAO-14-821

[a] All cost estimates were provided by BOP. We assessed the reliability of these estimates and found them sufficiently reliable to present as estimated savings.

[b] Federal Prison Industries is a federal government corporation overseen by BOP that, among other things, employs and provides job skills training to a number of federal inmates, and produces goods and services for sale to the federal government. Lean Six Sigma is a data-driven approach to process improvement based on the idea of eliminating defects and errors that contribute to losses of time, money, opportunities, or business.

[c] BOP states that it has a total of 14 psychiatrists (filling 20 allotted positions) providing virtual psychiatric services to inmates at 90 BOP institutions. The dermatologist participating in this program conducted 501 consultations with clinicians at 50 institutions during calendar year 2013.

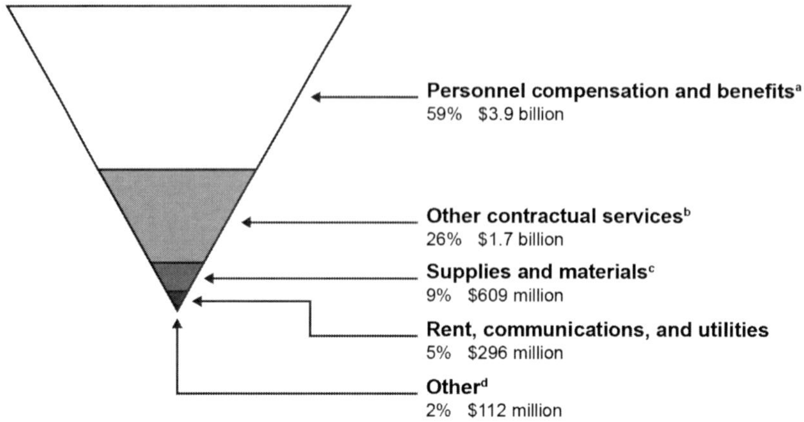

Source: GAO analysis of Bureau of Prisons data. | GAO-14-821

Notes: Totals do not add up to 100 percent because of rounding.

Included in these obligations are approximately $103 million in funds transferred to pay salaries and other costs associated with Public Health Services staff. According to BOP, these are medical professionals employed by the Department of Health and Human Services (HHS) who provide medical services to BOP institutions as needed. While these Public Health Services staff are technically paid by HHS, BOP transfers the necessary funds to HHS to pay for their services.

[a] Personnel compensation and personnel benefits are actually two separate object classifications, but were combined for the purposes of this figure.

[b] "Other contractual services" covers obligations for contractual services for advisory and assistance services (including contract staff), purchases of goods and services from government accounts; operation and maintenance of facilities and equipment; payments for medical care, research and development contracts; subsistence and support of persons; and other services not otherwise classified.

[c] "Supplies and materials" covers obligations for commodities whether acquired by formal contract or other form of purchase that are: ordinarily consumed or expended within 1 year after they are put into use, converted in the process of construction or manufacture, or used to form a minor part of equipment or fixed property. Examples include food, pharmaceuticals, clothing, and office supplies.

[d] Other object classifications include equipment, travel and transportation of persons, and other items.

Figure 3. Bureau of Prisons' (BOP) Fiscal Year 2013 Obligation Levels by Object Classification.

BOP Has Designed Internal Processes to Identify Opportunities for Additional Cost Efficiencies, but Could Improve the Monitoring of Corrective Actions

BOP Has Designed Mechanisms to Identify Opportunities for Cost Efficiencies

BOP has various mechanisms to identify opportunities for cost efficiencies, including the following:

- ***Strategic Plan.*** BOP's *Strategic Plan* helps guide its efforts in fulfilling its mission and achieving strategic goals. As one strategic goal, BOP states that it will manage its operations and resources in an effective manner that encourages innovation, and that it "continually strives toward improvements in its effective use of resources and its efficient delivery of services."[30] Further, BOP has developed a strategic objective focused on cost efficiency and innovation, stating that it will continue to focus on reducing costs using efficient and cost-effective methods to perform tasks. According to the *Strategic Plan*, it will accomplish this through, in part, "continued emphasis on financial planning, analyzing workload and staffing requirements, using consolidated and shared services, increasing the use of technology, and refining the processes of the BOP." In support of this strategic objective, BOP requires that institutions and regions submit to Central Office established local best practices or cost savings measures that can be shared and replicated at other institutions.
- ***Cost Efficiencies and Innovations Catalog.*** This product is a compendium of institution-level efficiency efforts and innovations that serves as a reference for other institutions. The catalog is a result of efforts to identify cost efficiencies as stated in BOP's *Strategic Plan.* To compile this catalog, BOP's Central Office surveys institutions twice a year regarding new or ongoing efforts that they consider to be local best practices in achieving cost efficiencies. After compiling the catalog, BOP distributes it bureau-wide, including to program managers at all institutions. Some examples of cost-efficiency efforts identified and shared throughout BOP via this catalog include efforts in recycling material and food waste, water and energy conservation, use of video conferencing, and inmate training and education. Institutional officials we spoke with reported that they were aware of and reviewed this catalog. BOP institution-level staff estimated that the catalog issued in March 2013 contained items saving tens of millions of dollars in expenses.[31]
- **Best practices internal site.** In April 2007, BOP implemented an internal information-sharing site designed to facilitate bureau-wide communication of efforts that have resulted in cost efficiencies to bureau staff or inmates. This reference tool includes links to cost reduction initiatives, energy conservation efforts, and other items that have been reviewed and vetted by subject matter experts as having demonstrated their value to BOP. The website includes institution-led efforts such as battery-recycling operations and improved efficiencies to water-heating systems.
- **General staff/program area meetings.** Officials at BOP's Central Office, regional offices, and selected institutions with whom we spoke all cited frequent communication between and among program officials and executive staff regarding items such as general operations, budget and cost levels, staffing levels and use of overtime, health care topics, and other items. These officials frequently cited the quarterly executive staff meeting, which includes assistant directors from Central Office and the six regional directors, as a key meeting for these discussions. At these meetings, among other things, officials present and discuss position papers that lay out information on initiatives that may have the potential for cost savings. For instance, at one meeting, the participants discussed a paper describing ongoing efforts to convert BOP's Inmate Case Files from a paper-based system to an electronic system, ultimately saving staff resources.

- **Internal control.** Internal control is an integral component of an organization's management that is to provide reasonable assurance that objectives are achieved, including the efficiency of operations. We focused our review on BOP's internal control objective related to achieving operational efficiencies. Given this, we reviewed the elements of BOP's internal control system that specifically provide BOP with opportunities to identify cost efficiencies, and found that BOP's internal control processes align with *Standards for Internal Control in the Federal Government.* Table 2 provides examples and descriptions of BOP's specific internal control processes, organized by internal control standard, that allow it to identify opportunities for cost efficiencies. We did not independently test BOP's internal controls to determine whether they mitigate all possible risks and are operating as intended.

BOP's Internal Control System Helps Identify Opportunities to Achieve Efficiencies, but Lacks a Mechanism to Consistently Monitor Bureau-wide Corrective Actions

We found that BOP's internal control system is designed to identify additional opportunities for cost efficiencies, but BOP did not provide specifics or documentation on a mechanism to consistently monitor bureau-wide corrective actions. Program reviews—which document the results of the Program Review Division's (PRD) internal reviews of programs and operations at each BOP institution—collectively cited repeated frequent control deficiencies and significant findings over multiple time periods that present inefficiencies or could increase costs.[32] However, for these repeated issues, BOP did not provide specifics or documentation for how its corrective actions were always monitored consistently to ensure that the actions addressed the issues bureau- wide.[33] Specifically, we reviewed BOP's quarterly program review summaries—which compile each quarter's internal review results and highlight frequent deficiencies and significant findings—for the years 2009-2013 to identify significant findings as well as the most frequent internal control deficiencies reported with respect to opportunities to achieve cost efficiencies in the highest-cost areas identified above. According to our review of these 20 quarterly summaries, frequent deficiencies or significant findings were repeatedly reported in three high- cost areas—time and attendance (14 of 20 quarters), food services (8 of 20 quarters), and RRC contract administration (6 of 20 quarters).

BOP has processes to identify and share information about these frequent and significant deficiencies. In particular, PRD disseminates its quarterly program review summaries to all BOP institutions and the other Central Office divisions to make them aware of these deficiencies. For instance, we found that officials from the Central Office Divisions with oversight over the repeated frequent deficiencies and significant findings that we analyzed—the Human Resource Management Division (HRMD), Health Services Division (HSD), and Reentry Services Division (RSD)— were aware of them.

Table 2. Bureau of Prisons' (BOP) Internal Control Processes That Provide Opportunities to Identify Cost Efficiencies by Internal Control Standard

Internal control standard	BOP process	BOP's use in identifying opportunities for cost efficiencies
Environment *Management and employees should establish and maintain an environment throughout the organization that sets a positive and supportive attitude toward internal control and conscientious management. It provides discipline and structure as well as the climate which influences the quality of internal control.*	• Central Office oversight	BOP Central Office's Program Review Division oversees compliance with the Office of Management and Budget's (OMB) Circular A-123 and conducts the internal review of administrative and operational functions bureau-wide.[a] As noted above, BOP's Strategic Plan also includes a strategic goal to continually strive toward improvements in effective use of resources and efficient delivery of services. As noted above, BOP's Director has stated BOP's commitment to stewardship of financial resources. For instance, in BOP's fiscal year 2015 Budget Request, the Director stated that the agency will continue to seek cost avoidance and find efficiencies throughout the agency.
Risk assessment *Internal control should provide for an assessment of the risks the agency faces from both external and internal sources.*	• Control Evaluation Template • Management Assessment	The Control Evaluation Template is a documented list of controls, and the risk each control is intended to mitigate, in compliance with OMB Circular A-123. For example, one identified risk is an error in payment. BOP's Management Assessment process includes documenting risks within BOP's major program areas (e.g. Food Services). Assessing risk informs the development of internal control and, consequently, guides the internal control review process. For instance, one identified risk is the probability of not conducting inventory properly, which could affect the accuracy of data used when formulating and submitting a budget. For each risk assessment tool, BOP assesses the magnitude and likelihood of each risk.
Control activities *Control activities help ensure that management's directives are carried out. The control activities should be effective and efficient in accomplishing the agency's control objectives, including achieving efficiencies.*	• Control Evaluation Template • Program statements (policy) • Program review guidelines (Internal control testing plan)	The Control Evaluation Template documents internal controls, designed to mitigate identified risks. The template also includes control testing results, in compliance with OMB Circular A-123. For example, certain BOP management review and approval chains are designed to mitigate the risk of improper payment. Program statements are internal policy documents that outline program requirements, including key internal control activities. For instance, program statements note that staff are to monitor the performance of and payments to contractors.

Table 2. (Continued)

Internal control standard	BOP process	BOP's use in identifying opportunities for cost efficiencies
		Program review guidelines serve as a guide to conducting internal reviews of program areas' operations and administrative activities, to ensure that key internal controls are strong and operated effectively (i.e., internal control testing). Program reviews document the results of this internal review process. For example, the guideline directs the reviewer to assess whether and how well staff conduct inventory and the program review documents the results of that assessment.
Information and communication *Information should be recorded and communicated to management and others within the entity who need it and in a form and within a time frame that enables them to carry out their internal control and other responsibilities.*	Program review results Quarterly program review summaries	BOP documents and shares internal review results with the organization that is reviewed, which are generally institutions. Quarterly program review summaries compile numerous internal review results and highlight frequent internal control deficiencies and other significant findings. BOP distributes these summaries bureau-wide. For example, if a significant finding related to an inventory process is identified at one institution, the summary would cite the issue anonymously for other institutions' awareness. As noted above, BOP also has two efforts—the Cost Efficiencies and Innovations Catalog and the best practices intranet site—to communicate efficiency and cost-saving efforts.
Monitoring Internal control monitoring should assess the quality of performance over time and ensure that the findings of audits and other reviews are promptly resolved.	Corrective action plan	Within BOP, the subject of an internal review is responsible for devising and completing a corrective action plan to resolve any internal control deficiency or other finding. For example, if an institution did not conduct a quarterly inventory of property in a certain program area, the institution is responsible for mitigating the risk of inaccurate agency records. BOP's Program Review Division monitors whether corrective action has been taken by the specific organization or program that is reviewed. A follow-up internal review eventually verifies whether the corrective action is adequate. The frequency with which a subsequent review occurs depends on the likelihood of risk as determined during the Management Assessment process. For example, BOP conducts internal reviews of certain institutions' operations, at a frequency ranging from once a year to once every 3 years.

Source: GAO analysis of BOP information. | GAO-14-821

[a] Office of Management and Budget, Circular A-123, *Management's Responsibility for Internal Control,* defines management's responsibility for internal control in federal agencies. The circular states that federal employees must ensure that resources are used efficiently and effectively to achieve desired objectives. Internal controls are the tools (organization, policies, and procedures) to help managers achieve results, including operational efficiency.

Moreover, one of the divisions, HRMD, formulated a corrective action plan and has systematically taken steps to address and monitor progress toward resolving reported deficiencies and findings related to time and attendance that were identified at multiple institutions across multiple time periods. For instance, BOP's program reviews identified control issues related to time and attendance in 14 of the 20 quarters from 2009 through 2013, such as inaccurate time and attendance records and the lack of appropriate documentation to support payment. These reported issues could lead to payment errors, such as incorrectly compensating staff for overtime. HRMD officials reported that, as a result of these issues, they implemented policy changes, such as developing mandatory training and requiring that each human resource office audit a representative sample of its time and attendance files annually. Further, BOP is currently transitioning to a web-based time and attendance reporting system, which includes information technology controls. Such information technology controls establish segregation of duties (e.g., the staff approving reported work hours is supervisory and different from the staff reporting the hours worked) and the retention of electronic records in compliance with rules and regulations, which officials report could help address the deficiencies. To consistently monitor progress toward resolving these issues bureau- wide, BOP's Central Office has conducted a number of audits of time and attendance records and reports that error rates in record accuracy have declined from about 5 percent in 2010 to less than 2 percent in 2014.

The other two Central Office divisions with oversight over the repeated frequent deficiencies and significant findings that we analyzed—HSD and RSD—have taken actions at the national level to attempt to address some of the deficiencies. However, they did not provide specifics or documentation for how the divisions would monitor progress toward correcting them. With respect to HSD, BOP's internal reviews identified findings related to the administration and management of resources in its Food Services Program (constituting $408 million, or 6 percent, of BOP's obligations in fiscal year 2013) in 8 of the 20 quarters from 2009 through 2013, such as incomplete inventories; not properly reporting lost, damaged, or stolen property; or failures to adjust inventory records referenced when formulating and submitting an institution's budget. At the national level, BOP is providing training on the use of the Food Services Program's information system that includes a quarterly inventory control function, and has formed support teams to provide assistance to institutions identified as having deficient programs. For the staff performing inventory control at the local level (e.g., warehouse staff), the division is requesting that they attend national training or a similar training program. However, HSD did not provide specifics or documentation for establishing a mechanism that would allow it to monitor whether the actions taken have produced needed improvements within Food Services comprehensively across institutions.

With respect to RSD, BOP's internal review identified findings related to RRC contract oversight and monitoring (RRC contracts constituting $296 million, or 4 percent, of BOP's obligations in fiscal year 2013) in 6 of 20 quarters from 2009 through 2013, such as monitoring reports not being completed on a timely basis and inaccurate payments being made to contractors. These reported issues could result in failing to address contractor performance or overpayments. In July 2013, Residential Reentry Management (RRM) offices nationwide were consolidated under the direct management of the Residential Reentry Management Branch (RRMB). Previously, the RRM field offices were under the operational control of the six BOP regional offices. According to BOP, this reorganization has allowed

BOP to implement and monitor consistent practices throughout the Residential Reentry offices. BOP also reported that, as a result of these findings, management teams within the Residential Reentry Management Branch provide guidance to individual field offices that require corrective actions. Additionally, they have scheduled a national-level training session in September 2014 to address repeated frequent deficiencies, share best practices in contract monitoring, and promote consistency and effective oversight of RRCs. Similar to Food Services, however, RSD did not provide specifics or documentation for establishing a mechanism that would allow it to monitor whether the actions taken have produced needed improvements with the Residential Reentry Program comprehensively across RRC contracts.

Internal control standards state that monitoring of internal controls should include policies and procedures for ensuring that the findings of audits and other reviews are promptly resolved. In particular, managers are to promptly evaluate findings from audits and other reviews, including those showing deficiencies and recommendations reported by auditors who evaluate agencies' operations; determine proper actions in response to findings and recommendations from audits and reviews; and complete, within established time frames, all actions that correct or otherwise resolve the matters brought to management's attention. According to the standards, the resolution is completed only after action that corrects identified deficiencies, produces improvements, or demonstrates the findings and recommendations do not warrant management action.[34]

For deficiencies and other findings associated with a particular institution, BOP has a mechanism to monitor corrective actions at the individual institution to help ensure that the deficiencies and findings do not reoccur at that specific location. Specifically, according to BOP, the responsible official of the entity reviewed (most often the warden of the institution) is responsible for developing and implementing the corrective action, and PRD monitors that specific institution's progress in implementing the corrective action. However, with respect to frequent deficiencies and significant findings across a number of institutions repeatedly reported over time, BOP did not provide specifics or documentation for establishing a mechanism to consistently monitor bureau-wide corrective actions to determine whether they are achieving desired results and helping to prevent similar deficiencies from occurring at different institutions over time. We found that in at least one instance in which deficiencies were repeatedly found across a number of institutions— HRMD's process for resolving deficiencies associated with time and attendance—a Central Office division did successfully take steps to consistently monitor the deficiencies bureau-wide. Specifically, for the repeated frequent deficiencies and significant findings associated with time and attendance, we found that HRMD's process for implementing and monitoring its corrective actions has resulted in fewer errors and stronger internal controls related to record retention and segregation of duties, which could reduce the risk of erroneous payments, thereby providing BOP with greater assurance that it is operating more efficiently with regard to its staff costs across its many institutions.

However, despite the repeated nature and recency of findings within the Food Services and Residential Reentry Programs, the relevant Central Office divisions did not provide specifics or documentation for how they have monitored their corrective actions to assess their progress toward addressing these findings across BOP institutions. As a result, BOP does not have reasonable assurance that actions taken are preventing certain frequent and significant findings from reoccurring at other institutions, thus hindering BOP's ability to achieve cost efficiencies in these two high- cost areas—accounting for spending of $408 million and $296.1 million in fiscal year 2013, respectively. By establishing a mechanism for relevant Central Office divisions to consistently monitor bureau-wide corrective actions and assess their progress in the presence of repeated frequent deficiencies or significant findings reported across multiple institutions, BOP could be better assured that it is resolving such deficiencies promptly and, ultimately, operating more efficiently. Further, although repeated frequent deficiencies and significant findings related to operational effectiveness and compliance-related issues were outside the scope of our review, such a mechanism would also better position BOP to resolve repeated deficiencies and significant findings in these areas.

AUTHORITIES WITHIN BOP'S CONTROL TO REDUCE COSTS ARE LIMITED; OPTIONS OUTSIDE OF BOP'S AUTHORITY COULD HAVE A LARGER IMPACT ON COSTS

BOP's Current Authority to Reduce Inmate Sentences Results in Limited Cost Savings Relative to Its Overall Budget

BOP has certain discretionary authorities that can affect the period for which an inmate is incarcerated or remains in BOP custody. We have previously reported on these in detail, and found that inmate eligibility for certain programs and lack of capacity affect BOP's use of them.[35] Among these discretionary authorities are those that permit BOP to

- determine the eligibility of a foreign national offender for transfer to the offender's home country to serve out his or her sentence;[36]
- reduce the length of the inmate's sentence, based on inmate "good conduct time (GCT);"[37]
- determine the eligibility of an offender for participation in a substance abuse program (which may result in a sentence reduction of up to 1 year);[38] and
- transfer an inmate out of prison to serve the remainder of his or her sentence in a residential reentry center or in home detention.[39]

Table 3 describes key statutory provisions in which BOP has a role in reducing a federal prisoner's period of incarceration in a BOP institution.

Of these authorities, two—IPTP and Compassionate Release—are programs that can result in a direct reduction of BOP's population and thus cost savings. The number of inmates released through these two programs annually is small, however, as are the estimated savings. For example, the estimated 2013 cost savings from these programs were about $2.6 million and $651,000, respectively, or about 0.04 and about 0.01 percent of BOP's total fiscal year 2013 appropriations of $6.44 billion.

- **IPTP.** As of June 28, 2014, BOP had about 54,000 foreign nationals in its custody. However, eligibility criteria constrain the number who can be transferred. Specifically, inmates must voluntarily request a transfer to their home countries to serve out the remainder of their sentences, the United States must have a treaty with the home country permitting repatriation, eligibility for transfer must be confirmed by BOP, the transfer request must be approved by DOJ's Office of Enforcement Operations, and the home country must agree to receive the prisoner. Further, while the United States has treaties with 94 foreign countries to permit IPTP transfers, the DOJ Inspector General (IG) reported that, as of 2010, about 22 percent of the foreign nationals in BOP come from countries with which there is no transfer agreement. In addition, as of late June 2014, almost 37,400 (17.3 percent) of all BOP inmates were Mexican nationals (or about 70 percent of all BOP foreign nationals). However, since 2001, Mexico has restricted eligibility for transfer from the United States, according to a 2011 DOJ IG report.[40]

In fiscal year 2013, DOJ approved 245 transfers out of BOP custody, representing less than 0.5 percent of BOP's foreign national population. Through these transfers, BOP estimates that it avoided costs of approximately $2.6 million in fiscal year 2013, or about 0.04 percent of BOP's fiscal year 2013 $6.44 billion appropriation.[41]

- **Compassionate Release.** We have previously reported on BOP's discretionary authority to request compassionate release for certain offenders—termed "reduction in sentence" by BOP—and found that BOP used this authority infrequently because of, among other things, BOP's eligibility criteria.[42] Specifically, compassionate release of an inmate historically has been limited by BOP to terminally ill patients with an incurable disease and short life expectancy or to those who are elderly with a profoundly debilitating medical condition. In April 2013, the DOJ IG reported that the existing BOP compassionate release program had been poorly managed and implemented inconsistently, likely resulting in eligible inmates not being considered for release and in terminally ill inmates dying before their requests were decided.[43] No cost savings estimate could be provided for earlier releases because, according to the IG report, BOP did not maintain cost data associated with the custody of inmates eligible for consideration under the program, and BOP had not conducted any analysis of cost savings achieved by releasing such inmates.

DOJ issued a revised program statement with less restrictive criteria for compassionate release in August 2013. The revisions included making terminally ill inmates with a life expectancy of up to 18 months eligible for consideration instead of maintaining the previous 12-month limit.[44]

According to BOP data, total releases under compassionate release increased from 29 inmates in calendar year 2011 to 39 in calendar year 2012, and to 61 in calendar year 2013 (including 11 released under the expanded criteria). An additional 2 had been released as of July 2014 under expanded nonmedical criteria. However, as a percentage of BOP's population and costs, the number of affected inmates and savings remains small given the numerous factors involved in determining eligibility. Inmates released under compassionate release in calendar year 2013 represented about 0.03 percent of the total BOP inmate population, and estimated savings from the releases amounted to about $651,000, or about 0.01 percent of BOP's fiscal year 2013 $6.44 billion appropriation.[45]

Table 3. Key Statutory Provisions Available to the Bureau of Prisons (BOP) to Reduce a Federal Prisoner's Period of Incarceration or Time in BOP Custody

Discretionary flexibilities	Description
International Prisoner Transfer Program (IPTP), 18 U.S.C. § 4102.	The Department of Justice (DOJ) is authorized to transfer offenders under a sentence of imprisonment, on parole, or on probation to the foreign countries of which they are citizens or nationals, provided that there is a current treaty between the United States and the other country that provides for such transfer, that the offender has voluntarily requested the treaty transfer, and that the home country agrees to the transfer. BOP determines whether an inmate meets specific minimum eligibility requirements; if these are met, BOP forwards the request to DOJ's Office of Enforcement Operations. DOJ is responsible for determining whether an inmate is approved or denied for treaty transfer.
Reduction in Sentence through Compassionate Release, 18 U.S.C. § 4205(g), 18 U.S.C. § 3582(c)(1)(A).	Upon motion of the Director of BOP, the court may reduce a term of imprisonment after considering certain factors if it finds that either (1) extraordinary and compelling reasons warrant such a reduction; or (2) the inmate is at least 70 years of age, has served at least 30 years in prison for the offense or offenses for which the inmate is imprisoned, and a determination has been made by the Director of BOP that the inmate is not a danger to the safety of any person or the community; and that such a reduction is consistent with applicable policy statements issued by the U.S. Sentencing Commission (USSC).
Good conduct time (GCT) 18 U.S.C. § 3624(b).	BOP is authorized to award credit toward the service of an inmate's sentence, beyond the time served, of up to 54 days per year of sentence served if the inmate has displayed exemplary compliance with institutional disciplinary regulations. To be eligible, the inmate must be serving a sentence of more than 1 year other than a term of imprisonment for life.
Residential Drug Abuse Treatment Program (RDAP), 18 U.S.C. § 3621(e).	BOP is required to provide substance abuse treatment for each inmate it determines has a treatable condition of substance abuse. BOP must, subject to the availability of appropriations, provide residential substance abuse treatment (and make arrangements for appropriate aftercare) for all eligible inmates, with priority provided based on proximity to release date. Through RDAP, BOP may reduce the sentence of an inmate convicted of a nonviolent offense who successfully completes the treatment program for a period of up to 1 year.
Residential Reentry Program 18 U.S.C. § 3624(c).	The Director of BOP must, to the extent practicable, ensure that an inmate spends a portion of the final months of that inmate's term (not to exceed 12 months), under conditions that will afford the inmate a reasonable opportunity to adjust to and prepare for reentry into the community. This may include a prisoner being placed in a residential reentry center (RRC, or halfway house).[a] As of April 2014, BOP supervised the operations of 200 RRCs nationwide; RRCs are operated by private contractors that have contracts with BOP.[b]

Source: GAO analysis of federal statutes and BOP information. See GAO-14-821.

[a] Home detention is an option for a limited number of offenders, and BOP requires that specific criteria be met, both with regard to the offender's eligibility and with having an acceptable home environment for home detention. By statute, an eligible offender may be placed in home detention for the shorter of 10 percent of the term of imprisonment or 6 months.

[b] BOP reported that it also has 49 intergovernmental agreements for "work release," which it includes under its count of RRCs (for a total of 249); of these agreements, 40 are with state and local governments, and 9 are with the U.S. Marshals Service.

Funding and eligibility constraints also limit BOP's use of RDAP and RRCs to affect costs related to the number of inmates in BOP custody. Some cost savings can result from inmates being able to reduce their sentences as a result of successfully completing the RDAP program; however, both RDAP and RRCs are types of rehabilitation programs intended to reduce recidivism rather than serving as cost-saving mechanisms.[46] Moreover, as RDAP and RRC are programs that require professional staff and resources, increasing the number of offender participants in either would require additional funding that could offset potential cost savings.[47]

- **RDAP.** We have previously reported that, according to BOP, delays resulting from system-wide demand for this treatment program have prevented timely inmate entry into RDAP and thereby reduced the number of eligible inmates receiving the maximum allowable sentence reduction. This is because by the time some inmates complete RDAP, they have fewer months remaining on their sentences than the maximum allowable reduction of 12 months.[48] According to BOP, the average participant reduced his or her sentence by about 10 months in fiscal year 2013.

As we have also previously concluded, increasing RDAP participation would cost more than the potential savings from reducing sentences by relatively small amounts. For example, if every eligible RDAP participant who completed the program in fiscal year 2011 had received his or her maximum sentence reduction, BOP would have been responsible for 15,729 fewer months of inmate incarceration, yielding an estimated cost savings of about $13.2 million. However, the fiscal year 2012 request for an additional $15 million to permit more offenders to enter RDAP "on time" and thereby to increase their allowable sentence reductions would not have been enough to achieve the full 12-month potential reduction, meaning that expanding RDAP would have cost at least $1.8 million more than it would have saved. Similarly, according to DOJ, BOP received an increase of $15 million in RDAP funding in fiscal year 2014 and this funding will, by fiscal year 2016, increase the average sentence reduction for RDAP participants from 10 months in fiscal year 2013 to an estimated 11.5 months.[49] BOP reported that reaching the full potential 12-month sentence reduction for all participants in fiscal year 2013 would have resulted in about $11 million in cost avoidance savings, but it did not provide a calculation of the cost of providing additional spaces and staff to permit the full sentence reduction for all participants.

These cost savings estimates do not take into account potential long-term savings to society from reducing substance abuse and recidivism among released inmates. While RDAP may contribute to achieving such savings, expanding it above current levels requires an up-front cost that exceeds its potential cost savings for BOP in the short term.

- **RRCs.** According to BOP, RRCs, or halfway houses, provide programs that are intended to help inmates rebuild their ties to the community and to thereby reduce the likelihood that they will recidivate. Run by private contractors, RRCs provide programs that help offenders find employment, and coordinate the provision of services to address substance abuse, medical, and mental health care with appropriate community providers. We have previously found that the use of RRCs is constrained by both eligibility criteria and funding.[50] For example, inmates with detainers (other crimes for which they were charged but were not yet sentenced), with sentences of 6 months or less, or who are in civil commitment status are all ineligible for RRC placement.[51] In addition, BOP officials stated that objections from local communities to halfway houses in residential neighborhoods have hindered expanding the RRC program, even when funds were available.

We have previously found that not all inmates are eligible to be sent to an RRC prior to their release from prison, and that for those who are eligible, some spend only a portion of the full 12 months' allowable time in an RRC because of a lack of bed space and because of eligibility criteria.[52] According to BOP, an increase in the number of offenders getting the full 12 months' allowable time would necessitate additional bed space, which would require both additional funding and additional RRC contracts. For example, in fiscal year 2013, BOP reported that it had 9,455 RRC beds available nationwide, but would have required about 30,000 beds to provide the maximum allowable 12 months in RRCs to all participants, or an addition of more than 20,500 beds above its current capacity. As noted above, and as we have previously reported, BOP officials explained that such an expansion could be challenged by local zoning restrictions and the unwillingness of many communities to accept nearby RRCs. Moreover, if such an expansion were to take place, BOP would need additional funding to pay for the new RRC bed space. For fiscal year 2013, BOP reports that the average daily cost per offender in an RRC was about $73, or $26,645 per year. This means that an increase of the more than 20,500 beds that would be required to achieve the allowable 12 months for all participants (at current program levels) would cost about $546 million annually.[53] Expanding RRCs might help reduce recidivism but would require a substantial funding increase, equal to almost 8 percent of BOP's entire $6.9 billion fiscal year 2015 budget request.

Potential Actions Outside of BOP's Authority Could Reduce Prison Populations and Costs, and Experts Say There Are Advantages and Disadvantages to These Options

We examined cost-saving options that are outside BOP's authority and that are widely discussed among criminal justice policy experts, the USSC, and DOJ, such as instructing federal prosecutors to decline to charge certain defendants in certain drug cases in such a manner as to trigger mandatory minimum prison sentences, reducing the lengths of sentences specified by federal guidelines for drug offenders, or applying the provisions of the Fair Sentencing Act of 2010 retroactively in order to provide sentences for cocaine base ("crack") offenders that are less disparate from those applied for possession of powder cocaine.[54] Toward this end, we reviewed selected reports and analyses from entities chosen for their expertise in criminal justice issues, and had discussions with officials from DOJ, BOP, and the USSC. See appendix VI for more information on the entities we selected. Through this review, we identified eight options outside BOP's authority that could reduce the size of the inmate population. These involve potential legislative actions by Congress, executive orders by the President, policy changes implemented by the Attorney General, or changes in sentencing guidelines that could be promulgated by the USSC.[55] For each of these options, we asked the USSC to calculate the estimated impact on the size of BOP's population and the potential savings that could result from implementation of each.[56] See appendix VII for the USSC analyses of these options. For the purposes of our analysis, we determined that the

USSC is an authoritative source for conducting such analysis; it has conducted similar analyses in recent years and published one on its website on July 25, 2014.[57] For each option, the time frame (number of years) over which the option would take effect may vary, as well as the number and type of offenders who would be eligible for a changed sentence under the option. In general, the majority of the impact of most options was estimated by the USSC to occur within 5 or 6 years of implementation. However, the options are not all directly comparable; some would have a greater impact more quickly than would others, depending on the option and the number of potentially eligible offenders. For options that apply only prospectively (that is, only to future offenders)—such as the Attorney General's August 2013 memorandum to U.S. Attorneys—the potential impact is typically less than for options that would apply to larger numbers of currently incarcerated offenders.

On the basis of analyses the USSC conducted of the potential results from implementing each of the eight options, which provided estimates of bed year savings, we then calculated the potential cost savings.[58] Implementation of the options could range from about $8.7 million to almost $4.1 billion, with the potential savings varying based on the option implemented and the duration of the option. Cost savings or cost avoidance savings were calculated using BOP's fiscal year 2014 estimated average annual marginal cost of approximately $11,000. Marginal costs covers such things as security, food, medical care, clothing, unit management, education, records, and maintenance associated with additional inmates entering existing BOP facilities. BOP officials stated that calculating cost savings using marginal cost was more appropriate than using per capita costs because BOP is about 36 percent overcrowded system-wide, and therefore BOP would have to reduce its existing population by that percentage (equal to about 78,000 offenders in July 2014) to eliminate overcrowding system-wide. Until that number is reached, BOP officials stated, they would not be closing existing prisons and therefore would expect savings only in marginal costs versus average per capita costs to be realized. However, the use of marginal cost in calculating savings does not take into account the possibility that reductions in BOP population could permit BOP to reduce the numbers of offenders sufficiently to reduce staff, close some existing facilities, or avoid opening additional ones that would otherwise have been required. If the options achieved population reductions resulting in reductions in fixed costs, such as reducing staff or closing existing prisons, calculating cost savings using average annual per capita costs—$29,291 in fiscal year 2013, according to BOP—would be appropriate. Three of the options could result in an estimated 78,000 or more offenders being eligible for release or eligible for sentence reductions over five years, which could greatly reduce or eliminate current overcrowding based on BOP's estimate within the same 5 years.[59] Given the size of these potential reductions in sentence lengths and the number of eligible offenders, we calculated per capita cost savings for three of these options, based on the USSC estimates for saved bed years. We did not calculate per capita savings for a fourth option—changing the way that BOP calculates the amount of "good conduct" time that offenders earn for each year served—because although the number of eligible inmates would be almost 180,000, the reduction in sentence for each inmate would be small in contrast to the other three options and would occur over 30 or more years. Therefore, this option may be less likely to allow BOP to reduce staffing levels or close facilities.[60]

Table 4. Options for Changes to Sentencing Processes, Number of Eligible Inmates, Estimated Cost of Options, and Assessment of Potential Advantages and Disadvantages by Expert Entities and Four States with Sentencing Change Experience

Option 1: Reduce the length of mandatory minimum sentences for incarcerated drug offenders[a]	
Description	Implementing this option would reduce the sentences of certain current incarcerated drug offenders convicted of an offense carrying a mandatory minimum sentence—for example, from 20 years to 10 years, 10 years to 5 years, and 5 years to 2 years—and would release incarcerated offenders if they had already completed their recalculated sentence (i.e., if the time served exceeded the new sentence length). Offenders with time remaining on their sentences would remain in prison until they met the new (shorter) sentence length requirement that applies to their cases. Implementing this option would mean an average reduction in sentence for eligible offenders of 57 months (44.2 percent).
Estimated number of inmates eligible for release or sentence reduction	This is estimated to be 78,102 inmates. Of these, 68,620 (88 percent) would be eligible for release during the first 5 years after implementation, and 9,482 in the sixth year and after.
Estimated bed year reduction and cost savings	It is estimated that 370,985 bed years would be saved, or $4.1 billion.[b] Savings would roughly match the released numbers—about 88 percent ($3.6 billion) in savings would occur in the first 5 years after implementation. Given the size of these potential reductions in offenders and required bed space, per capita savings could occur, which means savings could be as much as $10.231 billion over the first 5 years and an additional $1.395 billion in the sixth year after, or a total of $11.626 billion.[c]
Expert-identified potential advantages	• This could make sentences more proportionate to the crime committed. • This could significantly reduce Bureau of Prisons (BOP) population, thereby reducing overcrowding and improving prison safety for prisoners and staff, as well as reducing wait lists for anti-recidivism programs.
Expert-identified potential disadvantages	• Released offenders may recidivate, which could increase crime. The financial and societal costs of increased crime could eclipse cost savings. • This could reduce prosecutorial leverage to get plea bargains in exchange for evidence against those in higher positions in a criminal organization. • This could shorten sentences too much below original intent or shorter sentences may be too lenient.

[a] The Anti-Drug Abuse Act of 1986, Pub. L. No. 99-570, 100 Stat. 3207, established the basic framework of statutory penalties currently applicable to federal drug-trafficking offenses. The act specified statutory penalty ranges for manufacturing, distributing, or dispensing the drug, or possessing the drug with intent to manufacture, distribute, or dispense the drug. For each of several drug types, the act specified separate statutory ranges for such offenses involving various quantities of the drug. See 21 U.S.C. § 841.

[b] In developing its analysis, the USSC made a number of assumptions, including that Congress would authorize the courts (or the President using clemency powers) to reduce the sentences of offenders incarcerated on or after a specific date in a manner consistent with the *Guidelines Manual* and bound only by any mandatory minimum penalties that might apply in current law or as modified through the policy option. The bed year fiscal year 2014 average marginal cost of $11,000 was not adjusted for future inflation.

[c] Estimated per capita savings were calculated using BOP fiscal year 2014 average per capita costs of about $31,338. BOP's fiscal year 2014 enacted Salaries and Expenses appropriation of $6.769 billion was divided by the July 24, 2014 population of about 216,000. Future year savings were not adjusted for inflation.

Table 4. (Continued)

Option 2: Retroactively apply the Fair Sentencing Act of 2010 reductions in drug mandatory minimum penalties to offenders currently incarcerated for crack cocaine–related offenses	
Description	This option would retroactively apply to eligible incarcerated offenders the reductions in mandatory minimum penalties for crack cocaine- related offenses that are provisions of the Fair Sentencing Act (FSA) of 2010, which did not apply to offenders already sentenced under the original penalty guidelines.[a] The USSC amended the sentencing guidelines to implement these revisions effective November 1, 2011, and also voted to apply that amendment retroactively to those already sentenced under the guidelines that incorporated the original penalty structure. However, because Congress did not make the statutory changes to the mandatory minimum penalties retroactive, some offenders were unable to receive the full or, in some cases, any benefit from the commission's action. This option would have the effect of applying the new, lesser mandatory minimum penalties retroactively to currently incarcerated offenders.
Estimated number of inmates eligible for release or sentence reduction	An estimated 8,468 inmates would be eligible; 6685 (79 percent) would be eligible for release over a period of 5 years following implementation.[b]
Estimated bed year reduction and cost savings	It is estimated that 37,400 bed years would be saved, or about $411 million. Of the total, about $325 million would be saved over first 5 years; and about another $86 million in the sixth year and after.[c]
Expert-identified potential advantages	• This could enhance fairness in federal sentencing by making the sentence more commensurate with the crime. By applying the same sentences for the same crime retroactively, it could increase prison safety by reducing potential inmate conflict. • This could reduce BOP population, thereby reducing overcrowding and improving prison safety; it could allow BOP to shift fund to other priorities. • This could release offenders deemed to be at low risk for reoffending and at high likelihood for successful reentry; it could increase the likelihood of successful reentry and therefore save money.
Expert-identified potential disadvantages	• Released offenders may recidivate, which could increase crime. • Reductions in sentence length after conviction and sentencing could reduce prosecutors' ability to negotiate a plea bargain in future cases

[a] The mandatory minimums revised by the Fair Sentencing Act of 2010, Pub. L. No. 111-220, 124 Stat. 2372, had been enacted in the Anti-Drug Abuse Act of 1986, Pub. L. No. 99-570, 100 Stat. 3207, which included the federal criminal law distinction between "cocaine base" and other forms of cocaine. The thresholds triggering the 10-year penalty—5 kilograms of powder cocaine and 50 grams of cocaine base—created a 100-to-1 quantity ratio. The identical ratio was reflected in the 5-year mandatory minimum thresholds as well: 500 grams of powder cocaine and five grams of cocaine base both triggered the 5-year penalty. Among other things, the Fair Sentencing Act of 2010 increased the quantities of crack cocaine that trigger the 5- and 10-year statutory mandatory minimum penalties—from 5 grams to 28 grams for 5-year mandatory minimums and from 50 to 280 grams for 10-year mandatory minimums—and eliminated the 5-year mandatory minimum for simple possession of crack cocaine.

[b] USSC data permitted calculation of bed year savings based on 8,468 cases

[c] In developing its analysis, the USSC made a number of assumptions, including that Congress would authorize the courts by statute to reduce the sentences of offenders in accordance

with the *Guidelines Manual* in effect on a specific date and bound only by the mandatory minimum penalties as amended by the FSA. The bed year fiscal year 2014 average marginal cost of $11,000 was not adjusted for future inflation.	
Option 3: Avoid charging future low-level nonviolent drug offenders with a charge that results in a mandatory sentence	
Description	This option has been implemented as part of the August 2013 direction issued by the Attorney General instructing prosecutors in cases involving the applicability of drug law mandatory minimum sentences based on drug type and quantity to decline to charge the quantity necessary to trigger a mandatory minimum sentence if the defendant meets particular criteria.[a]
Estimated number of inmates eligible for release or sentence reduction	The Attorney General's August 2013 direction applies only to future offenders (i.e., it is not retroactive). The USSC estimates that it would be applicable to about 620 offenders annually each year for each of the next 5 years (or a total of about 3,100 offenders).
Estimated bed year reduction and cost savings	This would result in an estimated savings of 788 bed years over 5 years, or about $8.7 million.[b]
Expert-identified potential advantages	• This could help restore proportionality in federal drug sentences by ensuring that sentence length is more commensurate with offense severity. It also could serve to more often appropriately defer to local and state prosecution in many cases. • It could help reduce BOP overcrowding and thereby reduce costs. • It could allow for more judicial or prosecutorial discretion or alternative treatment opportunities. • It could allow more use of community punishments and treatment, which are more likely to reduce recidivism than the same programs in prison.
Expert-identified potential disadvantages	• Released offenders may recidivate, which could increase crime. • This could reduce prosecutorial leverage to get plea bargains in exchange for evidence against those higher up in a criminal organization. • A change in policy could be quickly reversed by a different administration or by Congress. • This could provide increased discretion to prosecutors, which could make it difficult to ensure consistency in application.
[a] According to the USSC, this option is comparable to making certain changes in application of the safety valve. [b] Bed year fiscal year 2014 average marginal cost of $11,000 was not adjusted for future inflation. USSC estimates for this option are based on the USSC's understanding of the implementation of the criteria established by DOJ in this policy; however, ultimate savings will depend on how DOJ personnel interpret and apply these criteria in practice.	
Option 4: Amend USSC sentencing guidelines for future drug offenders, reducing them two levels below current guidelines[a]	
Description	This option would reduce the potential sentences for all future drug offenders by two levels below current guidelines, resulting in a roughly 18 percent reduction of sentence length below current lengths.[b]
Estimated number of inmates eligible for release or sentence reduction	An estimated 87,285 inmates would be eligible, based on 17,457 annually for each of the next 5 years.
Estimated bed year reduction and cost savings	Approximately 17,990 bed years would be saved over 5 years, or $198 million. Given the size of these potential reductions in offenders' sentences and required bed space, per capita savings could occur; which means savings could be as much as $564 million over the first 5 years.[c]

Table 4. (Continued)

Expert-identified potential advantages	• This could significantly reduce average sentences, reducing BOP overcrowding and costs. • It could make sentences more proportionate to the crime. • It could result in sentences that are individualized to the risks and needs of the particular offender.
Expert-identified potential disadvantages	• Released offenders may recidivate, which could increase crime. • Overall reduction of guideline length does not address the specific offender risks and needs. Unilateral reduction in sentences could be a relatively blunt approach to reducing sentences for all types of drug offenders. • This may not address issues raised by statutory mandatory minimum sentences or differentiate among crimes committed by offenders receiving a reduced sentence.

[a] This option was approved by a vote of the USSC on April 10, 2014, and transmitted to Congress on April 30, 2014; the proposed amendment will go into effect on November 1, 2014, unless Congress acts to modify or disapprove the amendment to the sentencing guidelines.

[b] According to the USSC, if this option was implemented, and if the courts were to grant the full reduction possible in each case, the projected new average sentence for the eligible offenders would be 51 months versus a current average of 62 months, or a reduction of about 18 percent.

[c] Per capita savings were calculated using BOP fiscal year 2014 average per capita costs. BOP's fiscal year 2014 enacted Salaries and Expenses appropriation of $6.769 billion was divided by the July 24, 2014, population of about 216,000. Future-year savings were not adjusted for inflation.

Option 5: Apply the amendments to sentencing guidelines in option 4 also to incarcerated drug offenders—that is, to both new drug offenders and retroactively to incarcerated drug offenders[a]	
Description	Under this option, the provisions of option 4 would apply both to new drug offenders and also retroactively to incarcerated drug offenders. This would reduce the sentences for all future and currently incarcerated drug offenders by two levels below current USSC guidelines, resulting in a roughly 19 percent reduction below current lengths.[b]
Estimated number of inmates eligible for release or sentence reduction	An estimated 132,635 inmates would be eligible for sentence reductions (87,285 from option 4 and 45,350 from applying option 4 retroactively.)
Estimated bed year reduction and cost savings	This is estimated to save 81,303 bed years over the first 5 years, saving about $894.3 million. (17,990 bed years from future cost avoidance and 63,313 bed years saved from retroactively applying the reduction in sentence lengths). For retroactivity over a period of 6 or more years, an estimated additional 16,426 bed years would be saved, producing an additional $181 million in savings.[c] (Future-year cost avoidance savings beyond the first 5 years were not calculated.)
	Given the size of these potential reductions in offenders and required bed space, per capita savings could occur; which means savings could be as much as $2.548 billion over the first 5 years, and an additional $515 million in the sixth year and after. This would mean a total savings of about $3.1 billion.[d]

Expert-identified potential advantages[e]	• This could reduce BOP population, thereby reducing overcrowding and improving prison safety; it would increase the ability to shift (saved) funds to other priorities such as rehabilitation programs. • It could enhance fairness and proportionality in sentencing by ensuring that those in BOP custody for the same crime have similar sentences. • It could reduce BOP population and therefore save money.
Expert-identified potential disadvantages	• Released offenders may recidivate, which could increase crime. • This could reduce prosecutorial leverage to get plea bargains in exchange for evidence against those higher up in a criminal organization. • It could base release decisions solely upon guideline length reduction without a separate and current risk/needs assessment and without taking into consideration offender behavior and programming while incarcerated, which may result in increased recidivism.[f]

[a] Applying the sentencing guidelines in option 4 retroactively to eligible incarcerated offenders was approved by a vote of the USSC on July 18, 2014; the decision amended a policy statement related to the proposed amendment to the sentencing guidelines. As such, it corresponds to the April 30 USSC decision and does not require separate congressional action. Unless Congress acts to modify or disapprove the corresponding April 30 amendment, beginning November 1, 2014, eligible offenders can ask courts to reduce their sentences. Offenders whose requests are granted by the courts may not be released earlier than November 1, 2015. The Attorney General announced after the USSC vote that at his direction, BOP will begin notifying federal inmates of the opportunity to apply for a reduction in sentence immediately. BOP subsequently notified inmates about the USSC amendment.

[b] According to the USSC, retroactive application of option 4 would result in an average sentence for those eligible of 108 months, a reduction of 25 months from the current average of 133 months (18.8 percent less). The USSC also noted that sentences will be reduced retroactively only after consideration by a judge in each case.

[c] According to the USSC, 80 percent of the sentence reductions, and hence cost avoidance savings, would occur within the first 5 years of implementation. Fiscal year 2014 average marginal costs of $11,000 are not adjusted for future inflation. The remainder of the savings would occur over nearly 25 years, because of the length of the sentences of some of those potentially eligible.

[d] Per capita savings were calculated using BOP fiscal year 2014 average per capita costs. BOP's fiscal year 2014 enacted Salaries and Expenses appropriation of $6.769 billion was divided by the July 24, 2014, population of about 216,000. Future-year savings were not adjusted for inflation.

[e] Expert entities were asked to comment on this option before it was approved. The approved version delays implementation by 1 year (to November 2015). Since this did not affect the substance of the proposed change, we report the experts' comments as stated to us.

[f] The USSC notes that sentences will be reduced retroactively only after consideration by a judge in each case. The option reviewed by expert entities did not have this requirement as it was approved by the USSC after the list of options had been sent to the expert entities for review and comment.

Option 6: Increase good time credits for good conduct time (GCT)	
Description	BOP has discretionary authority to award credit toward the service of an inmate's sentence, beyond the time served, of up to 54 days per year of sentence served if the inmate has displayed exemplary compliance with institutional disciplinary regulations. As applied by BOP, this actually results in 47 days earned per year of sentence imposed because inmates do not earn GCT credit for years they do not ultimately serve because of being released early.[a] Under this option, the GCT credit would be awarded to current offenders using a formula that would result in 54 days' credit per year of sentence, rather than the current BOP interpretation that limits the GCT credit to 47 days per sentence year. This would result in eligible inmates serving 85 percent of their sentence, rather than the higher 87 percent average resulting from BOP's current interpretation of 18 U.S.C. § 3624(b).

Table 4. (Continued)

Estimated number of inmates eligible for release or sentence reduction	Approximately 179,265 inmates would be eligible.
Estimated bed year reduction and cost savings	This would save 34,359 bed years, saving $378 million, of which $246 million (65 percent) would occur during the first 5 years after implementation. The remaining $132 million would be saved in the sixth year and after. (According to a DOJ 2012 analysis of this potential change in calculating the GCT credit, it would take more than 30 years for all eligible inmates to be affected, given the length of some sentences.)
Expert-identified potential advantages[b]	• This could reduce BOP population/ overcrowding, which has positive consequences, such as decreasing wait lists for recidivism programs, increasing safety, or freeing up resources for other priorities. • It could incentivize participation in programming aimed at reducing recidivism, promoting successful reentry. • It could save money over the long term through reduced recidivism.
Expert-identified potential disadvantages	• It could require additional slots or spaces for inmates to participate in qualifying programming, thereby requiring more funding. • It could undermine "truth in sentencing," which was the goal of mandatory sentences and public confidence in the criminal justice system. • Released offenders may recidivate despite participation in programming, thus increasing crime. For instance, inmates could "game the system" to get admitted to antirecidivism programs in order to get a reduced sentence.
[a] See GAOor further discussion of these issues. [b] Expert entities were asked to comment on both good conduct time credits and credited time that might be earned through participation in anti-recidivism programs, including substance abuse programs. However, because such programs incur costs, rather than producing cost savings, and participation rates could not be specified, we asked the USSC to estimate the potential savings from a change in the way that GCT is credited by BOP for current federal inmates.	
Option 7: Make the current "safety valve" available to any drug offender with no offenses that receive 3 points under the criminal history point system[a]	
Description	Under this option, the current statutory requirements for eligibility for "safety valve" relief in drug cases involving a mandatory minimum penalty would be expanded to cover incarcerated offenders with any number of criminal history points under USSC guidelines, provided that the offender does not have a conviction for which the sentence imposed was a 3-point offense under USSC sentencing guidelines. The courts would be authorized to resentence all federal offenders convicted of a drug offense in a manner consistent with the revised statute.[b]
Estimated number of inmates eligible for release or sentence reduction	Approximately 11,949 inmates would be eligible (applies only retroactively). Of these, 10,259 (86 percent) would be released within the first 5 years following implementation.
Estimated bed year reduction and cost savings	This would save15,889 bed years, saving $175 million.[c] Of this, about $150.5 million (86 percent) would be saved within the first 5 years following implementation.
Expert-identified potential advantages	• It could reduce BOP population/overcrowding, which has positive consequences, such as decreasing wait lists for recidivism programs, increasing safety, or freeing up resources for other priorities.

	• It could increases judicial discretion, resulting in less severe and more proportionate and fair sentences. • It could help reduce BOP overcrowding and thereby reduce costs.
Expert-identified potential disadvantages	• Released offenders may recidivate, which could increase crime. • It could reduce prosecutorial leverage to get plea bargains in exchange for evidence against those higher up in a criminal organization. • It may not address issues raised by statutory mandatory minimum sentences or differentiate among crimes committed by offenders receiving a reduced sentence. For example, point systems are inflexible; change must recognize that three 1-point offenses are not the same as one 3-point offense.

"Source" | GAO-14-821

[a] The safety valve was created by the Violent Crime Control and Law Enforcement Act of 1994, Pub. L. No. 103-322, 108 Stat. 1796, which directed that certain defendants sentenced for certain drug offenses who meet specified criteria would not be subject to mandatory minimum penalties. Accordingly, only defendants sentenced after the guideline amendment's November 1, 1987, effective date who satisfy the safety valve requirements would be eligible for the reduced term of imprisonment.

[b] USSC guidelines are used to determine prison sentences based primarily on two factors: (1) the conduct associated with the offense (the offense conduct, which produces the offense level) and (2) the defendant's criminal history (the criminal history category). In general, criminal history points are calculated by adding 3 points for each prior sentence of imprisonment exceeding 1 year and 1 month; adding 2 points for each prior sentence of imprisonment of at least 60 days but not more than 13 months; adding 1 point for each prior sentence of less than 60 days, and so forth. This option would make more drug offenders eligible for sentencing by judges who would not be required to solely follow mandatory sentencing guidelines.

[c] The bed year fiscal year 2014 average annual marginal cost of $11,000 is not adjusted for future inflation.

Option 8: Expand the safety valve as described in option 7 to include both nonviolent drug offenders and any nonviolent offenders provided that they do not have a 3-point offense

Description	Under this option, the current statutory requirements for eligibility for "safety valve" relief in drug cases involving a mandatory minimum penalty would be expanded to cover both drug offenders and other nonviolent (nondrug) offenders. No offender could have a conviction for which the sentence imposed was a 3-point offense under USSC sentencing guidelines. The courts would be authorized to resentence all federal offenders convicted of a nonviolent offense in a manner consistent with the revised statute.
Estimated number of inmates eligible for release or sentence reduction	Approximately 38,930 inmates would be eligible.
Estimated bed year reduction and cost savings	This could save 40,552 bed years, saving about $446 million. Of this, about $397 million (89 percent) would be saved in the first 5 years following implementation. The remaining $49 million would be saved in the sixth year and after.
Expert-identified potential advantages	• This could reduce BOP population/overcrowding and would thus have positive consequences, such as decreasing wait lists for recidivism programs, increasing safety, or freeing up resources for other priorities. • It could result in sentences that are less severe and fairer, reducing prison overcrowding and improving prison safety; cost savings could permit shifting funds to other priorities, such as rehabilitation programs. • It could allow more judicial discretion (judges can render sentences focused upon the individual offender), thereby potentially increasing the likelihood of a successful outcome while simultaneously reducing the prison population.

Table 4. (Continued)

Expert-Identified Potential Disadvantages	• It could reduce prosecutorial leverage to get plea bargains in exchange for evidence against those higher up in a criminal organization. • It could lead to disparities in sentencing across multiple jurisdictions, which sentencing guidelines were intended to address. • It could shorten sentences too much below original intent.

Sources: USSC analysis, GAO analysis of USSC and BOP data, and GAO analysis of expert responses. | GAO-14-821

It is important to emphasize cost savings is one of many considerations. In particular, these options may have additional effects, such as on public safety. The expert entities we contacted identified potential advantages and disadvantages they believe could result from the implementation of each option, such as making sentences more commensurate with the crime or releasing inmates who may reoffend.

We are not taking a position on any of these options. We present the information we obtained from the USSC and the expert entities to inform policymakers as they weigh whether and how to address costs at BOP. Specifically, in table 4, we summarize each option we presented to the USSC, expert entities, and the four states selected because of their experience with criminal justice sentencing initiatives. For each option, we show the USSC estimate of the number of BOP offenders who would likely be eligible for release or for a reduced sentence (leading to release) as a result of implementation. The table also shows the USSC estimates, if available, of the bed year savings that would result from implementation of each option, and our calculation of the cost savings that would result.[61] In addition, we summarize the comments from the responding states and the expert entities with regard to potential advantages and disadvantages that could result from implementing these options.

As the Attorney General has noted, without action to reduce the current size of BOP's population, and projected future growth, BOP will continue to require an ever greater share of DOJ's budget, having increased from about 14 percent of that budget in 1980 to nearly 25 percent in the fiscal year 2015 request. As table 4 shows, a number of options outside of BOP's current authority exist by which the sentence lengths of prospective and incarcerated offenders could be reduced (producing bed year savings), as well as the number of offenders to be incarcerated, such as under the Attorney General's August 2013 Smart on Crime direction (option 3). Hence, BOP's costs could be reduced, but the range of potential savings from these options is great. As illustrated in table 4, actual savings are greater for options that apply to current offenders compared with those that apply only prospectively. For example, retroactively reducing drug sentences by about 44 percent (option 1) would have the greatest estimated cost savings: $4.1 billion using marginal cost savings, or $11.626 billion if per capita savings were to occur. Other options would have a lesser impact, such as avoiding charging future low-level, nonviolent drug offenders with charges that result in mandatory minimum sentences, which could be a savings of $8.7 million in marginal costs over 5 years (option 3). However, as discussed earlier, cost savings is one of many considerations in weighing which, if any, option could be adopted. Equally important is consideration of the advantages and disadvantages associated with each option.

CONCLUSION

According to BOP officials, BOP's biggest challenges are managing the continually increasing federal inmate population while providing for inmates' care and safety, as well as the safety of BOP staff and surrounding communities, within budgeted levels. BOP has made improvements in its effective use of resources a strategic goal. Toward that end, BOP has implemented mechanisms that allow it to identify opportunities for cost savings, such as an internal website through which BOP staff can view cost efficiency efforts being implemented across BOP, and undertaken cost-savings efforts, such as in energy conservation. However, establishing a mechanism for relevant Central Office divisions to consistently monitor bureau-wide corrective actions and assess their progress in the presence of repeated frequent or significant findings could help BOP better ensure that it is resolving such deficiencies promptly and, ultimately, operating more efficiently.

BOP's inmate population is its primary cost driver; however, BOP's ability to reduce its population, and thus its costs, are limited. Potential changes outside of BOP's authority could substantially reduce both BOP's population and its costs. Expert entities and states from which we obtained views reported that there are potential trade-offs to implementing these options. Some expert entities observed that release of offenders poses the risk of recidivism and that reductions in sentence length could reduce prosecutors' leverage in extracting information from low-level criminals that is used to prosecute higher-level ones. At the same time, other expert entities reported potential advantages to these options, such as making sentence lengths more commensurate with the crime committed. These experts' analyses of the possible savings and the potential advantages and disadvantages, beyond cost savings, of these options may be useful for policymakers to consider as they weigh whether and how to address BOP's population and, ultimately, its costs.

Recommendation for Executive Action

To enable BOP to promptly address repeated frequent deficiencies and other significant findings it identifies through its program reviews in areas of high cost across multiple institutions, we recommend that the Director of the Bureau of Prisons establish a mechanism for relevant Central Office divisions to consistently monitor bureau-wide corrective actions.

Agency Comments and Our Evaluation

We requested comments on a draft of this report from DOJ. In an email received September 17, 2014, the DOJ liaison stated that DOJ concurred with our recommendation. The Department did not provide official written comments to include in our report, but did provide written technical comments, which we incorporated as appropriate. The U.S. Sentencing Commission also provided written technical comments, which we incorporated as appropriate.

David C. Maurer
Director, Homeland Security and Justice Issues

Appendix I. Objectives, Scope, and Methodology

We addressed the following questions as part of this review:

1) What are the major costs for Bureau of Prisons (BOP) operations, and what actions has BOP taken to implement cost savings?

2) To what extent does BOP have mechanisms to identify opportunities for cost efficiencies and to take corrective actions that may improve cost efficiency?
3) What potential changes, both within and outside of BOP's authority, could lead to cost reductions or improved efficiencies in BOP operations, and what might be the potential impact of these changes?

To address the first question, we obtained historical obligation data from BOP's Financial Management Information System for fiscal years 2009-2013—a 5-year time frame to provide us with an adequate understanding of trends in BOP obligation levels—to identify the major costs incurred by BOP for its Salaries and Expenses account, which generally represents 98 percent of BOP's budget.[62] We have assessed the reliability of these data and determined them to be reliable for the purposes of this report. This assessment included performing checks on the data received and interviewing officials responsible for compiling and maintaining these data. We also collected data (e.g., cost savings estimates prepared by BOP) and documentation, such as memos and concept papers approved by executive staff from fiscal years 2009 through 2013; through review of these data and documents and interviews with relevant agency officials, we determined that these data are also reliable for the purposes of this report. In addition, we interviewed Central Office-, regional-, and institutional-level officials to identify to the extent possible all existing cost efficiency and savings initiatives adopted by BOP and their impact on its overall budget.

To address the second question, we reviewed the processes and tools at BOP during the same time period (fiscal years 2009-2013) that identify, implement, and promote cost-efficiency and savings initiatives throughout its institutions, such as executive staff meetings and a catalog compiling cost-savings initiatives. With respect to identifying additional opportunities to realize cost efficiencies or reduce costs, using our financial analysis as context, we analyzed elements of BOP's internal control system related to the control objective of achieving operational efficiencies and interviewed relevant officials to assess whether BOP has a management structure and processes to routinely assess its administrative and operational activities for possible corrective action. Specifically, we reviewed BOP's mechanisms and processes leading to its internal review of operational and administrative functions, including its process for taking corrective action, related to high-cost areas and compared these characteristics with those called for in *Standards for Internal Control in the Federal Government.*[63]

To address the third question, on potential policy changes both within and outside BOP's authority that could lead to BOP cost savings, we collected analysis and documentation from the Department of Justice (DOJ), BOP, the U.S. Sentencing Commission (USSC), and entities selected for their expertise in criminal justice issues, and, in particular, potential changes to federal sentencing policies.[64] We identified these expert entities through several means, including (1) asking officials at both the USSC and the Urban Institute who have previously worked on analyses and reports relevant to prison population data and criminal justice to identify entities they considered as expert in the field of sentencing reform and criminal justice, (2) conducting a literature search to identify publications issued by some of the entities on sentencing reform or corrections, and (3) identifying entities with known expertise and authoritativeness (e.g., the ABA) in the criminal justice field through literature searches. These entities may not be representative of the universe of expert entities in the criminal justice field and therefore may not represent all views on this topic; however, their views provide insights. We obtained data from calendar year 2011 through July 2014 from BOP on the impact on BOP's population and costs resulting from changes implemented by BOP to broaden the criteria for compassionate release of offenders, as well as analyses from the USSC on the estimated impact of the memorandum accompanying the Attorney General's August 2013 DOJ Smart on Crime initiative that instructed prosecutors to decline to charge certain defendants in certain types of drug cases in such a manner as to trigger mandatory minimum sentences. For data on efforts taken under BOP's authority, we assessed the reliability by reviewing documentation and interviewing knowledgeable officials; we determined the data to be sufficiently reliable for the purposes of this report. For data on the impact of policy changes outside BOP's authority, we obtained analyses from the USSC. According to our audit objectives, we determined based on its expertise that the evidence obtained from the USSC provides a reasonable basis for our findings and conclusions.

We reviewed sentencing reform options identified by the expert entities, as well as analyses of these options from these entities. We identified these entities on the basis of their demonstrated expertise as well as to ensure that a wide range of views on the advantages or disadvantages of potential changes to existing sentencing guidelines was covered. GAO is not taking a position on any of these options, but presents information on estimated cost savings and experts' views of advantages and disadvantages for such options to inform policymakers as they weigh whether and how to address rising costs at BOP.

On the basis of the options we identified, we compiled a list of seven sentencing guideline and related changes that were being widely considered and discussed among expert entities at the time we began our review and during the course of the review. We also included one change resulting from a memorandum issued by the Attorney General in August 2013 to U.S. Attorneys instructing them to decline to charge certain defendants in certain types of drug cases in such a manner as to trigger mandatory minimum sentences. These selected options were based on our assessment of proposals put forward by several sources, including the Attorney General, expert entities, states with experience with criminal justice reform, and advocacy entities with a range of views on criminal justice reform. See appendix II for the letter sent to expert entities asking for their assessment of options, which provides a list of the proposals that were used to develop the selected options. During the course of our review, two of these options were approved by the USSC, with the amendment to the sentencing guidelines forwarded to Congress. This amendment will become effective on November 1, 2014, unless Congress acts to modify or disapprove the amendment. The two options approved are closely related—the first, approved by the USSC on April 10, 2014, reduces the sentences for future (federal) drug offenders, such that there would be an approximately 18 percent reduction in the average length of such sentences compared with sentences under current guidelines. The second was approved on July 18, 2014, by USSC, and applies the reduction retroactively—that is, to currently incarcerated drug offenders.[65] After the USSC July 18 vote to make the drug sentence reductions retroactive (if eligibility criteria are met), the Attorney General issued a statement that, at his direction, BOP will begin notifying federal inmates of the opportunity to apply for a reduction in sentence immediately. Unless Congress modifies or disapproves the amendment to the sentencing guidelines submitted by the USSC, beginning November 1, 2014, eligible offenders can ask courts to reduce their sentences. Offenders whose requests are granted by the courts can be released no earlier than November 1, 2015, under the USSC provision. For the purposes of this report, we refer to these two changes by the USSC, and the Attorney General's August 2013 directive to U.S. Attorneys, and to the other options collectively as eight options.

For each of these eight options, we asked the USSC to estimate the impact on the size of the BOP inmate population. The USSC calculates such impact in bed years; 1 bed year is defined by the USSC as 12 months of prison time (e.g., one offender in prison for 1 year, or three offenders in prison for 4 months each, and so forth). Using the USSC bed years'savings estimates, we then calculated cost savings or cost avoidance that could result from implementing a given option.[66] The USSC analyses of these eight options are reproduced in appendix VII.

In addition, we asked the 14 expert entities to comment on the options with regard to their view of the advantages or disadvantages of implementation of the eight options. We also identified 4 states (Texas, Louisiana, Ohio, and North Carolina) that have had at least 1 year's experience in implementing state-level sentencing and criminal justice changes similar to the ones being discussed for federal offenders, and asked them to comment on the potential options for change.[67] We selected Louisiana, Ohio, and North Carolina also because they are participants in the joint DOJ-Pew Charitable Trust Justice Reinvestment Initiative (JRI), which funds implementation of changes to state sentencing and criminal justice policies intended to reduce prison populations and recidivism, and these states were also the largest in terms of annual spending on corrections among the JRI states with at least 1 year's experience in implementing JRI-related initiatives.[68] We selected Texas because, as of 2012, it had both the largest state prison population in the United States and was cited by the Urban Institute as an early leader in criminal justice reform initiatives that DOJ used as a model for the Justice Reinvestment Initiative program. We received responses from 17 of the 18 entities (the 14 expert entities and 4 states) to which we sent the letter.[69]

We conducted this performance audit from July 2013 to September 2014 in accordance with generally accepted government auditing standards. Those standards require that we plan and perform the audit to obtain sufficient, appropriate evidence to provide a reasonable basis for our findings and conclusions based on our audit objectives. We believe that the evidence obtained provides a reasonable basis for our findings and conclusions based on our audit objectives.

Appendix II. Letter Sent to Select States and Expert Entities

March 24, 2014

The U.S. Government Accountability Office (GAO), the investigative arm of the U.S. Congress, is carrying out a research engagement (GAO job #441173) on ways in which the Federal Bureau of Prisons (BOP) can achieve cost efficiencies. As part of this work, we will be listing select options that would require action by entities other than BOP—such as changes enacted by Congress and the President that could affect the size of the BOP prison population, or changes in sentencing guidelines that could be promulgated by the U.S. Sentencing Commission (USSC) and possibly also applied retroactively. These options include proposals identified by a number of experts or included in pending legislation that would likely help reduce costs at BOP. We are writing you to ask for your comments or observations on these select options.

These options are based on an assessment of varying proposals put forward by several sources:

- Proposals and guidance from the U.S. Attorney General on sentencing reform, including changes to charging procedures ordered in August 2013 as part of the DOJ Smart on Crime Initiative to avoid incarceration of low-level, non-violent drug offenders.
- Potential cost-saving changes or concepts identified by expert entities, including the USSC; the Pew Charitable Trusts; the Urban Institute; the Heritage Foundation; the Vera Institute of Justice; the Council of State Governments/Justice Center; and the American Bar Association, some of which are also included in pending legislation.
- The experiences of various states in recent years with criminal justice reform, often intended to reduce prison populations and recidivism, including Texas and 17 states involved in the DOJ Justice Reinvestment Initiative (JRI) and as reported on in the January 2014 joint DOJ-Urban Institute report, *Justice Reinvestment Initiative State Assessment Report.*[70]
- Comments and analyses by several expert/advocacy entities with a range of views on criminal justice reform including the National Association of Assistant United States Attorneys; the National Association of Former United States Attorneys; the Brennan Center for Justice at New York University School of Law; Families Against Mandatory Minimums; and Right on Crime: A project of the Texas Public Policy Foundation in cooperation with Justice Fellowship.

Based on common policy themes assessed or reported by the aforementioned sources, the options listed below are grouped into three broad categories (in most cases, there are several related proposals or concepts that have been put forth by various expert entities or experts):

1) Sentencing Reform—Proposals to Reduce Length of Mandatory Sentences;
2) Enhancement of "Good Conduct Time" reduction-in-sentence through good behavior by inmates and/or through participation in programs intended to reduce recidivism, enhance post-release employment chances, and/or reduce substance abuse; and
3) Proposals to expand the safety valve for offenders. A "safety valve" is a statutory exception to mandatory minimum sentencing laws that authorizes a judge to sentence a person below a mandatory minimum term if certain conditions are met. The current federal sentencing guidelines provide for a reduced sentence for persons who meet the current federal safety valve criteria (which apply only to drug trafficking cases) even in cases where a mandatory minimum penalty would not otherwise apply.

Instructions

For each option, we would like to ask you to briefly identify any potential "advantage" or "disadvantage", based on your organization's expertise or, for states, based on your experience in implementing some version of them (we recognize these vary considerably in detail). For example, an "advantage" for most of these proposals is sometimes stated to be to reduce overcrowding of prisons, or to reduce the waiting list for anti- recidivism educational or substance abuse programs. Alternatively, a "disadvantage" for some of these, as identified by some experts, is that a certain percentage of those released may commit crimes again and that, therefore, early release (v. serving the full sentence) may put someone back into society who may become a recidivist earlier than would otherwise have occurred.

GAO will generally present only the aggregate results of the responses to these questions in our report to Congress. Although in some cases individual responses may be discussed, the report will not include any information that could be used to identify individual respondents. Identifying information will not be released outside of GAO, unless compelled by law or pursuant to a Congressional request. See 31 U.S.C. §716.

Please start by saving the document as a Microsoft Word file to a hard drive before completing it, as your comments will otherwise not be saved. There are comment boxes below each of the options. Please type your responses in the space provided, which will expand automatically to accommodate your comments.

Group 1: Proposals to Reduce Length of Mandatory Sentences

Option A: Reduce the length of mandatory minimum sentences for drug- related offenses –for example, reduce the mandatory minimum sentences in drug trafficking cases from 20 years to 10 years; 10 years to 5 years; and 5 years to 2 years.

Your Comments Advantage: Disadvantage: Additional: ☐ Please check box if Not Applicable or Not Enough Information to Comment

Option B: Make the amendments to drug mandatory minimum penalties of the Fair Sentencing Act of 2010 retroactive to those offenders currently incarcerated for crack cocaine-related offenses.

Your Comments Advantage: Disadvantage: Additional: ☐ Please check box if Not Applicable or Not Enough Information to Comment

Option C: Avoid charging low-level non-violent drug offenders with a charge which results in a mandatory sentence.

Your Comments Advantage: Disadvantage: Additional: ☐ Please check box if Not Applicable or Not Enough Information to Comment

Option D: Amend sentencing guidelines for all drug offenders—for example, reduce such sentences by a given percentage below current lengths (e.g., by 20 percent; by 10 percent).

Your Comments Advantage: Disadvantage: Additional: ☐ Please check box if Not Applicable or Not Enough Information to Comment

Option E: Apply the amendments to sentencing guidelines in Option D to both new drug offenders and retroactively to incarcerated drug offenders.

Your Comments Advantage: Disadvantage: Additional: ☐ Please check box if Not Applicable or Not Enough Information to Comment

Group 2: Proposals to Reduce Sentence Time Based on Good Conduct and/or Participation in Anti-Recidivism and Substance Abuse Programs

Option F: Increase good time credits for good conduct and/or participation in anti-recidivism programs, including substance abuse programs.

Your Comments Advantage: Disadvantage: Additional: ☐ Please check box if Not Applicable or Not Enough Information to Comment

Group 3: Proposals to Expand the Safety Valve for Drug and/or Other Offenders

Overview: The "safety valve" was created by the Violent Crime Control and Law Enforcement Act of 1994, which directed that lower-level defendants sentenced for certain drug offenses who meet specified criteria will not be subject to mandatory minimum penalties. Accordingly, only defendants sentenced after the guideline amendment's November 1, 1995 effective date who satisfy the safety valve requirements are eligible for the reduced term of imprisonment.

Select Options:

Option G: Expand the current "safety valve" for drug offenders to make it available to offenders with more than one prior minor offense up to a certain limit (for instance, up to three criminal history points.)[71]

Your Comments
Advantage:
Disadvantage:
Additional:
□ Please check box if Not Applicable or Not Enough Information to Comment

Option H: Expand the safety valve as described in Option G to include both drug offenders and other non-violent offenders (this would not apply to any sex offenders).

Your Comments
Advantage:
Disadvantage:
Additional:
□ Please check box if Not Applicable or Not Enough Information to Comment

Information to Comment

Additional Comments or Suggested Options

Finally, in the box below, please make any other comments or suggestions you may have, especially with regard to whether there are any other options for making cost effective changes to criminal justice rules or processes that you wish to bring to our attention.

Additional Comments or Observations: Other Options to Consider

This completes the requested assessment of potential options we are considering. Thank you for your time in providing your input on these options with regard to the federal criminal justice system.

APPENDIX III. DATA ON THE FEDERAL BUREAU OF PRISONS' (BOP) LARGEST COST CENTERS

Table 5 presents annual obligations data for fiscal years 2009 through 2013 for BOP's 20 largest cost centers during fiscal year 2013.

Table 5. Annual Obligations for Each of the Bureau of Prisons' (BOP) 20 Largest Cost Centers, Fiscal Years 2009 through 2013

Cost center	2009	2010	2011	2012	2013
Correctional Services	$1,349,084,739	$1,429,586,006	$1,469,511,315	$1,495,434,551	$1,513,151,472
Privately Operated Secure Contract Facilities	$486,680,887	$544,310,237	$556,674,258	$625,636,747	$624,456,406
BOP Medical Care[a]	$493,979,657	$518,183,641	$545,304,468	$565,568,091	$595,492,696
Non-BOP Medical Care	$319,585,026	$351,572,156	$362,448,629	$385,865,248	$419,927,987
Food Service	$354,285,520	$366,808,966	$386,830,370	$403,446,856	$408,021,963
Unit Management	$287,515,668	$296,250,747	$300,984,838	$304,402,809	$305,156,264
Contract Residential Reentry Centers	$244,444,527	$259,937,098	$271,605,677	$280,878,201	$296,123,954
Construction and Mechanical Services	$246,547,837	$258,751,128	$270,133,073	$283,939,306	$283,682,155
Purchased Utilities	$231,373,396	$238,163,022	$239,485,407	$285,387,855	$250,421,579
Uncontrollables-Administrative	$120,313,499	$138,476,463	$167,144,272	$177,159,116	$177,549,624
Education	$108,573,667	$115,174,065	$120,343,124	$125,397,895	$125,822,670
Chief Executive Officer	$103,826,162	$108,540,721	$109,648,711	$108,185,902	$110,346,853
Financial Management	$97,038,156	$101,538,642	$103,963,681	$103,675,217	$107,468,147
Management and Administrative Support	$90,888,006	$96,183,777	$99,626,401	$101,044,832	$103,648,380
Inmate Services	$63,743,317	$79,161,534	$72,535,791	$86,344,508	$85,059,211
Leisure Time Activities	$65,441,546	$70,407,608	$73,291,323	$74,274,020	$76,032,065
Drug Abuse Program	$58,528,233	$64,109,527	$66,826,055	$69,733,453	$75,883,387
Psychology Services	$44,748,555	$47,206,056	$49,624,556	$51,534,118	$52,438,931
Power Plant	$45,741,334	$48,326,306	$49,020,235	$49,020,897	$50,507,908
Employee Services Department	$39,935,664	$41,446,038	$43,837,987	$44,717,642	$44,002,882

Source: GAO analysis of BOP data. | GAO-14-821

Notes: All program areas above represent obligations incurred at the institutional level, except for the following:

Privately Operated Secure Contract Facilities (Contract Confinement Cost Centers, nationwide)

Contract Residential Reentry Centers (Contract Confinement Cost Centers, nationwide).

Uncontrollables-Administrative (National Programs). This cost center represents items that are tracked and funded out of the Central Office on behalf of the institutions, such as DOJ phone services, National Finance Center payroll processing, mail services, transit subsidies, and other items.

[a] BOP Medical care includes costs of salaries and other costs associated with Public Health Services staff. According to BOP, these are medical professionals employed by the Department of Health and Human Services (HHS) who provide medical services to BOP institutions. While these Public Health Services staff are technically paid by HHS, BOP transfers the necessary funds over to HHS to pay for their services.

APPENDIX IV. DATA ON THE FEDERAL BUREAU OF PRISONS' (BOP) LARGEST SUBOBJECT CLASS EXPENSES

Table 6 presents annual obligations data for fiscal years 2009 through 2013 for BOP's 20 largest subobject classes in fiscal year 2013. Compensation for full-time permanent staff has consistently been the greatest area of expense; personnel compensation and benefits account for most of the subobject classes listed below.

Table 6. Bureau of Prisons' (BOP) Obligations by Its 20 Largest Subobject Classes, Fiscal Years 2009 through 2013

Object/subobject class	2009	2010	2011	2012	2013
Personnel Compensation and Benefits[a]					
Full Time-Permanent Appointment	$1,843,183,744	$1,935,330,619	$1,982,819,749	$1,984,097,551	$2,012,540,824
Federal Employees' Retirement System Retirement, Law Enforcement Officers, and Firefighters	$493,494,905	$521,660,581	$553,491,039	$569,164,019	$542,789,373
Federal Employees Health Benefits Act	$213,563,268	$232,974,957	$258,500,221	$272,741,587	$269,165,149
Wage Board-Permanent Appointment	$222,097,563	$232,822,515	$239,808,681	$242,571,507	$245,682,761
Federal Insurance Contributions Act	$133,085,312	$140,256,606	$142,415,468	$143,237,577	$136,549,567
Overtime, Other than Wage Board	$86,672,551	$85,966,848	$78,938,623	$89,297,894	$90,438,851
Contribution Accrual[b]	$1,197	$4,181			$72,455,016
Thrift Savings Plan Matching Government Contribution	$65,858,897	$71,003,306	$73,361,984	$73,567,039	$69,859,878
Employee Compensation (Injury or Death)	$50,387,420	$54,276,066	$59,573,568	$60,616,186	$63,622,470
Holiday Pay	$36,006,208	$36,497,469	$35,959,582	$36,253,718	$39,779,485
Other contractual services					

Table 6. (Continued)

Object/subobject class	2009	2010	2011	2012	2013
Contract Servicesc	$640,758,937	$751,876,304	$781,896,029	$861,571,108	$936,791,945
Housing of Prisoners, Temporary Housing for Federally Assisted Witnesses[d]	$309,231,120	$290,455,682	$307,978,195	$282,334,113	$250,236,250
Medical Hospital	$187,987,798	$190,474,836	$180,663,439	$196,405,226	$195,153,846
ServicesOther Services[e]	$125,846,279	$133,993,847	$154,818,892	$154,593,414	$153,185,222
Supplies and materials					
Supplies/Purchase Card[f]	$290,468,851	$303,532,259	$321,588,084	$334,613,110	$346,619,862
Food	$92,074,252	$90,759,178	$101,156,094	$104,630,698	$108,460,308
Pharmaceutical, Other	$62,758,400	$62,558,146	$63,259,284	$71,464,265	$75,396,816
Other Materials and Supplies[g]	$35,919,356	$48,650,402	$34,869,912	$44,093,428	$42,889,721
Rent, communications, and utilities					
Electricity	$99,700,242	$103,055,828	$106,759,993	$103,184,518	$105,136,797
Water	$32,981,285	$34,776,915	$37,104,912	$38,153,278	$41,942,871

Source: GAO analysis of BOP data. | GAO-14-821.

Notes: The obligations above do not include funds to pay salaries and other costs associated with Public Health Services staff. According to BOP, these are medical professionals employed by the Department of Health and Human Services (HHS) who provide medical services to BOP institutions. BOP tracks these obligations only by object classification and does not break them down by subobject class. For fiscal year 2013, the object class obligations were approximately as follows: Personnel Compensation, $71 million; Personnel Benefits, $31 million; Transportation of Things, $437,000; Travel and Transportation of Persons, $133,000; Other Contractual Services $100,000.

[a] Items under the Personnel Compensation and Personnel Benefits object classifications are combined in this table.

[b] Contribution Accrual—month-end accrual of DOJ contributions chargeable to other subobject classes, such as Federal Employees Health Benefits Act and Federal Insurance Contributions Act contributions. The accrual is reversed in the following month.

[c] Contract Services—contractual charges for consultants and other contractors, such as doctors, dentists, teachers, chaplains, legal advisors, architects, engineers, surveyors, appraisers, inmate commissary clerks, etc.

[d] Housing of Prisoners, Temporary Housing for Federally Assisted Witnesses—charges for the housing of federal prisoners under the jurisdiction of the United States Marshals Service who are being held in nonfederal jail facilities. Charges for housing and moving expenses for witnesses under the Emergency Witness Assistance Program. Includes, but is not limited to, prisoners being held in state/local facilities, unsentenced prisoners, detained witnesses, the

expense of 1 month's deposit on a rental property, moving expenses, truck rentals, etc., if such expenses are more cost-effective than hotel/motel stays; it may also include dependents and other family members, as appropriate.

[e] Other Services—charges for services not otherwise classified. Includes premiums for surety bonds, money order fees, registration and license fees, charges for sanitation and towel service, charges for General Services Administration information centers and water cooler services.

[f] Supplies/Purchase Card —purchases made with the government-issued credit card (nontravel) for supplies not to exceed $3,000. BOP officials noted that some contracting officers can use the cards to make payments of up to $30,000.

[g] Other Materials and Supplies—charges for materials and supplies not otherwise classified.

Appendix V. Additional Federal Bureau of Prisons' (BOP) Efforts to Achieve Cost Savings and Efficiencies

In addition to efforts discussed earlier, BOP also reports pursuing the following initiatives that could provide current and future cost savings, shown in Table 7.

Table 7. Additional Cost-Savings Efforts Under Way or Being Pursued by the Bureau of Prisons (BOP)

Cost savings initiative	Description
Electronic Inmate Central File project	This is an ongoing effort in BOP to convert inmate paper records to electronic files. In 2010, BOP estimated that the logistics of moving, managing, and accounting for inmate paper files required approximately 1.2 million staff hours annually. BOP began this project to modernize bureau operations and repurpose the time spent managing these paper files back to focusing on the custody and care of inmates. BOP is currently testing an approach to integrate its data with that from the U.S. Marshals Service that it plans to complete by the end of August 2014. If successful, BOP officials state that they would then transfer documents from shared directories into the electronic files, which would be complete by the end of September 2014.
Program and administrative reductions	BOP's fiscal year 2015 Congressional Budget Justification contains $157 million in program offsets through program and administrative reductions, which BOP officials reported will not be identified until 2015 funds are appropriated. According to BOP, these funds are necessary to pay for increases in costs, including pay raises, retirement contributions, and General Services Administration rent, among other things.
Medical Claims Adjudication	A contractor reviews the accuracy of payments for medical services provided through contractual agreements with health care providers, currently in place at 25 BOP facilities. BOP does not routinely track cost savings of these adjudications as they are considered more of an operational efficiency effort; however, officials stated that when this effort began at Federal Medical Center Butner, about $1.3 million in savings was originally identified. As this effort has grown in scope, according to BOP officials, cost savings are difficult to quantify as service providers become more focused on accurate billings.
Medical Contracting Initiatives for Residential Reentry Center (RRC) Inmates	BOP is examining the feasibility of regional contracting options at specific locations for medical, dental, and mental health services for inmates at RRCs. Specifically, BOP acquisition staff are formulating a procurement strategy and engaged in informal discussions with vendors to identify an approach that will reduce medical costs while assisting RRC inmates' transition into their community. At this point, BOP has not established any time frames for this acquisition of services. In addition, BOP is hiring three Health Service Specialists to conduct medical bill adjudication for these services.
Mail order pharmacy	BOP is pursuing a Mail Order Pharmacy program to consolidate prescription drugs into one main inventory and buy the least expensive generic medications, as well as automate prescriptions, pending funding. However, this program has been on hold as BOP is working to identify potential new sites for this inventory, and funding for building renovation has been unavailable.

Cost savings initiative	Description
National contracts for medical resources	Through representation on the interagency Strategic Sourcing Leadership Council, BOP is pursuing use of a Department of Defense prime vendor contract to purchase medical and surgical supplies.[a]
Measuring cost effectiveness of health services	BOP's Health Services Division has tentatively identified nine metrics related to evaluating efficiency of health care services to report to its National Governing Board. These metrics will provide data on top diagnostic codes, top procedural codes, rate of rejected medical claims, drug expenditures, catastrophic care costs, outside medical trips, hospital readmission rates (catastrophic), annual health care expenditures, and average annual percentage growth in health care expenditures. BOP reports that all nine cannot be gathered in a systematic way, so the Health Services Division is researching alternative or proxy measures, with no current projected implementation date.
Purchase of garbage trucks	Over the last 3 years, BOP has purchased and provided 26 new garbage trucks, and estimates that about one-third of all institutions haul away garbage on their own, rather than paying contractors.

Source: GAO analysis of BOP information. | GAO-14-821.

[a] The Strategic Sourcing Leadership Council was formed to lead governmental efforts in increasing the use of government-wide management and sourcing of goods and services in order to save money in contracting. This council is chaired by the Administrator for Federal Procurement Policy and contains representatives from a number of federal agencies.

APPENDIX VI. EXPERT ENTITIES PROVIDING INPUT ON PRISON POPULATION REDUCTION OPTIONS

The expert sources that provided us with analysis or information on sentencing issues are listed in table 8.

Table 8. Expert Entities That GAO Consulted in Reviewing Selected Policy Options

Organization	Description
American Bar Association	A professional organization with nearly 400,000 voluntary members that supports the legal profession with resources for legal professionals while working to improve the administration of justice, accredit law schools, establish model ethical codes, and more.
Association of State Correctional Administrators	An organization consisting of state and Bureau of Prisons (BOP) officials focused on improving correctional practices. Among other things, the Association of State Correctional Administrators works to identify and promulgate correctional practices that are likely to reduce the number of offenders returning to prison after release.
Brennan Center for Justice, New York University School of Law	A nonpartisan law and policy institute that provides legal strategy and empirical research for legal and policy efforts in areas including mass incarceration.

Table 8. (Continued)

Organization	Description
Council of State Governments/Justice Center	A region-based forum that fosters the exchange of insights and ideas to help state officials shape public policy. The Council of State Governments' Justice Center is a national nonprofit organization that provides evidence-based strategies and advice to policymakers at the local, state, and federal government levels with the goal of increasing public safety—including work on reentry issues and reducing spending on corrections.
Families Against Mandatory Minimums	A nonprofit organization that advocates for federal and state prison sentencing reforms.
Fraternal Order of Police	With over 325,000 sworn law enforcement officers as members, this organization works to improve the working conditions of law enforcement officers and the safety of communities through education, information, community involvement, and employee representation.
Heritage Foundation	An independent, tax-exempt research and education institution that studies and advises policymakers on a variety of issues, such as federal spending and criminal law.
National Association of Assistant U.S. Attorneys	Formed to protect, promote, and advance the mission of Assistant U.S. Attorneys; their membership contains experts in a number of fields such as gang and narcotics prosecutions, among other things.
National Association of Former U.S. Attorneys	Established to promote the litigating authority and independence of the office of the U.S. Attorney, the association provides education and continuing professional relationships for former U.S. Attorneys.
Pew Charitable Trusts	An independent, nonprofit research and public policy organization focused on issues such as family financial security and various legal issues, among other things.
"Right on Crime," a project of the Texas Public Policy Foundation in cooperation with Justice Fellowship	The Texas Public Policy Foundation is a nonprofit, independent research institute focused on issues of personal responsibility and free enterprise. Right on Crime is an initiative focused on conservative ideas for criminal justice and prison reform in Texas and the nation.
The Sentencing Project	Conducts research and advocates for criminal sentencing reform.
Urban Institute	An organization that gathers data, conducts research, evaluates programs, offers technical assistance overseas, and educates the public on social and economic issues to foster public policy developments in areas such as justice, health care, and housing.
Vera Institute of Justice	An independent, nonpartisan organization that conducts data and policy analysis to provide assistance to government agencies on issues such as relations between police and immigrant communities and policy options to safely reduce prison and jail populations, among other things.

Source: GAO analysis of information from each entity listed above. | GAO-14-821.

APPENDIX VII. ANALYSES OF OPTIONS PROVIDED BY THE U.S. SENTENCING COMMISSION (USSC)

This appendix reproduces the methodology and analyses prepared by the U.S. Sentencing Commission (USSC) in developing estimates of the impact on the Federal Bureau of Prisons (BOP) inmate population of eight options for cost saving that are outside BOP's authority and that are widely discussed among criminal justice policy experts and entities. GAO identified these eight options based on our assessment of proposals put forward by several sources, including the Attorney General, expert entities, states with experience with criminal justice reform, and advocacy entities with a range of views on criminal justice reform. GAO is not taking a position on any of these options, but presents information on them to inform policymakers as they weigh whether and how to address rising costs at BOP. The USSC estimates on the inmate population are reported in the full report.

For options 1, 2, 5, 6, 7 and 8, the USSC prepared a written analysis describing its estimate of the impact of changes specified by the option. For options 3 and 4, the USSC provided tables showing estimated impact. A description of the option analyzed by the USSC and further information relevant to specific analyses are included with each analysis or table below.

1. USSC analysis of option 1: Reduce the length of mandatory minimum sentences for incarcerated drug offenders.

Under this option, the sentences of certain incarcerated drug offenders convicted of an offense carrying a mandatory minimum sentence would be reduced by an average of about 44 percent—for example, from 10 years to 5 years and from 5 years to 2 years. Incarcerated offenders who have completed their recalculated sentence (i.e., if the time served exceeded the new sentence length) would be released.

***

UNITED STATES SENTENCING COMMISSION
ONE COLUMBUS CIRCLE, N.E.
SUITE 2-500, SOUTH LOBBY
WASHINGTON, D.C. 20002-8002
(202) 502-4500
FAX (202) 502-4699

April 11, 2014

Jonathan R. Tumin
Senior Analyst

U.S. Government Accountability Office
441 G St., NW
Washington, DC 20548

Dear Mr. Tumin:

The Government Accountability Office has asked the U.S. Sentencing Commission to assist it in connection with its engagement (number 441173). We understand that through this engagement the GAO is examining ways in which the operating costs of the Federal Bureau of Prisons (BoP) can be reduced. As we have previously discussed with you and your colleagues, the Commission has agreed to analyze on GAO's behalf several policy options which could reduce the overall size of the prison population that the BoP administers. Specifically, our analyses of these policy options will consider the effect on the federal prison population if the policies were implemented in such a way that the options would apply to inmates currently incarcerated in the BoP system.

In this memorandum, we provide to you another of these estimates. Here we provide our estimate of the impact on the federal prison population if the current statutory mandatory minimum penalties for drug offenses of 5, 10 and 20 years were reduced to 2, 5, and 1 0 years, respectively, and the courts were authorized to resentence all federal offenders convicted of an drug offense carrying one of these mandatory minimum penalties under a sentencing framework that incorporated the new minimum penalties.

As we discuss more fully below, we estimate that 78,106 offenders who are incarcerated and would still be in prison as of October 1, 2014 would be eligible for a sentence reduction. The average reduction in sentence for these offenders would be 57 months (44.2 percent). The estimated total savings to the BoP from such a policy change applied retroactively would be 370,985 bed years.

I. The Policy Option We Considered

One of the policy options that we have agreed to examine on behalf of the GAO is the impact of a policy change in current law whereby the current statutory mandatory minimum penalties for drug offenses of 5, 10 and 20 years were reduced to 25, and 10 years, respectively (the "Policy Option"). [72] As part of our analysis, we have assumed that the courts would be authorized (most likely by statute[73]) to resentence all federal offenders convicted of a drug offense carrying one of these mandatory minimum penalties under a sentencing framework that incorporated the new minimum penalties.

II. What We Found

Applying the Policy Option to offenders in the custody of the BoP, we estimate that there are 78,106 offenders who would be incarcerated on October 1, 2014 who would be eligible for a reduction in their current sentence if the Policy Option were to be retroactively applied. If the courts were to grant each of these offenders the full reduction in their sentence we estimate that the total savings to the BoP would be 370,985 bed years.[74]

Table 1 provides information on some of the demographic characteristic of the offenders eligible for a sentence reduction pursuant to the Policy Option. Table 2 provides an estimate of the number of offenders who would be released each year if the Policy Option was applied retroactively compared to the number of offenders who will be released each year pursuant to their current sentence. As can be seen on this table, if the Policy Option were fully retroactive on October 1, 2014, more than 24,600 offenders would be eligible for immediate release. Within the first year of the effective date of the Policy Option, another 8,221 offenders would be eligible for release above the number who will be released under their current sentence. Table 3 provides information on selected sentencing guideline characteristics and the criminal history category of these offenders.

For the 78,102 offenders who would be eligible to receive a sentence reduction under the Policy Option, the current average sentence is 129 months. If the courts (or the President) were to grant the full reduction possible in each case, the projected new average sentence for these offenders would be 72 months, a reduction of 57 months (or 44.2 percent). Based on this reduction, the estimated total savings to the BoP from the retroactive application of the Policy Option would be 37,400 bed years. This savings would not be realized in any single year but is the cumulative savings realized over several years.

III. How We Conducted This Analysis

A. Methodology

The methodology for this analysis is based on the Commission's Prison Impact Model, which has been in use in some form since the guidelines were first developed. This model is used to estimate the impact of proposed statutory and guideline amendments on newly sentenced offenders and to project the future impact those amendments will have on bed space in the BoP. For this analysis, those offenders who appear to be eligible to receive a reduced sentence were hypothetically "resentenced" with the computer program as if the proposed policy change had been in effect in the year in which they were sentenced. A new release date for each offender also was calculated in order to determine when the offender would be eligible for release if he or she were provided the full reduction in sentence provided by the proposed policy change.

B. The Offender Population We Studied

The Bureau of Prisons provided the Commission with a datafile of inmates who were in the custody of the BoP on Jan 25, 2014. That file contained approximately 189,000 offenders. Approximately 184,000 of these offenders were sentenced between fiscal year 1992 and fiscal2013.[75] USSC staff was able to match 171,765 of these offenders to Commission records. Of these, 138,894 were estimated to remain incarcerated on October 1, 2014.

In order to approximate the group of offenders who will be sentenced in fiscal year 2014, the Commission used the FY2013 datafile and moved all sentence dates forward by one year. Staff then determined which of these offenders would be incarcerated on October 1, 2014. This process added another 40,178 offenders into the analysis. Between the two groups, the Commission's analysis included data on 179,072 offenders.

C. Our Assumptions

In performing our analysis, we have been required to make some assumptions (set forth below) concerning the decisions that Congress and the courts (or the President) would make in determining whether, and to what extent, to reduce the sentences of offenders eligible to receive a modification of sentence pursuant to the Policy Option discussed above. These assumptions may not hold in every case.

1. Procedural assumptions

Specifically, we have assumed that Congress would authorize the courts (or the President would issue an order) to reduce the sentences of offenders incarcerated on or after a specific date (discussed below) in a manner consistent with the *Guidelines Manual* and bound only by any mandatory minimum penalties that might apply in current law or as modified through the Policy Option being discussed. We also assumed that the Commission would make no further changes to the *Guidelines Manual* in light of the Policy Option, so that the provisions of the 2013 *Guidelines Manual* would apply in these cases. Finally, we assumed that the effective date of any such Policy Option would be October 1, 2014. Therefore, only offenders incarcerated as of that date would be eligible to seek a reduction in sentence pursuant to the Policy Option discussed in the memorandum.

2. Substantive assumptions

The policy we analyzed would have the effect of lowering the current statutory mandatory minimum penalties in drug cases from 5, 10, and 20 years to 2, 5, and 10 years, respectively. In fiscal year 2010, approximately 66 percent of all drug offenders were convicted of an offense carrying a mandatory minimum penalty.[76] Of those, approximately 46 percent remain subject to the penalty at the time of sentencing.[77] Some offenders receive relief from the effect of any such penalty by providing substantial assistance to the government in the investigation or prosecution of another offender.[78] Others receive relief from such a penalty through the statutory "safety valve" provision which authorizes courts to sentence drug offenders without regard to any mandatory minimum penalty provided the offender meets several criteria designed to identify low level, non-violent offenders with little or no prior criminal history.[79] Some offenders are eligible for both provisions.

In our analysis, we provide a full reduction for all offenders who remained subject to a mandatory minimum penalty at the time of sentencing. That is, we reduce sentences by 60 percent for all offenders convicted of a 5-year mandatory minimum who remained subject to that mandatory minimum at sentencing. Similarly, we reduce sentences by 50 percent for all offenders convicted of a 10-year or a 20-year mandatory minimum penalty and who remained subject to that penalty at sentencing.

Drug offenders who receive relief from a mandatory minimum penalty by providing substantial assistance to the government have sentences that are, in general, 46 percent below the applicable guideline minimum sentence,[80] which often is the mandatory minimum penalty.[81] Drug offenders who receive relief from a mandatory minimum penalty through the statutory safety valve provision have sentences that are, in general, 39 percent below the applicable guideline minimum sentence.[82] The extent of these reductions fluctuates somewhat each year. Because these offenders benefitted from substantial reductions in their sentence at the time of the original sentence, we have assumed that any benefit to them from the Policy Option would not be as great as it would be for those offenders who remained subject to a mandatory minimum penalty at sentencing. Therefore, for this analysis, we made additional assumptions for these offenders, as follows:

- offenders who were convicted of a drug offense carrying a 5-year mandatory minimum penalty, but who were not subject to any mandatory penalty at sentencing due to relief through substantial assistance or the safety valve would receive a further reduction of 30 percent under the Policy Option (i.e., 50% of the 60% reduction that offenders received if they remained subject to that mandatory minimum penalty at sentencing);
- offenders who were convicted of a drug offense carrying a 10-year or 20-year mandatory minimum penalty, but who were not subject to any mandatory penalty at sentencing due to relief through substantial assistance or the safety valve would receive a further reduction of25 percent under the Policy Option (i.e., 50% of the 50% reduction that offenders received if they remained subject to either of those mandatory minimum penalties at sentencing).

This analysis does not assume any change in sentence for offenders who were not convicted of a drug offense carrying a mandatory minimum penalty. It is possible, of course, that Congress (of the President) might authorize a reduction in sentence for drug offenders currently incarcerated but who were not convicted of an offense carrying a mandatory minimum penalty. Any such reduction would likely be tied to a change in the *Guidelines Manual* that incorporated the Policy Option. We are unable to model any change to the sentencing guidelines from a statutory enactment of the Policy Option, and so have excluded from this analysis any consideration of a change in sentence for drug offenders who were not convicted of an offense carrying a mandatory minimum penalty.

Additional assumptions we have made for this analysis are that the sentence for each offender would be reduced based on the maximum good conduct credit allowed by the Bureau of Prisons, and offenders would serve the lesser of the newly calculated sentence or their life expectancies.

If you have any questions about our analysis, please do not hesitate to contact the Commission. We continue to work to analyze the other policy options that we discussed with you and your colleagues. We will provide our analyses of these options as they are completed.

Sincerely,

Noah D. Bookbinder
Director, Office of Legislative and Public Affairs

Glenn R. Schmitt
Director, Office of Research and Data
Attachments

Table 1. Demographic Characteristics of Drug Offenders Convicted of a Drug Offense Carrying a 5,10. or 20-Year Mandatory Minimum Penalty Eligible for 2, 5, and 10-Year Mandatory Minimums

DEMOGRAPHICS Race/Ethnicity			
	Whitt:	14,773	19.0%
	Black	27,512	35.3%
	Hispanic	34,096	43.7%
	Other	1,590	2.0%
	Total	**77,971**	**100.0%**
Citizenship			
	U.S. Citizen	57,783	74.1%
	Non-Citizen	20,242	25.9%
	Total	**78,025**	**100.0%**
Gender			
	Male	72,257	92.5%
	Female	5,845	7.5%
	Total	**78,102**	**100.0%**
Average Age			
	35 (as of October I, 2014)		

[1] The analysis involves n total of 78,106 cases in which the offender was identified as eligible to seek a sentence reduction if the drug mandatory minimum changes were made retroactive. Cases missing information for any specific analysis are excluded from that analysis.

Total percentages may not add to exactly 100% due to rounding.

Source: U.S. Sentencing Commission, 1992 - 2013 Datafiles, USSCFY92 - USSCFY13 and projected 2014 Datafile.

Table 2. Estimated Projected Year of Release for Drug Offenders Potentially Eligible for Mandatory Minimum Sentence Reduction

Release Date	If Policy Option Applied Retroactivly N	CURRENT SENTENCE N
immediate	24,601	
within 1 yr	12,515	4,294
within 2 yr	12,191	9,223
within 3 yr	8,546	10,166
within 4 yr	6,404	9,256
within 5 yr	4,363	7,852
within 6 yr +	9,482	37,311

[1] Of the 78,106 offenders who appear to be eligible for relief if the Policy Option was applied retroactivly, Commission records contained sufficient information to perform this a analysis for 78,102 offenders.

Source: U.S. Sentencing Commission, 1992 - 2012 Datafiles,USSCFY92 - USSCFY13 and projecte.

Table 3. Guideline Sentencing Characteristics and Criminal History of Drug Offenders Potentially Eligible for Mandatory Minimum Sentence Reduction

CHARACTERISTICS		
Average Base Offense Level	**32**	
Weapon Specific Offense Characteristic	14,729	18.9%
Firearms Mandatory Minimum Applied	7,433	9.5%
Safety Valve §5C1.2	14,042	18.1%
Aggravating Role §3B1.1	11,549	14.8%
Mitigating Role §3B1.2	6,675	8.6%
Obstruction Adjustment §3C1.1	3,660	4.7%
Career Offender Status §4B1.1	10,982	14.1%
Criminal History Category		
I	28,925	37.0%
II	9,652	12.4%
Ill	12,995	16.6%
IV	6,853	8.8%
v	4,079	5.2%
VI	15,602	20.0%
Total	**78,106**	**100%**

[1] The analysis involves a total of 78,106 cases in which the offender was identified as eligible to seek a sentence reduction if the drug mandatory minimum changes were made retroactive. Cases missing information for any specific analysis are excluded from that analysis.

[2] The average base offense level was excluded from this analysis due to missing guideline relevant statutory information from the new sentence.

Total percentages may not add to exactly 100% due to rounding.

Source: U.S. Sentencing Commission, 1992-2012 Datafiles, USSCFY92 - USSCFY13 and projected 2014 Datafile.

2. USSC analysis of option 2: Retroactively apply the Fair Sentencing Act (FSA) of 2010 reductions in drug mandatory minimum penalties to offenders currently incarcerated for crack cocaine-related offenses.

This option would retroactively apply to eligible incarcerated offenders the reductions in mandatory minimum penalties for crack cocaine-related offenses that are provisions of the Fair Sentencing Act of 2010, Pub. 1. No. 111-220, 124 Stat. 2372, which did not apply to offenders already sentenced under the original penalty guidelines.

UNITED STATES SENTENCING COMMISSION
ONE COLUMBUS CIRCLE, N.E.
SUITE 2-500, SOUTH LOBBY
WASHINGTON, D.C. 20002-8002
(202) 502-4500
FAX (202) 502-4699

February 20, 2014

Jonathan R. Tumin
Senior Analyst
U.S. Government Accountability Office
441 G St., NW
Washington, DC 20548

Dear Mr. Tumin:

The Government Accountability Office has asked the U.S. Sentencing Commission to assist it in connection with its engagement (number 441173). We understand that through this engagement the GAO is examining ways in which the operating costs of the Federal Bureau of Prisons (BoP) can be reduced. As we have previously discussed with you and your colleagues, the Commission has agreed to provide to the GAO the results of our analyses of several policy options which could reduce the overall size of the prison population that the BoP administers. Specifically, our analyses of these policy options will consider the effect on the federal prison population if the policies were implemented in such a way that the options would apply to inmates currently incarcerated in the BoP system.

In this memorandum, we provide to you the first of these estimates. Here we provide our estimate of the impact on the federal prison population if the provisions of the Fair Sentencing Act of 2010[83] (the "FSA") were authorized to apply to persons currently incarcerated and sentenced before the enactment of that law. As we discuss more fully below, we estimate that 8,829 offenders who were incarcerated on January 1, 2014 would be eligible for a sentence reduction if the FSA were applied retroactively beginning on that date. If the courts were to reduce the sentence of each eligible offender in accordance with the FSA and the current *Guidelines Manual,* the average reduction in sentence for these offenders would be 53 months (28.8 percent). The estimated total savings to the BoP would be 37,400 bed years.

I. Statutory Changes in the FSA and the Conforming Guideline Amendment

A. Statutory Changes in the FSA

The FSA changed the quantities of crack cocaine that trigger the five- and ten year statutory mandatory minimum penalties. As a consequence, first-time trafficking offenses involving less than 28 grams of crack cocaine are subject to a statutory penalty range of zero to 20 years of imprisonment. First-time trafficking offenses involving between 28 and 280 grams of crack cocaine are subject to a statutory penalty range of five to 40 years of imprisonment?[84] A first-time trafficking offense involving 280 or more grams of crack cocaine is subject to a statutory penalty range of 10 years to life imprisonment.[85] The FSA did not make any of the statutory changes retroactive. Therefore, offenders sentenced before the effective date of the FSA[86] continue to be subject to the mandatory minimum penalties in effect on the date of sentencing.[87]

B. Temporary and Permanent Amendments to the Guidelines Manual in Response to the FSA

On October 15, 2010, the Commission promulgated a temporary, emergency amendment to the guidelines that implemented the emergency directive in section 8 of the FSA.[88] On April 6, 2011, the Commission re-promulgated the temporary amendment as a permanent multipart amendment, which became effective on November 1, 2011.[89] (In this memorandum, the several modifications to the drug guidelines promulgated in response to the FSA are referred to collectively as the "FSA Guideline Amendment.")

Part A of the FSA Guideline Amendment modified the base offense level for various quantities of crack cocaine assigned by the Drug Quantity Table.[90] Part B of the FSA Guideline Amendment added both new mitigating and aggravating provisions to USSG §2D1.1 for offenses involving drugs, regardless of drug type. Part C of the FSA Guideline Amendment eliminated a provision in the guidelines under which an offender who possessed more than 5 grams of crack cocaine was sentenced under the drug trafficking guideline.

C. Retroactive Application of the FSA Guideline Amendment

The Commission voted to authorize courts to retroactively apply Parts A and C of the FSA Guideline Amendment to offenders currently incarcerated.[91] Pursuant to 18 U.S.C. § 3582(c)(2), courts were then authorized to reduce the sentences of those offenders consistent with the amended sentencing guidelines. To date, the courts have reduced the sentences of more than 7,500 offenders pursuant to retroactive application of the FSA Guideline Amendment.[92] In more than 5,000 other cases, the courts have denied relief to offenders seeking a reduction in sentence under the FSA Guideline Amendment. The courts found that the offender was not eligible for any sentence reduction in more than 3,700 of those cases. For example, in 1,458 cases, the court found that the offender was ineligible because the applicable mandatory minimum penalty controlled the sentence and prevented the court from reducing the sentence.

In more than 1,045 other cases, the offender was found ineligible because the Career Offender guideline (USSG §4B1.1), and not the drug trafficking guideline (USSG §2D1.1), determined the guideline range at sentencing. As discussed above, the mandatory minimum penalties applicable to offenders sentenced prior to the FSA were unchanged by the act. The Career Offender guideline is linked to statutory maximum penalties which, in drug cases, are also linked to statutory mandatory minimum penalties. Because neither the FSA nor the FSA Guideline Amendments had the effect of lowering the Career Offender guideline, the provisions of 18 U.S.C. § 3582(c)(2) allowing courts to reduce the sentences of incarcerated offenders when their sentencing guideline is lowered do not apply to offenders whose guideline range is determined under that provision.

Finally, in some additional cases, the offender received only a partial reduction in sentence under the FSA Guideline Amendment. This was because a mandatory minimum penalty prevented the court from lowering the sentence to a point within the amended guideline range.

II. Retroactive Application of the FSA

One of the policy options that we have agreed to examine on behalf of the GAO is the impact of applying the provisions of the FSA retroactively to offenders in the custody of the BoP. We estimate that there are 8,829 offenders incarcerated on January 1, 2014 who would be eligible for a reduction in their current sentence if the FSA were to be retroactively applied. If the courts were to grant each of these offenders the full reduction in their sentence in accord with the *Guideline Manual,* we estimate that the total savings to the BoP would be 37,400 bed years.[93]

Table GAO-l provides an estimate of the number of offenders who would be released each year if the FSA were fully retroactive compared to the number of offenders who will be released each year pursuant to their current sentence. As can be seen on this table, if the FSA were fully retroactive on January 1, 2014, more than 3,000 offenders would be released in 2014 in addition to those who would be released if the current sentences of these offenders remains unchanged.

Of the 8,829 offenders who appear eligible for retroactive application of the FSA, Commission records contained sufficient information to perform an analysis of the amount of reduction in sentence for 8,468 offenders. For those 8,468 offenders, the current average sentence is 184 months. If the courts were to grant the full reduction possible in each case in accordance with the *Guidelines Manual,* the projected new average sentence for these offenders would be 131 months, a reduction of 53 months (or 28.8 percent). Based on this reduction, the estimated total savings to the BoP from the retroactive application of the FSA would be 37,400 bed years. This savings would not be realized in any single year but is the cumulative savings realized over several years.

III. How We Conducted This Analysis

A. Methodology

The methodology for this analysis is based on the Commission's Prison Impact Model, which has been in use in some form since the guidelines were first developed. This model is used to estimate the impact of proposed statutory and guideline amendments on newly sentenced offenders and to project the future impact those amendments will have on bed space in the BoP. For this analysis, those offenders who appear to be eligible to receive a reduced sentence were hypothetically "resentenced" with the computer program as if the proposed policy change had been in effect in the year in which they were sentenced. A new release date for each offender also was calculated in order to determine when the offender would be eligible for release if he or she were provided the full reduction in sentence provided by the proposed policy change.

B. Our Assumptions

In performing our analysis, we have been required to make some assumptions (set forth below) concerning the decisions that Congress and the courts would make in determining whether, and to what extent, to reduce the sentences of offenders eligible to receive a modification of sentence pursuant to the FSA if it were retroactively applied. These assumptions may not hold in every case.

Specifically, we have assumed that Congress would authorize the courts by statute to reduce the sentences of offenders in accordance with the *Guidelines Manual* in effect on a specific date and bound only by the mandatory minimum penalties as they were amended by the FSA. We also assumed that the Commission would make no further changes to the *Guidelines Manual* regarding crack cocaine offenses in response to Congress' action, so that the provisions of the 2012 *Guidelines Manual* would apply in these cases.[94] Finally, we assumed that the effective date of any such statutory change would be no earlier than January 1, 2014.

Additional assumptions we have made for this analysis are as follows:

(1) offenders sentenced within the applicable guideline range when they were first sentenced would be sentenced at the same point in the range under the *Guidelines Manual* in effect on January 1, 2014;

(2) offenders sentenced outside the applicable guideline range when they were first sentenced would be sentenced to a new position outside the guideline range under the *Guidelines Manual* in effect on January I, 2014 that is the same proportional distance above or below the amended guideline range as their original sentence was from the guideline range in effect at the original sentencing;

(3) offenders for whom the new estimated sentence is below the applicable mandatory minimum (all cases in this analysis have five grams triggering a five-year mandatory minimum or 50 grams triggering a 10-year mandatory minimum), and where no safety valve or substantial assistance reduction was applied when the offender was originally sentenced, would be sentenced at the new applicable mandatory minimum;

(4) offenders classified as Career Offenders would be sentenced pursuant to the Career Offender provision of the guidelines in accordance with the statutory maximums as amended by the FSA.
(5) the "mitigating role cap" on the base offense level of the guidelines would be applied, if appropriate, based upon the new base offense level;
(6) offenders originally receiving relief from a mandatory minimum penalty by operation of the safety valve provision would continue to receive relief but, if the applicable statutory minimum is at least five years, the offense level determined after applying Chapters Two (Offense Conduct) and Three (Adjustments) of the guidelines would not be less than level 17 (pursuant to USSG §5C1.2(b));
(7) for offenders with an original combined offense level (after application of Chapters Two and Three) of level 16 or greater but having a new combined offense level below level 16, the applicable reduction for Acceptance of Responsibility would be reduced from three levels to two levels in accordance with that guideline provision;
(8) the sentence for each offender would be reduced based on the maximum good conduct credit allowed by the Bureau of Prisons; and
(9) offenders would serve the lesser of the newly calculated sentence or their life expectancies.

C. Limitation as to Application of New Mitigating Provisions of the FSA

As discussed above, Part B of the FSA Guideline Amendment added both new mitigating and aggravating provisions to USSG §2D1.1 for offenses involving drugs, regardless of drug type. The Commission did not vote to allow those provisions to be applied retroactively. We are unable to assess the extent to which the courts might apply these new mitigating provisions were the FSA to be applied retroactively as those provisions involve the consideration of facts that are not readily available in the sentencing documents provided to the Commission in all cases. To the extent that the courts might consider these provisions in resentencing offenders when applying the FSA retroactively, the sentences for some offenders could be reduced below the point determined in our estimate, which would accelerate the release of those offenders from incarceration.

D. The Offender Population We Studied

In conducting this analysis, the Commission requested and received a datafile from the BoP which identified a total of 135,536 offenders in the BOP's custody at that time who the BoP estimated would still be incarcerated on January 1, 2014 (the proposed retroactivity date we used for this analysis.). These offenders were those sentenced between FY1992 and FY2012 and whose BoP record could be matched with USSC records.[95] Of those, 19,154 offenders were identified as 1) having been sentenced under the drug trafficking guideline,[96] 2) having crack cocaine as one of the drug types involved in the offense, and 3) having sufficient information for analysis by the Commission's prison and sentencing impact model.

The Commission's retroactivity analysis determined that of these 19,154 offenders, 10,325 would not experience a change in their sentence if the FSA were fully retroactive. These offenders were excluded from the analysis. The majority of the offenders (n = 9,741) were excluded because they would not experience the proposed statutory change - either because no statutory mandatory minimum penalty applied in their cases or the offender already was sentenced below the FSA mandatory minimum thresholds.[97] Another 362 offenders were sentenced under the Career Offender provision and, despite a change to their drug statutory minimum penalty, their guideline range under the Career Offender provision did not change. In another 191 cases, the current sentence is greater than both the guideline minimum and the FSA statutory minimum, therefore no change in their sentence would result. A small number of offenders (n=30) were excluded because their guideline range was determined under the Armed Career Criminal provision, which would be unaffected by the retroactive application of the FSA. Lastly, one offender had a base offense level of 38, the top of the Drug Quantity Table, and the quantity of drugs involved in that case continued to place the offender at that level, so therefore no change in his or her guideline range would occur.

After these offenders were excluded, there remained 8,829 offenders who were projected to be incarcerated on January I, 2014 and who appeared eligible to seek a reduced sentence if the provisions of the FSA were to be made retroactive as described above.

If you have any questions about our analysis please do not hesitate to contact the Commission. We continue to work to analyze the other policy options that we discussed with you and your colleagues. We will provide our analyses of these options as they are completed.

Sincerely,

Noah D. Bookbinder
Director, Office of Legislative and Public Affairs

Glenn R. Schmitt
Director, Office of Research and Data
Attachment

Table GAO-1. Estimated Projected Year of Release for Crack Cocaine Offenders Potentially Eligible for FSA Retroactivity[1]

	IF FSA RETROACTIVITY GRANTED	CURRENT SENTENCE
Release Date	**N**	**N**
within 1 yr	3,695	682
within 2 yr	999	847
within 3 yr	806	951
within 4 yr	682	996
within 5 yr	503	958
within 6 ya· +	1,783	4,034

[1] Of the 8,829 offenders who appear to be eligible for relief if the Fair Sentencing Act of 2010 were retroactive, Commission records contained sufficient information to perform this analysis for 8,468 offenders.

Source: U.S. Sentencing Commission, 1992-2012 Data files, USSCFY92- USSCFYI2.

3. USSC table with data for impact of option 3: Instruct U.S. Attorneys to decline to charge certain defendants in certain types of drug cases in such a manner as to trigger mandatory minimum sentences.

This option has been implemented as part of the August 2013 direction issued by the Attorney General instructing prosecutors in cases involving the applicability of drug law mandatory minimum sentences based on drug type and quantity to decline to charge the quantity necessary to trigger a mandatory minimum sentence if the defendant meets particular criteria.

For option 3, the USSC provided a table composed of six subtables that show the USSC's analysis of the estimated impact of the changes discussed in option 3. According to the USSC, the total number of offenders estimated to be affected annually by option 3 can be found in line 1, column 2, of the first table (i.e., 620). For the first 5 years' estimated impact, we multiplied 620 by 5. According to the USSC, the bed years saved over the first 5 years of implementation can be found by adding the numbers shown in the first line of the third table, which total 788.

Comparison of Prison Impact Analysis – Safety Valve Expansion with Statutory Trumps FY2012 Cases

Change in Sentences Imposed							
	Total Cases[1]	Number Affected[2]	Percent Affected	Current Average Sentence for Affected Cases	New Average Sentence for Affected Cases	Number of Months Change	Percent Change
2 pts	841	620	73.7	46	37	-9	-19.6
2-3 pts	2,242	1,636	73.0	49	40	-9	-18.4

Change in Incarceration Levels Change in total years of incarceration for offenders sentenced in one fiscal year[3]								
	1st Year	2nd Year	3rd Year	4th Year	5th Year	10th Year	15th Year	Total[4]
2 pts	-51	-46	-64	-47	-64	-6	-1	-372
2-3 pts	-115	-119	-167	-142	-181	-34	-3	-1,065

Change in Total BOP Population in Future Years[5]					
	1st Year After Effective Date	2nd Year After Effective Date	3rd Year After Effective Date	4th Year After Effective Date	5th Year After Effective Date
2 pts	-51	-97	-161	-208	-271
2-3 pts	-115	-234	-401	-543	-724

[1]**Total Cases** are those with a particular sentencing factor being analyzed.

[2]**Affected Cases** are those in which the sentence is estimated to change as a result of the sentencing factor being analyzed. Not all cases will change as a result of the application of the sentencing factor being analyzed.

[3]This table represents the number of prison beds saved each year by a cohort of offenders sentenced in a single year.

[4]This is the total number of prison beds that will be saved when all offenders who were sentenced in the same year are ultimately released from prison.

[5]This is the annual number of prison beds saved as ongoing cohorts of offenders enter the Bureau of Prisons who have been sentenced under the changed guideline.

Source: U.S. Sentencing Commission Prison and Sentencing Impact Assessment Model, FY2012 datafile.

Comparison of Prison Impact Analysis – Safety Valve Expansion without Statutory Trumps FY2012 Cases

Change in Sentences Imposed							
	Total Cases[1]	Number Affected[2]	Percent Affected	Current Average Sentence for Affected Cases	New Average Sentence for Affected Cases	Number of Months Change	Percent Change
2 pts	841	787	93.6	53	42	-11	-20.8
2-3 pts	2,242	2,090	93.2	56	45	-11	-19.6

Change in Incarceration Levels Change in total years of incarceration for offenders sentenced in one fiscal year[3]								
	1st Year	2nd Year	3rd Year	4th Year	5th Year	10th Year	15th Year	Total[4]
2 pts	-52	-49	-67	-163	-61	-8	-3	-617
2-3 pts	-116	-126	-173	-447	-170	-36	-12	-1,731

Change in Total BOP Population in Future Years[5]					
	1st Year After Effective Date	2nd Year After Effective Date	3rd Year After Effective Date	4th Year After Effective Date	5th Year After Effective Date
2 pts	-52	-101	-168	-330	-392
2-3 pts	-116	-242	-415	-862	-1,032

[1]**Total Cases** are those with a particular sentencing factor being analyzed.

[2]**Affected Cases** are those in which the sentence is estimated to change as a result of the sentencing factor being analyzed. Not all cases will change as a result of the application of the sentencing factor being analyzed.

[3]This table represents the number of prison beds saved each year by a cohort of offenders sentenced in a single year.

[4]This is the total number of prison beds that will be saved when all offenders who were sentenced in the same year are ultimately released from prison. [5]This is the annual number of prison beds saved as ongoing cohorts of offenders enter the Bureau of Prisons who have been sentenced under the changed guideline.

Source: U.S. Sentencing Commission Prison and Sentencing Impact Assessment Model, FY2012 datafile.

4. USSC table with data for impact of option 4: Amend USSC sentencing guidelines for future drug offenders, reducing them two levels below current guidelines.

This option reduces the potential sentences for all future drug offenders by two levels below current guidelines, resulting in a roughly 18 percent reduction of sentence length below current lengths. It was approved by the USSC and forwarded to Congress on April 30, 2014; it will apply to future eligible drug offenders effective November 1, 2014, in connection with option 5 (see next option) unless amended or rejected by Congress.

For option 4, the USSC provided a table composed of 2 subtables; the overall table is labeled "Table 5" by the USSC and shows the USSC estimate of the changes discussed in option 4. According to the USSC, the number of offenders estimated to be affected annually by the option (17,457) can be found in line 1 of the first table. Some other data in the two subtables were updated as a result of USSC actions that made option 4 retroactive (i.e., option 5), but which also delayed implementation of retroactivity until November 1, 2015, unless amended or rejected by Congress.

Table 5. Estimated Effect on Sentencing and Incarceration of Decreasing the Drug Quantity Table by Two Levels FY2012 Cases

Change in Sentences Imposed						
Total Cases[1]	**Number Affected[2]**	**Percent Affected**	**Current Average Sentence for Affected Cases**	**New Average Sentence for Affected Cases**	**Number of Months Change**	**Percent Change**
24,968	17,457	69.9	62	51	-11	-17.7

Change in Sentences Served							
Change in years of incarceration served for offenders sentenced in a single fiscal year[3]							
1st Year	**2nd Year**	**3rd Year**	**4th Year**	**5th Year**	**10th Year**	**15th Year**	**Total[4]**
-894	-1,083	-1,667	-1,281	-1,625	-634	-256	-13,938

	Change in total BOP Population in Future Years[5]			
1st Year After Effective Date	**2nd Year After Effective Date**	**3rd Year After Effective Date**	**4th Year After Effective Date**	**5th Year After Effective Date**
-894	-1,977	-3,644	-4,925	-6,550

[1] Total Cases are those with a particular sentencing factor being analyzed.

[2] Affected Cases are those in which the sentence is estimated to change as a result of the sentencing factor being analyzed. Not all cases will change as a result of the application of the sentencing factor being analyzed.

[3] This table represents the number of prison beds saved each year by a cohort of offenders sentenced in a single year.

[4] This is the total number of prison beds that will be saved when all offenders who were sentenced in the same year are ultimately released from prison.

[5] This is the annual number of prison beds saved as ongoing cohorts of offenders enter the Bureau of Prisons who have been sentenced under the changed guideline.

Source: U.S. Sentencing Commission Prison and Sentencing Impact Assessment Model, FY2012 datafile.

5. USSC analysis of option 5: Apply the amendments to sentencing guidelines in option 4 also to incarcerated drug offenders—that is, to both new drug offenders and retroactively to incarcerated drug offenders.

Under this option, the provisions of option 4 apply to both new drug offenders and also retroactively to eligible incarcerated drug offenders. It reduces the sentences for all future and currently incarcerated drug offenders by two levels below current USSC guidelines, resulting in a roughly 19 percent reduction below current lengths. It was approved by the USSC in July 2014 as an amendment to option 4; as such, it corresponds to the April 2014 USSC decision and does not require separate congressional action. Unless Congress acts to modify or disapprove the corresponding April 30 amendment, beginning November 1, 2014, eligible incarcerated offenders can ask courts to reduce their sentences. Incarcerated offenders whose requests are granted by the courts may not be released earlier than November 1, 2015.

This analysis (which also includes information relevant to option 4, to which it is closely related) was posted to the USSC website on July 25, 2014. (http://www.ussc.gov/research-and-publications/retroactivity-analyses-and-data-reports/retroactivity-analyses-and-data-reports)

***

UNITED STATES SENTENCING COMMISSION
ONE COLUMBUS CIRCLE, NE
SUITE 2-500, SOUTH LOBBY
WASHINGTON, DC 20002-8002
(202) 502-4500
FAX (202) 502-4699

July 25, 2014

MEMORANDUM

TO: Chair Saris
Commissioners
Kenneth Cohen

FROM: Office of Research and Data

SUBJECT: Summary of Key Data Regarding Retroactive Application of the 2014 Drug Guidelines Amendment

I. Introduction

On April30, 2014, the United States Sentencing Commission submitted to Congress an amendment to the federal sentencing guidelines that would revise the guidelines applicable to drug trafficking offenses by changing how the base offense levels in the drug quantity tables in sections 2D1.1 and 2D1.11 of the *Guidelines Manual*[98] incorporate the statutory mandatory minimum penalties for drug trafficking offenses (Amendment 782).[99] Specifically, the amendment would reduce by two levels the offense levels assigned to the quantities that trigger the statutory mandatory minimum penalties, resulting in corresponding guideline ranges that include the mandatory minimum penalties, and make confirming changes to section 2D2.11. On July 18, the Commission voted to give retroactive effect to Amendment 782 beginning on the effective date of the amendment, which will be November 1, 2014, unless Congress acts to modify or disapprove the amendment.

As part of the Commission's decision to retroactively apply Amendment 782, it required that no offender may be released pursuant to the retroactive application of the amendment until November 1, 2015 or later. This memorandum provides information concerning the effect of this limitation.

II. Further Analyses of the Impact of Retroactive Application of the 2014 Drug Guidelines Amendment

A. Summary of Data on the Eligible Offenders

ORD previously estimated that 51,141 offenders sentenced between October 1, 1991 and October 31, 2014,[100] would be eligible to seek a reduction in their current sentence if the Commission were to make the 2014 drug guidelines amendment retroactive.[101] Of this group, there are 46,376 offenders who would not be released under their current sentence until on or after November 1, 2015, and so could benefit from the Commission's decision to retroactively apply Amendment 782.

The current average sentence for the 46,376 offenders who could benefit under retroactive application of the amendment is 133 months. Applying the amendment retroactively to these offenders the new average sentence would be 108 months. This is a difference of 25 months, which represents an 18.8 percent reduction in the sentence. The number of bed years saved by this reduction is 79,740 bed years, which would be realized by the Bureau of Prisons over a period of years, of course.

The most common drug types involved in these cases are methamphetamine (28.8%), powder cocaine (27.8%), crack cocaine (19.3%), marijuana (11.6%), heroin (7.6%), and other drugs (5.0%). Attached to this memorandum is a summary of selected offender characteristics about these offenders as well as information about their criminal history.

B. Summary of Data on the Projected Release Dates of the Eligible Offenders

We estimate that on November 1, 2015 there would be 7,953 offenders eligible for immediate release. Another 8,550 offenders would be released during the year that begins on November 1, 2015 and ends on October 31, 2016. That is, a total of 16,503 offenders will be released during the first year in which offenders may be released pursuant to retroactive application of the amendment. If the Commission had not authorized the amendment to be applied retroactively, we estimate that 7,609 offenders would still have been released during that year, as their current terms of incarceration expired. Attached to this memorandum is a table that provides additional information concerning the release years of these offenders and the districts in which they were sentenced.

Selected Characteristics of Eligible Offenders Retroactive Application of Amendment 782 with Release on or after November 1, 2015 (FY1992 through FY2015)

Race/Ethnicity		
White	10,734	23.2%
Black	14,427	31.2%
Hispanic	19,958	43.1%
Other	1,171	2.5%
Total	**46,290**	**100.0%**
Citizenship		
U.S. Citizen	34,928	75.4%
Non-Citizen	11,411	24.6%
Total	**46,339**	**100.0%**
Gender		
Male	42,759	92.2%
Female	3,615	7.8%
Total	**46,374**	**100.0%**
Criminal History Category		
I	17,580	37.9%
II	6,320	13.6%
III	9,232	19.9%
IV	5,473	11.8%
V	3,417	7.4%
VI	4,354	9.4%
Total	**46,376**	**100.0%**
Projected Year of Release	**Retroactive***	**If Not Retroactive**
November 1, 2015	7,953	--
within 1 yr	8,550	7,609
within 2 yr	6,938	7,461
within 3 yr	5,473	6,207
within 4 yr	4,177	5,291
within 5 yr	2,909	3,923
more than 5 yr	9,350	14,859
Total	**45,350**	**45,350**

The analysis involves a total of 46,376 cases, however, cases missing information for any specific analysis are excluded from that analysis. Total percentages may not add to exactly 100% due to rounding.

* A total of 16,503 offenders are estimated to be eligible for release during the first year in which offenders may be released under retroactive application of the amendment. This is 8,894 more than will be released upon expiration of their current sentence.

Source: U.S. Sentencing Commission, 1992 - 2005 Datafiles, USSCFY92- USSCFY13.

Possible Release Timing for Retroactive Eligible Offenders by District (FY1992 through FY2015)

CIRCUIT	Eligible for Immediate Release 11/01/15		Eligible for Release in Year One*		Eligible for Release in Year Two		Eligible for Release in Year Three		Eligible for Release in Year Four		Eligible for Release in Year Five		Eligible for Release in Six or More Years		TOTAL
District	N	%	N	%	N	%	N	%	N	%	N	%	N	%	N
TOTAL	**7,953**	**17.5**	**8,550**	**18.9**	**6,938**	**15.3**	**5,473**	**12.1**	**4,177**	**9.2**	**2,909**	**6.4**	**9,350**	**20.6**	**45,350**
D.C. CIRCUIT	25	12.7	37	18.8	38	19.3	27	13.7	12	6.1	8	4.1	50	25.4	197
District of Columbia	25	12.7	37	18.8	38	19.3	27	13.7	12	6.1	8	4.1	50	25.4	197
FIRST CIRCUIT	231	10.8	412	19.3	387	18.1	342	16.0	256	12.0	147	6.9	364	17.0	2,139
Maine	30	18.1	45	27.1	31	18.7	22	13.3	19	11.4	7	4.2	12	7.2	166
Massachusetts	27	14.9	37	20.4	33	18.2	19	10.5	16	8.8	9	5.0	40	22.1	181
New Hampshire	11	17.7	21	33.9	14	22.6	5	8.1	1	1.6	3	4.8	7	11.3	62
Puerto Rico	149	9.1	295	17.9	290	17.6	280	17.0	214	13.0	122	7.4	294	17.9	1,644
Rhode Island	14	16.3	14	16.3	19	22.1	16	18.6	6	7.0	6	7.0	11	12.8	86
SECOND CIRCUIT	344	17.2	380	19.0	328	16.4	264	13.2	196	9.8	118	5.9	371	18.5	2,001
Connecticut	45	16.7	67	24.8	51	18.9	31	11.5	32	11.9	18	6.7	26	9.6	270
New York															
Eastern	51	17.4	49	16.7	66	22.5	43	14.7	21	7.2	14	4.8	49	16.7	293
Northern	48	17.9	58	21.6	53	19.8	39	14.6	29	10.8	10	3.7	31	11.6	268
Southern	136	18.0	132	17.4	104	13.7	101	13.3	65	8.6	48	6.3	171	22.6	757
Western	55	16.3	52	15.4	43	12.8	43	12.8	37	11.0	22	6.5	85	25.2	337
Vermont	9	11.8	22	28.9	11	14.5	7	9.2	12	15.8	6	7.9	9	11.8	76
THIRD CIRCUIT	207	15.8	267	20.4	198	15.1	160	12.2	120	9.2	74	5.6	284	21.7	1,310
Delaware	9	22.5	9	22.5	8	20.0	2	5.0	1	2.5	0	0.0	11	27.5	40
New Jersey	54	17.1	82	26.0	58	18.4	38	12.1	26	8.3	16	5.1	41	13.0	315
Pennsylvania															
Eastern	55	11.7	73	15.5	64	13.6	64	13.6	46	9.8	33	7.0	135	28.7	470
Middle	65	23.1	59	21.0	40	14.2	36	12.8	31	11.0	7	2.5	43	15.3	281
Western	19	11.1	38	22.2	23	13.5	15	8.8	12	7.0	15	8.8	49	28.7	171
Virgin Islands	5	15.2	6	18.2	5	15.2	5	15.2	4	12.1	3	9.1	5	15.2	33

FOURTH CIRCUIT	1,028	17.0	954	15.8	812	13.5	683	11.3	559	9.3	454	7.5	1,545	25.6	6,035
Maryland	85	15.3	102	18.3	102	18.3	80	14.4	49	8.8	37	6.6	102	18.3	557
North Carolina															
Eastern	140	12.6	147	13.2	143	12.8	122	10.9	112	10.0	111	10.0	340	30.5	1,115
Middle	86	20.1	89	20.8	50	11.7	44	10.3	36	8.4	29	6.8	93	21.8	427
Western	150	23.1	118	18.2	82	12.6	60	9.2	63	9.7	40	6.2	137	21.1	650
South Carolina	133	14.1	117	12.4	116	12.3	118	12.5	109	11.6	85	9.0	264	28.0	942
Virginia															
Eastern	170	14.9	127	11.1	145	12.7	121	10.6	98	8.6	85	7.4	396	34.7	1,142
Western	134	20.8	100	15.6	83	12.9	73	11.4	49	7.6	44	6.8	160	24.9	643
West Virginia															
Northern	88	26.4	87	26.1	51	15.3	37	11.1	29	8.7	13	3.9	28	8.4	333
Southern	42	18.6	67	29.6	40	17.7	28	12.4	14	6.2	10	4.4	25	11.1	226

* For example, in the District of Columbia, 62 offenders are eligible for release between November 1, 2015 and October 31, 2016.

FIFTH CIRCUIT	1,853	18.3	2,023	20.0	1,562	15.4	1,180	11.6	901	8.9	608	6.0	2,013	19.9	10,140
Louisiana															
Eastern	46	14.8	56	18.0	46	14.8	38	12.2	31	10.0	28	9.0	66	21.2	311
Middle	22	19.3	24	21.1	20	17.5	12	10.5	8	7.0	6	5.3	22	19.3	114
Western	57	21.3	35	13.1	49	18.4	29	10.9	19	7.1	14	5.2	64	24.0	267
Mississippi															
Northern	34	21.4	33	20.8	23	14.5	22	13.8	14	8.8	7	4.4	26	16.4	159
Southern	46	13.8	52	15.6	52	15.6	44	13.2	24	7.2	24	7.2	92	27.5	334
Texas															
Eastern	210	14.8	209	14.8	203	14.3	183	12.9	142	10.0	101	7.1	367	25.9	1,415
Northern	220	16.1	179	13.1	183	13.4	150	11.0	124	9.1	109	8.0	403	29.5	1,368
Southern	559	19.5	680	23.7	462	16.1	334	11.6	255	8.9	145	5.1	432	15.1	2,867
Western	659	19.9	755	22.8	524	15.9	368	11.1	284	8.6	174	5.3	541	16.4	3,305
SIXTH CIRCUIT	739	17.9	913	22.1	709	17.1	514	12.4	362	8.7	265	6.4	637	15.4	4,139
Kentucky															
Eastern	92	16.8	123	22.5	116	21.2	64	11.7	48	8.8	30	5.5	73	13.4	546
Western	49	19.9	61	24.8	37	15.0	34	13.8	23	9.3	12	4.9	30	12.2	246
Michigan															
Eastern	73	19.3	77	20.3	52	13.7	57	15.0	32	8.4	16	4.2	72	19.0	379
Western	55	15.9	61	17.6	48	13.8	39	11.2	27	7.8	30	8.6	87	25.1	347

(Continued)

Ohio															
Northern	95	18.6	131	25.6	90	17.6	63	12.3	45	8.8	29	5.7	59	11.5	512
Southern	87	20.3	101	23.5	76	17.7	57	13.3	36	8.4	27	6.3	45	10.5	429
Tennessee															
Eastern	179	16.2	231	20.9	203	18.4	131	11.9	104	9.4	88	8.0	168	15.2	1,104
Middle	32	21.2	30	19.9	21	13.9	23	15.2	17	11.3	6	4.0	22	14.6	151
Western	77	18.1	98	23.1	66	15.5	46	10.8	30	7.1	27	6.4	81	19.1	425
SEVENTH CIRCUIT	455	16.7	437	16.0	389	14.3	292	10.7	252	9.3	210	7.7	689	25.3	2,724
Illinois															
Central	79	19.4	51	12.5	38	9.3	32	7.9	30	7.4	29	7.1	148	36.4	407
Northern	123	18.2	93	13.7	101	14.9	75	11.1	59	8.7	55	8.1	171	25.3	677
Southern	51	10.6	63	13.1	48	10.0	58	12.0	77	16.0	58	12.0	127	26.3	482
Indiana															
Northern	56	17.0	73	22.2	68	20.7	28	8.5	21	6.4	20	6.1	63	19.1	329
Southern	63	14.7	53	12.4	72	16.8	56	13.1	35	8.2	23	5.4	126	29.4	428
Wisconsin															
Eastern	45	17.9	76	30.2	48	19.0	30	11.9	10	4.0	16	6.3	27	10.7	252
Western	38	25.5	28	18.8	14	9.4	13	8.7	20	13.4	9	6.0	27	18.1	149
EIGHTH CIRCUIT	742	17.5	739	17.5	628	14.8	501	11.8	401	9.5	285	6.7	933	22.1	4,229
Arkansas															
Eastern	51	15.5	75	22.7	45	13.6	45	13.6	42	12.7	21	6.4	51	15.5	330
Western	45	17.4	44	17.0	47	18.1	42	16.2	21	8.1	19	7.3	41	15.8	259
Iowa															
Northern	123	19.8	80	12.9	74	11.9	65	10.5	80	12.9	47	7.6	152	24.5	621
Southern	82	15.0	85	15.6	78	14.3	63	11.6	41	7.5	38	7.0	158	29.0	545
Minnesota	75	24.1	55	17.7	39	12.5	36	11.6	23	7.4	22	7.1	61	19.6	311
Missouri															
Eastern	130	23.4	123	22.1	96	17.3	53	9.5	42	7.6	24	4.3	88	15.8	556
Western	89	16.4	88	16.2	86	15.8	70	12.9	47	8.7	43	7.9	120	22.1	543
Nebraska	91	12.6	127	17.6	113	15.7	93	12.9	73	10.1	47	6.5	176	24.4	720
North Dakota	30	14.2	38	18.0	32	15.2	21	10.0	17	8.1	12	5.7	61	28.9	211
South Dakota	26	19.5	24	18.0	18	13.5	13	9.8	15	11.3	12	9.0	25	18.8	133

NINTH CIRCUIT	889	17.2	1,153	22.3	873	16.9	667	12.9	465	9.0	273	5.3	849	16.4	5,169
Alaska	36	19.9	34	18.8	27	14.9	24	13.3	19	10.5	11	6.1	30	16.6	181
Arizona	172	25.3	223	32.7	111	16.3	59	8.7	33	4.8	14	2.1	69	10.1	681
California															
Central	114	15.7	134	18.5	103	14.2	88	12.2	72	9.9	44	6.1	169	23.3	724
Eastern	92	13.4	132	19.2	124	18.1	98	14.3	82	12.0	44	6.4	114	16.6	686
Northern	58	20.1	52	18.0	49	17.0	37	12.8	28	9.7	20	6.9	45	15.6	289
Southern	77	11.2	176	25.7	135	19.7	128	18.7	68	9.9	33	4.8	69	10.1	686
Guam	6	16.2	9	24.3	5	13.5	5	13.5	1	2.7	1	2.7	10	27.0	37
Hawaii	55	19.7	54	19.4	37	13.3	29	10.4	28	10.0	15	5.4	61	21.9	279
Idaho	48	16.6	60	20.8	43	14.9	37	12.8	23	8.0	10	3.5	68	23.5	289
Montana	49	13.2	65	17.5	60	16.1	50	13.4	34	9.1	19	5.1	95	25.5	372
Nevada	55	18.9	56	19.2	59	20.3	36	12.4	17	5.8	18	6.2	50	17.2	291
Northern Mariana Islands	0	0.0	3	50.0	0	0.0	0	0.0	2	33.3	1	16.7	0	0.0	6
Oregon	40	18.9	50	23.6	43	20.3	28	13.2	13	6.1	14	6.6	24	11.3	212
Washington															
Eastern	39	19.1	41	20.1	35	17.2	23	11.3	24	11.8	17	8.3	25	12.3	204
Western	48	20.7	64	27.6	42	18.1	25	10.8	21	9.1	12	5.2	20	8.6	232
TENTH CIRCUIT	419	18.5	428	18.9	322	14.2	263	11.6	186	8.2	151	6.7	492	21.8	2,261
Colorado	37	14.6	48	19.0	46	18.2	33	13.0	18	7.1	17	6.7	54	21.3	253
Kansas	84	13.7	104	17.0	81	13.2	76	12.4	64	10.4	46	7.5	158	25.8	613
New Mexico	89	23.3	92	24.1	61	16.0	39	10.2	21	5.5	23	6.0	57	14.9	382
Oklahoma															
Eastern	21	19.3	20	18.3	8	7.3	14	12.8	14	12.8	5	4.6	27	24.8	109
Northern	24	16.7	31	21.5	21	14.6	22	15.3	9	6.3	9	6.3	28	19.4	144
Western	51	22.3	40	17.5	29	12.7	23	10.0	15	6.6	16	7.0	55	24.0	229
Utah	72	23.3	64	20.7	53	17.2	39	12.6	23	7.4	16	5.2	42	13.6	309
Wyoming	41	18.5	29	13.1	23	10.4	17	7.7	22	9.9	19	8.6	71	32.0	222
ELEVENTH CIRCUIT	1,021	20.4	807	16.1	692	13.8	580	11.6	467	9.3	316	6.3	1,123	22.4	5,006
Alabama															
Middle	45	26.3	17	9.9	29	17.0	21	12.3	18	10.5	5	2.9	36	21.1	171
Northern	78	26.9	40	13.8	34	11.7	33	11.4	31	10.7	17	5.9	57	19.7	290
Southern	80	23.3	70	20.3	49	14.2	29	8.4	31	9.0	25	7.3	60	17.4	344

(Continued)

Florida															
Middle	235	17.6	207	15.5	196	14.7	155	11.6	128	9.6	115	8.6	298	22.3	1,334
Northern	97	21.5	48	10.6	43	9.5	45	10.0	37	8.2	28	6.2	153	33.9	451
Southern	249	19.4	234	18.2	198	15.4	152	11.8	115	9.0	69	5.4	266	20.7	1,283
Georgia															
Middle	31	13.1	57	24.2	45	19.1	37	15.7	21	8.9	9	3.8	36	15.3	236
Northern	100	19.3	61	11.8	49	9.5	67	13.0	55	10.6	32	6.2	153	29.6	517
Southern	106	27.9	73	19.2	49	12.9	41	10.8	31	8.2	16	4.2	64	16.8	380

Of the 46,376 offenders identified as eligible for relief under the amendment, Commission records contained sufficient information to perform this analysis for 45,350 offenders.

Estimated release dates are determined using the Commission's prison and sentencing impact model **which applies proposed guideline** changes to **affected offenders and re-sentences these offenders** in a proportional manner. **Under the model, affected offenders:** 1) receive a new offense level; 2) have a new sentencing range **determined (using the ranges** from the **Sentencing Tables**); **3) are resentenced to the same relative** position within **(or outside) the original guideline range** (e.g., an offender currently sentenced at the midpoint of the original **guideline range then** will be sentenced to the **midpoint of the new guideline range**); **and 4)** receive statutory and guideline trumps when applicable. Other assumptions incorporated into the model include: 1) offenders earn the maximum allowable good-time (currently 54 days per year served for imposed sentences greater than one year but not life imprisonment); and 2) offenders serve the lesser of A) the sentence imposed less the maximum allowable good conduct time, or B) their estimated remaining life expectancy, based upon an actuary table incorporating age, race, and sex.

SOURCE: U.S. Sentencing Commission, 1992 - 2013 Datafiles, USSCFY92 - USSCFY13.

6. USSC analysis of option 6: Increase good time credits for good conduct time (GCT).

Under this option, a credit for GCT would be awarded to current offenders using a formula that would result in 54 days' credit per year of sentence, rather than the current BOP interpretation that limits the GCT credit to 47 days per served sentence year. This would result in eligible inmates serving 85 percent of their sentences, rather than the higher 87 percent average resulting from BOP's current interpretation of 18 U.S.C. § 3624(b).

***

UNITED STATES SENTENCING COMMISSION
ONE COLUMBUS CIRCLE, N.E.
SUITE 2-500, SOUTH LOBBY
WASHINGTON, D.C. 20002-8002
(202) 502-4500
FAX (202) 502-4699

June 12, 2014

Jonathan R. Tumin
Senior Analyst
U.S. Government Accountability Office
441 G St., NW
Washington, DC 20548

Dear Mr. Tumin:

The Government Accountability Office has asked the U.S. Sentencing Commission to assist it in connection with its engagement (number 441173). We understand that through this engagement the GAO is examining ways in which the operating costs of the Federal Bureau of Prisons (BoP) can be reduced. As we have previously discussed with you and your colleagues, the Commission has agreed to analyze on GAO's behalf several policy options which could reduce the overall size of the prison population that the BoP administers. Specifically, our analyses of these policy options will consider the effect on the federal prison population if the policies were implemented in such a way that the options would apply to inmates currently incarcerated in the BoP system.

In this memorandum, we provide to you another of these estimates. Here we provide our estimate of the impact on the federal prison population if the current method of determining "good time credit" were to be changed so that offenders could earn up to 54 days per year for good conduct and the BoP would be authorized to apply that expanded credit to all offenders currently incarcerated.

As we discuss more fully below, we estimate that 179,265 offenders who are incarcerated and would still be in prison on October 1, 2014 would be eligible to receive additional good conduct credit under such a policy change. The average increase in good conduct credit for these offenders would be 2.3 months (2.2%). The estimated total savings to the BoP from such a policy change applied retroactively would be 34,359 bed years.

I. The Policy Option We Considered

Under current law, [102] a prisoner who is serving a term of imprison of more than one year may receive credit to the service of a sentence if they behave satisfactorily while incarcerated. Section 3624(b) of title 18 provides:

> A prisoner may receive credit toward the service of the prisoner's sentence, beyond the time served, of up to 54 days at the end of each year of the prisoner's term of imprisonment, beginning at the end of the first year of the term .. .. [C]redit for the last year or portion of a year of the term of imprisonment shall be prorated and credited within the last six weeks of the sentence.[103]

The goal of this provision is, in essence, that offenders serve at least 85 percent of the sentence imposed. The BoP currently uses a formula to determine good conduct credit that results in a maximum of 47 days of credit being given for each year of incarceration served. The difference between the BoP approach and the 54 days described in the statute occurs because of the BOP's interpretation of when the good conduct credit is accrued (following the service of each year) and how the credit is to be applied to the partial year remaining at the end of an offender's sentence.

An alternate method of calculating the good conduct credit could be to simply award 54 days of credit for each year of sentence imposed at the beginning of the sentence. Although the BOP's current interpretation of the statute has been upheld by the Supreme Court,[104] the Department of Justice has proposed to Congress that it amend the governing statute so as to allow the BoP to award up to 54 days per year.[105]

You have asked us to consider a change to the statute whereby the calculation of the good conduct credit is changed to authorize 54 days per year to be awarded (the "Policy Option").

II. What We Found

Applying the Policy Option to offenders in the custody of the BoP, we estimate that there are 179,265 offenders who would be incarcerated on October 1, 2014 who would be eligible for a reduction in the time they have left to serve on the sentence imposed if the Policy Option were to be retroactively applied. If the BoP were to grant each of these offenders the full good time credit of the Policy Option we estimate that the total savings to the BoP would be 34,359 bed years.[106]

Table 1 provides information on some of the demographic characteristic of the offenders eligible for a sentence reduction pursuant to the Policy Option. Table 2 provides an estimate of the number of offenders who would be released each year if the Policy Option was applied retroactively compared to the number of offenders who will be released each year pursuant to their current sentence. As can be seen on this table, if the Policy Option were fully retroactive on October 1, 2014, there would be 819 offenders eligible for immediate release. Within the first year of the effective date of the Policy Option, another 25,918 offenders would be eligible for release. In total, the number of offenders eligible for release under the Policy Option in the first year is 2,878 more than the number who will be released under their current sentence. Table 3 provides information on selected sentencing guideline characteristics and the criminal history category of these offenders.

For the 179,265 offenders who would be eligible to receive additional good conduct credit under the Policy Option, the current average time served is 103.3 months. If the BoP were to award the maximum good time credit under the Policy Option, the projected average time served would be 101.0 months, a reduction of 2.3 months (or 2.2%). Based on this reduction, the estimated total savings to the BoP from the retroactive application of the Policy Option would be 34,359 bed years. This savings would not be realized in any single year but is the cumulative savings realized over several years.

III. How We Conducted This Analysis

A. Methodology

The methodology for this analysis is based on the Commission's Prison Impact Model, which has been in use in some form since the guidelines were first developed. This model is used to estimate the impact of proposed statutory and guideline amendments on newly sentenced offenders and to project the future impact those amendments will have on bed space in the BoP. For this analysis, those offenders who appear to be eligible to receive a reduced sentence were hypothetically "resentenced" with the computer program as if the proposed policy change had been in effect in the year in which they were sentenced. A new release date for each offender also was calculated in order to determine when the offender would be eligible for release if he or she were provided the full reduction in sentence provided by the proposed policy change.

B. The Offender Population We Studied

The Bureau of Prisons provided the Commission with a datafile of inmates who were in the custody of the BoP on Jan 25, 2014. That file contained approximately 189,000 offenders. Approximately 184,000 of these offenders were sentenced between fiscal year 1992 and fiscal 2013.[107] USSC staff was able to match 171,765 of these offenders to Commission records. Of these, 138,894 were estimated to remain incarcerated on October 1, 2014.

In order to approximate the group of offenders who will be sentenced in fiscal year 2014, the Commission used the FY2013 datafile and moved all sentence dates forward by one year. Staff then determined which of these offenders would be incarcerated on October 1, 2014. This process added another 40,178 offenders into the analysis. Between the two groups, the Commission's analysis included data on 179,072 offenders.

C. Our Assumptions

In performing our analysis, we have been required to make some assumptions (set forth below) concerning the decisions that Congress and the courts would make in determining whether, and to what extent, to reduce the sentences of offenders eligible to receive a modification of sentence pursuant to the Policy Option discussed above. These assumptions may not hold in every case.

1. Procedural assumptions

Specifically, we have assumed that Congress would amend the provisions of 18 U.S.C. § 3624(b) in such a way that the BoP would award a maximum of good conduct credit of 54 days per year of sentence imposed. We have also assumed that Congress would authorize the statutory change to be applied retroactively to offenders incarcerated in the BoP.

2. Substantive assumptions

We have assumed that the sentence for each offender would be reduced based on the maximum good conduct credit allowed under the Policy Option. This assumption may not hold for every offender, as some offenders lose a portion or all of their earned good conduct credit as a sanction for unacceptable behavior. As a result, our estimate of the impact of the Policy Options may be overbroad, but not to an extent we can determine. We have also assumed that offenders would serve the lesser of the newly calculated sentence or their life expectancies.

If you have any questions about this analysis, or any of our prior analyses that we have provided to the GAO, please do not hesitate to contact the Commission. This analysis completes the list of analyses we have agreed to provide to you. We hope that the information the Commission has provided has been useful to the GAO in its work.

Sincerely,

Noah D. Bookbinder
Director
Office of Legislative and Public Affairs

Glenn R. Schmitt
Director
Office of Research and Data

Attachments

Table 1. Demographic Characteristics of Eligible Offenders (FY1992 through FY2014)

DEMOGRAPHICS		
Race/Ethnicity		
White	47,363	26.5%
Black	58,531	32.7%
Hispanic	67,051	37.5%
Other	6,045	3.4%
Total	**178,990**	**100.0%**
Citizenship		
U.S. Citizen	133,096	74.3%
Non-Citizen	46,073	25.7%
Total	**179,169**	**100.0%**
Gender		
Male	166,582	92.9%
Female	12,675	7.1%
Total	**179,257**	**100.0%**
Average Age		
	39 (as of November 1, 2014)	**36** (at sentencing)

The analysis involves a total of 179,265 cases, however, cases missing information for any specific analysis are excluded from that analysis.

Total percentages may not add to exactly 100% due to rounding.

Source: U.S. Sentencing Commission, 1992-2013 Datafiles, USSCFY92- USSCFYI3.

Table 2. Projected Year of Release for· Retroactive Eligible Offenders (FY1992 through FY2014)

	If Option Retroactive	If Option Not Retroactive
Release Date	**N**	**N**
Immediate Release	819	--
within 1 yr	25,918	23,859
within 2 yr	31, Ill	30,901
within 3 yr	24,980	24,972
within 4 yr	19,287	19,395
within 5 yr	14,841	15,063
within 6 yr +	62,309	65,075

Of the 179,265 offenders who appear to be eligible to benefit under the Policy Option, Commission records contained sufficient information to perform this analysis for 179,265 offenders.

Source: U.S. Sentencing Commission, 1992 - 2013 Datafiles, USSCFY92 - USSCFY13.

Table 3. Guideline Sentencing Characteristics, Criminal History, and Position Relative to the Guideline Range of Eligible Offenders (FY1992 through FY2014)

CHARACTERISTICS		
Average Base Offense Level		
Weapon Specific Offense Characteristic	23,888	1 3.3%
Firearms Mandatory Minimum Applied	21,962	12.3%
Safety Valve §5C1.2	15,970	16.3%
Aggravating Role §3B1.J	17,959	10.0%
Mitigating Role §3B1.2	8,705	4.9%
Obstruction Adjustment §3C1.J	8,416	4.7%
Career Offender Status §4B1.1	19,532	10.9%
Criminal History Category		
I	58,109	32.4%
n	19,809	11.1%
III	28,548	15.9%
IV	19,857	11.1%
v	13,790	7.7%
VI	39,152	21.8%
Total	**179,265**	**100%**
Sentence Relative to the Guideline Range		
Within Range	97,940	54.7%
Above Range	5,615	3.1%
Substantial Assistance §5K1.1	25,871	14.5%
Otherwise Below Range	49,478	27.7%
Total	**178,904**	**100%**

The analysis involves a total of 179,265 cases, however, cases missing information for any specific analysis are excluded from that analysis.
Total percentages may not add to exactly 100% due to rounding.
Source: U.S. Sentencing Commission, 1992 ·2013 Datafiles, USSCFY92- USSCFY 13.

7. USSC analysis of option 7: Make the current "safety valve" available to any drug offender with no offenses that receive 3 points under the criminal history point system.

Federal law generally requires a sentencing judge to impose a minimum sentence of imprisonment following conviction for any number of federal offenses; however, there are two statutorily provided exceptions. One of these exceptions, commonly referred to as the "safety valve," was created by the Violent Crime Control and Law Enforcement Act of 1994, Pub. 1. No. 103-322, 108 Stat. 1796, and is available for certain types of defendants for certain offenses that carry minimum sentences. Under this option, the current statutory requirements for eligibility for safety valve relief in drug cases involving a mandatory minimum penalty would be expanded to cover incarcerated offenders with any number of criminal history points, provided that the offender does not have a conviction for which the sentence imposed was a 3-point offense under USSC sentencing guidelines. Under USSC sentencing guidelines, 3 criminal history points are assigned if an offender has been previously sentenced or is being sentenced to a prison term of 13 months or more.

UNITED STATES SENTENCING COMMISSION
ONE COLUMBUS CIRCLE, N.E.
SUITE 2-500, SOUTH LOBBY
WASHINGTON, D.C. 20002-8002
(202) 502-4500
FAX (202) 502-4699

April 24, 2014

Jonathan R. Tumin
Senior Analyst
U.S. Government Accountability Office
441 G St., NW
Washington, DC 20548

Dear Mr. Tumin:

The Government Accountability Office has asked the U.S. Sentencing Commission to assist it in connection with its engagement (number 441173). We understand that through this engagement the GAO is examining ways in which the operating costs of the Federal Bureau of Prisons (BoP) can be reduced. As we have previously discussed with you and your colleagues, the Commission has agreed to analyze on GAO's behalf several policy options which could reduce the overall size of the prison population that the BoP administers. Specifically, our analyses of these policy options will consider the effect on the federal prison population if the policies were implemented in such a way that the options would apply to inmates currently incarcerated in the BoP system.

In this memorandum, we provide to you another of these estimates. Here we provide our estimate of the impact on the federal prison population if the current statutory requirements for eligibility for "safety valve" relief in drug cases involving a mandatory minimum penalty[108] were to be expanded. Specifically, you have asked us to consider a change to current law whereby offenders with any criminal history not involving a conviction for which the sentence imposed exceeded 13 months would be eligible for such relief and the courts would be authorized to resentence all federal offenders convicted of a drug offense in a manner consistent with the revised statute.

As we discuss more fully below, we estimate that 11,949 offenders who are incarcerated and would still be in prison as of October 1, 2014 would be eligible for a sentence reduction. The average reduction in sentence for these offenders would be 18 months (19.1 percent). The estimated total savings to the BoP from such a policy change applied retroactively would be 15,889 bed years.

I. The Policy Option We Considered

One of the policy options that we have agreed to examine on behalf of the GAO is the impact of a policy change in current law whereby the current statutory requirements for eligibility for "safety valve" relief from the application of mandatory minimum penalties in drug cases would be expanded. That provision currently requires courts to sentence offenders who have been convicted of a drug offense carrying a mandatory minimum penalty without regard for that penalty when all of several criteria are met.[109] One of those criteria involves the criminal history score[110] of the offender. Currently, offenders are eligible for safety valve relief only if they have been assessed no more than one criminal history point under the sentencing guidelines.[111] You have asked us to consider a change to the statute whereby offenders would be eligible for safety valve relief regardless of their criminal history score provided that none of their criminal history involves a conviction for which the sentence imposed exceeded one year and one month,[112] and further provided they meet the remaining safety valve criteria (the "Policy Option").

II. What We Found

Applying the Policy Option to offenders in the custody of the BoP, we estimate that there are 11,949 offenders who would be incarcerated on October 1, 2014 who would be eligible for a reduction in their current sentence if the Policy Option were to be retroactively applied. Ifthe courts were to grant each of these offenders the full reduction in their sentence we estimate that the total savings to the BoP would be 15,889 bed years.[113]

Table 1 provides information on some of the demographic characteristic of the offenders eligible for a sentence reduction pursuant to the Policy Option. Table 2 provides an estimate of the number of offenders who would be released each year if the Policy Option was applied retroactively compared to the number of offenders who will be released each year pursuant to their current sentence. As can be seen on this table, if the Policy Option were fully retroactive on October 1, 2014, more than 1,123 offenders would be eligible for immediate release. Within the first year of the effective date of the Policy Option, another 865 offenders would be eligible for release above the number who will be released under their current sentence. Table 3 provides information on selected sentencing guideline characteristics and the criminal history category of these offenders.

For the 11,949 offenders who would be eligible to receive a sentence reduction under the Policy Option, the current average sentence is 94 months. If the courts were to grant the full reduction possible in each case, the projected new average sentence for these offenders would be 76 months, a reduction of 18 months (or 19.1 percent). Based on this reduction, the estimated total savings to the BoP from the retroactive application of the Policy Option would be 15,889 bed years. This savings would not be realized in any single year but is the cumulative savings realized over several years.

III. How We Conducted This Analysis

A. Methodology

The methodology for this analysis is based on the Commission's Prison Impact Model, which has been in use in some form since the guidelines were first developed. This model is used to estimate the impact of proposed statutory and guideline amendments on newly sentenced offenders and to project the future impact those amendments will have on bed space in the BoP. For this analysis, those offenders who appear to be eligible to receive a reduced sentence were hypothetically "resentenced" with the computer program as if the proposed policy change had been in effect in the year in which they were sentenced. A new release date for each offender also was calculated in order to determine when the offender would be eligible for release if he or she were provided the full reduction in sentence provided by the proposed policy change.

B. The Offender Population We Studied

The Bureau of Prisons provided the Commission with a datafile of inmates who were in the custody of the BoP on Jan 25, 2014. That file contained approximately 189,000 offenders. Approximately 184,000 of these offenders were sentenced between fiscal year 1992 and fiscal 2013.[114] USSC staff was able to match 171,765 of these offenders to Commission records. Of these, 138,894 were estimated to remain incarcerated on October 1, 2014.

In order to approximate the group of offenders who will be sentenced in fiscal year 2014, the Commission used the FY2013 datafile and moved all sentence dates forward by one year. Staff then determined which of these offenders would be incarcerated on October 1, 2014. This process added another 40,178 offenders into the analysis. Between the two groups, the Commission's analysis included data on 179,072 offenders.

C. Our Assumptions

In performing our analysis, we have been required to make some assumptions (set forth below) concerning the decisions that Congress and the courts would make in determining whether, and to what extent, to reduce the sentences of offenders eligible to receive a modification of sentence pursuant to the Policy Option discussed above. These assumptions may not hold in every case.

1. Procedural assumptions

Specifically, we have assumed that Congress would amend the provisions of 18 U.S.C. § 3553(f)(1) to the effect that "the defendant does not have a criminal history score, as determined under the sentencing guidelines, that includes points added for any conviction for which the sentence imposed exceeded one year and one month." We have further assumed that the Commission would amend USSG §5C1.3 to conform it to the provisions of the amended statutory safety valve provision[115] but make no further changes to the *Guidelines Manual,* so that the remaining provisions of the 2013 *Guidelines Manual* would apply in these cases. Further, we have assumed that Congress would authorize the statutory change to be applied retroactively to offenders incarcerated in the BoP and that the Commission would amend USSG §1B1.10 to authorize courts to apply the amendment to USSG §5C1.3 retroactively to those offenders on some specific date.[116] We also assumed that the courts would resentence offenders in a manner that is consistent with the amended *Guidelines Manual*[117] Finally, we assumed that the effective date of any such Policy Option would be October 1, 2014. Therefore, only offenders incarcerated as of that date would be eligible to seek a reduction in sentence pursuant to the Policy Option discussed in this memorandum.

2. Substantive assumptions

In fiscal year 2010, approximately 66 percent of all drug offenders were convicted of an offense carrying a mandatory minimum penalty.[118] Of those, approximately 46 percent remain subject to the penalty at the time of sentencing.[119] Some offenders receive relief from the effect of any such penalty by providing substantial assistance to the government in the investigation or prosecution of another offender.[120] Others receive relief from such a penalty through the statutory "safety valve" provision.[121] Some offenders are eligible for both provisions.

Under the sentencing guidelines, drug offenders who meet the requirements of the statutory safety valve provision, which is incorporated into the guidelines at USSG 5C1.3, are entitled to a two-level reduction in offense level.[122] This provision applies regardless of whether the offender was convicted of an offense carrying a mandatory minimum penalty. That is, for offenders who are convicted of an offense carrying a mandatory minimum penalty, eligibility for the safety valve provides two benefits: 1) statutory relief from application of the mandatory minimum penalty, and 2) a two-level reduction in the offense level calculated under the sentencing guidelines. For drug offenders who were not convicted of an offense carrying a mandatory minimum penalty, eligibility for safety valve relief also results in the two-level reduction in offense level. For the analysis described in this memorandum, we have assumed that this structure would be unchanged, so that all drug offenders could benefit from the Policy Option if they meet the revised safety valve criteria and regardless of whether a mandatory minimum penalty had ever applied in the case.

Additional assumptions we have made for this analysis are that the sentence for each offender would be reduced based on the maximum good conduct credit allowed by the Bureau of Prisons, and offenders would serve the lesser of the newly calculated sentence or their life expectancies.

If you have any questions about our analysis, please do not hesitate to contact the Commission. We continue to work to analyze the other policy options that we discussed with you and your colleagues. We will provide our analyses of these options as they are completed.

Sincerely,

Noah D. Bookbinder

Noah D. Bookbinder
Director, Office of Legislative and Public Affairs

Glenn R. Schmitt
Director
Office of Research and Data
Attachments

Table 1. Demographic Characteristics of Drug Offenders Potentially Eligible for Retroactive Expanded Safety Va lve (No 3-Point Events)

DEMOGRAPHICS			
Race/Ethnicity			
	White	3,496	29.3%
	Black	3,463	29.0%
	Hispanic	4,667	39.1%
	Other	309	2.6%
	Total	**11,935**	**100.0%**
Citizenship			
	U.S. Citizen	9,639	80.7%
	Non-Citizen	2,308	19.3%
	Total	**11,947**	**100.0%**
Gender			
	Male	10,458	87.5%
	Female	1,490	12.5%
	Total	**11,948**	**100.0%**
Average Age		**33**	

[1] The analysis involves a total of 11,949 cases in which the offender was identified as eligible to seek a sentence reduction if the drug mandatory minimum changes were made retroactive. Cases missing information for any specific analysis are excluded from that analysis.

Total percentages may not add to exactly I 00% due to rounding.

Source: U.S. Sentencing Comm ission, 1992-2013 Datafiles, USSCFY92- USSCFY13 and projected 2014 Datafile.

Table 2. Estimated Projected Year of Release for Drug Offenders Potentially Eligible for Retroactive Expansion of Safety Valve (No 3-Point Events)

	If Policy Option Applied Retroactivly	Current Sentence
Release Date	N	N
immediate	1,123	
within 1 yr	2,108	1,243
within 2 yr	2,520	2,242
within 3 yr	2,118	2,009
within 4 yr	1,446	1,888
within 5 yr	912	1,327
within 6 yr +	1,690	3,208

[1] Of the 11,949 offenders who appear to be eligible for relief if the Policy Option was applied retroactively, Commission records contained sufficient information to perform this analysis for 11,917 offenders.

Source: U.S. Sentencing Commission, 1992-2013 Datafiles, USSCFY92- USSCFY13 and projected 2014 Datafile.

Table 3. Guideline Sentencing Characteristics and Criminal Historv of Drug Offenders Potentia lly Eligible for Retroactive Expanded Safety Valve (No 3-Point Events)

CHARACTERISTICS	N	%
Average Base Offense Level	**30**	
Weapon Specific Offense Characteristic	0	0.0%
Firearms Mandatory Minimum Applied	0	0.0%
Safety Valve §5C1.2	0	0.0%
Aggravating Role §3B1.1	0	0.0%
Mitigating Role §3B1.2	1,339	11.2%
Obstruction Adjustment §3C1.1	0	0.0%
Career Offender Status §4B1.1	0	0.0%
Criminal History Category		
I	0	0.0%
II	4,658	39.0%
III	4,936	41.3%
IV	1,452	12.2%
v	599	5.0%
VI	304	2.5%
Total	**11,949**	**100%**

[1] The analysis involves a total of 11,949 cases in which the offender was identified as eligible to seek a sentence reduction if the expanded safety valve changes were made retroactive. Cases missing information for any specific analysis are excluded from that analysis.

Total percentages may not add to exactly 100% due to rounding.

Source: U.S. Sentencing Commission, 1992-2013 Datafiles, USSCFY92 - USSCFYI3 and projected 2014 Datafile.

8. USSC analysis of option 8: Expand the safety valve as described in option 7 to include both non-violent drug offenders and any nonviolent offenders provided that they do not have a 3-point offense.

Under this option, the current statutory requirements for eligibility for "safety valve" relief in drug cases involving a mandatory minimum penalty would be expanded to cover both drug offenders and other non-violent (non-drug) offenders. No offender could have a conviction for which the sentence imposed was a 3-point offense under USSC sentencing guidelines.

***

UNITED STATES SENTENCING COMMISSION
ONE COLUMBUS CIRCLE, N.E.
SUITE 2-500, SOUTH LOBBY
WASHINGTON, D.C. 20002-8002
(202) 502-4500
FAX (202) 502-4699

June 11, 2014

Jonathan R. Tumin
Senior Analyst
U.S. Government Accountability Office
441 G St., NW
Washington, DC 20548

Dear Mr. Tumin:

The Government Accountability Office has asked the U.S. Sentencing Commission to assist it in connection with its engagement (number 441173). We understand that through this engagement the GAO is examining ways in which the operating costs of the Federal Bureau of Prisons (BoP) can be reduced. As we have previously discussed with you and your colleagues, the Commission has agreed to analyze on GAO's behalf several policy options which could reduce the overall size of the prison population that the BoP administers. Specifically, our analyses of these policy options will consider the effect on the federal prison population if the policies were implemented in such a way that the options would apply to inmates currently incarcerated in the BoP system.

In this memorandum, we provide to you another of these estimates. Here we provide our estimate of the impact on the federal prison population if the current statutory requirements for eligibility for "safety valve" relief in drug cases involving a mandatory minimum penalty[123] were to be expanded to all offenders regardless of the type of offense committed, subject to some limitations. Specifically, you have asked us to consider a change to current law whereby any non-violent offender would be eligible for safety valve relief regardless of the offender's criminal history, provided that the offender had not been convicted of any offense for which the sentence imposed exceeded 13 months, and the courts would be authorized to resentence those offenders in a manner consistent with the revised statute.

As we discuss more fully below, we estimate that 38,930 offenders who are incarcerated and would still be in prison as of October 1, 2014 would be eligible for a sentence reduction under such a policy change. The average reduction in sentence for these offenders would be 15 months (20.5%). The estimated total savings to the BoP from such a policy change applied retroactively would be 40,552 bed years.

I. The Policy Option We Considered

One of the policy options that we have agreed to examine on behalf of the GAO is the impact of a policy change in current law whereby the current statutory requirements for eligibility for "safety valve" relief from the application of mandatory minimum penalties in drug cases would be expanded. That provision currently requires courts to sentence offenders who have been convicted of a drug offense carrying a mandatory minimum penalty without regard for that penalty when all of several criteria are met.[124] One of those criteria involves the criminal history score[125] of the offender. Currently, offenders are eligible for safety valve relief only if they have been assessed no more than one criminal history point under the sentencing guidelines.[126]

You have asked us to consider a change to the statute whereby the safety valve would be available to all offenders, not just those committing drug offenses, provided that they offender was not a violent offender. You also asked us to consider a further change to the statute so that any such non-violent offender would be eligible regardless of their criminal history score, provided that none of their criminal history involves a conviction for which the sentence imposed exceeded one year and one month,[127] and further provided they meet the remaining safety valve criteria (the "Policy Option").

II. What We Found

Applying the Policy Option to offenders in the custody of the BoP, we estimate that there are 38,930 offenders who would be incarcerated on October 1, 2014 who would be eligible for a reduction in their current sentence if the Policy Option were to be retroactively applied. If the courts were to grant each of these offenders the full reduction in their sentence we estimate that the total savings to the BoP would be 40,552 bed years.[128]

Table 1 provides information on some of the demographic characteristic of the offenders eligible for a sentence reduction pursuant to the Policy Option. Table 2 provides an estimate of the number of offenders who would be released each year if the Policy Option was applied retroactively compared to the number of offenders who will be released each year pursuant to their current sentence. As can be seen on this table, if the Policy Option were fully retroactive on October 1, 2014, more than 5,623 offenders would be eligible for immediate release. Within the first year of the effective date of the Policy Option, another 12,067 offenders would be eligible for release. In total, the number of offenders eligible for release under the Policy Option in the first year is 6,321 more than the number who will be released under their current sentence. Table 3 provides information on selected sentencing guideline characteristics and the criminal history category of these offenders.

For the 38,931 offenders who would be eligible to receive a sentence reduction under the Policy Option, the current average sentence is 73 months. If the courts were to grant the full reduction possible in each case, the projected new average sentence for these offenders would be 58 months, a reduction of 15 months (or 20.5%). Based on this reduction, the estimated total savings to the BoP from the retroactive application of the Policy Option would be 40,552 bed years. This savings would not be realized in any single year but is the cumulative savings realized over several years.

III. How We Conducted This Analysis

A. Methodology

The methodology for this analysis is based on the Commission's Prison Impact Model, which has been in use in some form since the guidelines were first developed. This model is used to estimate the impact of proposed statutory and guideline amendments on newly sentenced offenders and to project the future impact those amendments will have on bed space in the BoP. For this analysis, those offenders who appear to be eligible to receive a reduced sentence were hypothetically "resentenced" with the computer program as if the proposed policy change had been in effect in the year in which they were sentenced. A new release date for each offender also was calculated in order to determine when the offender would be eligible for release if he or she were provided the full reduction in sentence provided by the proposed policy change.

B. The Offender Population We Studied

The Bureau of Prisons provided the Commission with a datafile of inmates who were in the custody of the BoP on Jan 25, 2014. That file contained approximately 189,000 offenders. Approximately 184,000 of these offenders were sentenced between fiscal year 1992 and fiscal2013.[129] USSC staff was able to match 171,765 of these offenders to Commission records. Of these, 138,894 were estimated to remain incarcerated on October 1, 2014.

In order to approximate the group of offenders who will be sentenced in fiscal year 2014, the Commission used the FY2013 datafile and moved all sentence dates forward by one year. Staff then determined which of these offenders would be incarcerated on October 1, 2014. This process added another 40,178 offenders into the analysis. Between the two groups, the Commission's analysis included data on 179,072 offenders.

C. Our Assumptions

In performing our analysis, we have been required to make some assumptions (set forth below) concerning the decisions that Congress and the courts would make in determining whether, and to what extent, to reduce the sentences of offenders eligible to receive a modification of sentence pursuant to the Policy Option discussed above. These assumptions may not hold in every case.

1. Procedural Assumptions

Specifically, we have assumed that Congress would amend the provisions of 18 U.S.C. § 3553(f) to provide that the subsection would apply at sentencing in any case in which the offender was not convicted of a violent offense and had not used violence in the commission of the offense. We have also assumed that Congress would amend 18 U.S.C. § 3553(f)(l) to expand eligibility under that section to any federal offender to the extent that: "the defendant does not have a criminal history score, as determined under the sentencing guidelines, that includes points added for any conviction for which the sentence imposed exceeded one year and one month."

We have further assumed that the Commission would amend USSG §5C1.3 to conform it to the provisions of the amended statutory safety valve provision[130] but make no further changes to the *Guidelines Manual,* so that the remaining provisions of the 2013 *Guidelines Manual* would apply in these cases. Further, we have assumed that Congress would authorize the statutory change to be applied retroactively to offenders incarcerated in the BoP and that the Commission would amend USSG §1B1.10 to authorize courts to apply the amendment to USSG §5C1.3 retroactively to those offenders on some specific date.[131] We also assumed that the courts would resentence offenders in a manner that is consistent with the amended *Guidelines Manua1.*[132] Finally, we assumed that the effective date of any such Policy Option would be October 1, 2014. Therefore, only offenders incarcerated as of that date would be eligible to seek a reduction in sentence pursuant to the Policy Option discussed in this memorandum.

2. Substantive Assumptions

In fiscal year 2010, approximately 66 percent of all drug offenders were convicted of an offense carrying a mandatory minimum penalty.[133] Of those, approximately 46 percent remain subject to the penalty at the time of sentencing.[134] Some offenders receive relief from the effect of any such penalty by providing substantial assistance to the government in the investigation or prosecution of another offender.[135] Others receive relief from such a penalty through the statutory "safety valve" provision.[136] Some offenders are eligible for both provisions.

Under the sentencing guidelines, drug offenders who meet the requirements of the statutory safety valve provision, which is incorporated into the guidelines at USSG 5C1.3, are entitled to a two-level reduction in offense level.[137] This provision applies regardless of whether the offender was convicted of an offense carrying a mandatory minimum penalty. That is, for offenders who are convicted of an offense carrying a mandatory minimum penalty, eligibility for the safety valve provides two benefits: 1) statutory relief from application of the mandatory minimum penalty, and 2) a two-level reduction in the offense level calculated under the sentencing guidelines. For drug offenders who were not convicted of an offense carrying a mandatory minimum penalty, eligibility for safety valve relief also results in the two-level reduction in offense level.

For the analysis described in this memorandum, we have assumed that this structure would be unchanged, but now would be applied in all cases (not just drug cases) in which the offender was not convicted of a violent offense and had not used violence in connection with the offense. As a result, all non-violent offenders could benefit from the Policy Option if they meet the revised safety valve criteria and regardless of whether a mandatory minimum penalty had ever applied in the case.

We made several assumptions in for the purpose of determining which offenders were violent offenders. Specifically, we considered any of the following to be a violent offense or an indication that violence had been used in connection with the offense:

the guideline applied in the case was from Part A of Chapter 2 of the Guidelines Manual (which involves crimes against the person);

the guideline applied was USSG §2B2.1 (burglary of a residence);

the guideline applied was USSG §2B3.1 (robbery);

the guideline applied was USSG §2B3.2 (extortion by force or threat of injury);

the guideline applied was USSG §2D1.9 (placing dangerous devices to protect drug production);

the guideline applied was from Subpart 1 of Part E of Chapter 2 (racketeering);

the guideline applied was from Subpart 1 of Part G of Chapter 2 (promoting commercial sex acts or other prohibited sexual conduct);

the guideline applied was from Subpart 2 of Part G of Chapter 2 and the conduct involved the production of child pornography;

the guideline applied was USSG §2H4.1 (peonage, slave trade);

the guideline applied was from Part K of Chapter 2 (firearms);

the guideline applied was from Subparts 1, 2, 3, 5, or 6 of Part M of Chapter 2 (treason, sabotage, espionage, and cases involving nuclear, biological and chemical weapons and materials);

the guideline applied was USSG §2N1.1 (tampering with consumer products with risk of death);

the guideline applied was USSG §2P1.3 (prison riot);

the guideline applied was USSG §2Q1.1 (knowing endangerment from HAZMATs);

the guideline applied was USSG §2Q1.4 (tampering with public water system); or the guideline applied was USSG §2X6.1 (use of a minor in a crime of violence).

Additional assumptions we have made for this analysis are that the sentence for each offender would be reduced based on the maximum good conduct credit allowed by the Bureau of Prisons, and offenders would serve the lesser of the newly calculated sentence or their life expectancies.

If you have any questions about our analysis, please do not hesitate to contact the Commission. We continue to work to analyze the other policy options that we discussed with you and your colleagues. We will provide our analyses of these options as they are completed.

Sincerely,

Noah D. Bookbinder
Director, Office of Legislative and Public Affairs

Glenn R. Schmitt
Director, Office of Research and Data

Attachments

Table 1. Demographic Characteristics of Eligible Offenders (FY1992 through FY2014)

DEMOGRAPHICS			
Race/Ethnicity			
	White	13,640	35.2%
	Black	6,540	16.9%
	Hispanic	17,586	45.4%
	Other	997	2.6%
	Total	**38,763**	**100.0%**
Citizenship			
	U.S. Citizen	25,707	66.1%
	Non-Citizen	13,211	33.9%
	Total	**38,918**	**100.0%**

Table 1. (Continued)

DEMOGRAPHICS			
Gender			
	Male	34,574	88.8%
	Female	4,341	11.2%
	Total	**38,915**	**100.0%**
Average Age			
		38 (as of November 1, 2014)	**37 (at sentencing)**

The analysis involves a total of 38,931 cases, however, cases missing information for any specific analysis are excluded from that analysis.

Total percentages may not add to exactly 100% due to rounding.

Source: U.S. Sentencing Commission, 1992-2013 Datafiles, USSCFY92- USSCFY13.

Table 2. Projected Year of Release for Retroactive Eligible Offenders (FY1992 through FY2014)

Release Date	IF AMENDMENT RETROACTIVE N	IF AMENDMENT NOT RETROACTIVE N
Immediate Release	5,623	--
within 1 yr	12,067	11,369
within 2 yr	7,113	7,605
within 3 yr	4,724	5,476
within 4 yr	3,168	4,115
within 5 yr	1,975	2,816
within 6 yr +	4,260	7,549

Of the 38,931 offenders who appear to be eligible for relief under the amendment, Commission records contained sufficient information to perform this analysis for 38,930 offenders.

SOURCE: U.S. Sentencing Commission, 1992 - 2013 Datafiles, USSCFY92- USSCFY13.

Table 3. Guideline Sentencing Characteristics, Criminal History, and Position Relative to the Guideline Range of Eligible Offenders (FY1992 through FY2014)

CHARACTERISTICS		
Average Base Offense Level	--	
Weapon Specific Offense Characteristic	0	0.0%
Firearms Mandatory Minimum Applied	0	0.0%

CHARACTERISTICS		
Safety Valve §5C1.2	0	0.0%
Aggravating Role §3B1.1	0	0.0%
Mitigating Role §3B1.2	2,108	5.4%
Obstruction Adjustment §3C1.1	0	0.0%
Career Offender Status §4B1.1	845	2.2%
Criminal History Category		
I	17,290	44.4%
II	7,895	20.3%
III	8,492	21.8%
IV	2,848	7.3%
v	1,095	2.8%
VI	1,311	3.4%
Total	**38,931**	**100%**
Sentence Relative to the Guideline Range		
Within Range	20,748	53.3%
Above Range	823	2.1%
Substantial Assistance §5K1.1	4,895	1 2.6%
Otherwise Below Range	12,438	32.0%
Total	**38,904**	**100%**

The analysis involves a total of 38,931 cases, however, cases missing information for any specific analysis are excluded from that analysis.

Total percentages may not add to exactly 100% due to rounding.

Source: U.S. Sentencing Commission, 1992-2013 Datafiles, USSCFY92- USSCFY13.

End Notes

[1] BOP per capita annual cost per prisoner increased from about $13,400 in fiscal year 1980 to about $31,338 in fiscal year 2014 in nominal terms. However, after adjustment for inflation, BOP spending per capita for salaries and expenses in 2014 is about 6.1 percent less than in 1980. According to the chain-weighted gross domestic product price index, if BOP spending per capita had kept even with inflation since 1980, annual cost per prisoner would be about $33,251 for fiscal year 2014 (about 6.1 percent higher than $31,338). Annual per capita cost per prisoner for fiscal year 2014 was calculated by dividing BOP's enacted fiscal year 2014 budget for Salaries and Expenses of $6.769 billion by total prisoner population of about 216,000 as of July 24, 2014. BOP excludes appropriations for Buildings and Facilities from its calculation of per capita costs because these may vary substantially year to year. These costs are also excluded from our calculation of fiscal year 2014 per capita costs. Prisoner population data are from BOP's inmate tracking database, the SENTRY Inmate Management System.

[2] The DOJ Fiscal Year 2015 Performance Budget Congressional Submission projects BOP's population to increase by 2,500 (about 1 percent) for 2015 over the fiscal year 2014 level—which is forecast to be the same as the fiscal year 2013 level—and by about 8.5 percent by fiscal year 2019 over the July 2014 level. As a result of these projected increases, system-wide overcrowding is estimated to increase from 36 percent in fiscal year 2013 to 41 percent by fiscal year 2019. We have previously reported on these issues in GAO, *Bureau of Prisons: Growing Inmate Crowding Negatively Affects Inmates, Staff, and Infrastructure,* GAO-12-743 (Washington, D.C.: Sept. 12, 2012).

[3] See GAO, *Bureau of Prisons: Eligibility and Capacity Impact Use of Flexibilities to Reduce Inmates' Time in Prison,* GAO-12-320 (Washington, D.C.: Feb. 7, 2012).

[4] Pub. L. No. 98-473, 98 Stat. 1987. The act was effective for convictions on or after November 1, 1987. Prior to the act, federal judges generally had broad discretion in sentencing. Most criminal statutes provided only broad maximum terms of imprisonment. Federal law outlined the maximum sentence, federal judges imposed a

sentence within a statutory range, and the federal parole official eventually determined the actual duration of incarceration.

[5]18 U.S.C. § 3621(e). We have previously reported on BOP's use of these discretionary authorities. See GAO

[6] Under 18 U.S.C. § 3624(b), a "prisoner who is serving a term of imprisonment of more than 1 year other than a term of imprisonment for the duration of the prisoner's life, may receive credit toward the service of the prisoner's sentence, beyond the time served, of up to 54 days at the end of each year of the prisoner's term of imprisonment, beginning at the end of the first year of the term, subject to determination by the Bureau of Prisons that, during that year, the prisoner has displayed exemplary compliance with institutional disciplinary regulations."

[7] The USSC is an independent agency in the judicial branch of government. It was created by the Sentencing Reform Act provisions of the Comprehensive Crime Control Act of 1984, Pub. L. No. 98-473, 98 Stat. 1976. The sentencing guidelines established by the commission are designed to incorporate the purposes of sentencing (i.e., just punishment, deterrence, incapacitation, and rehabilitation).

[8] According to the memorandum, a defendant must be someone (1) whose relevant conduct does not involve the use of violence, the credible threat of violence, the possession of a weapon, the trafficking of drugs to or with minors, or the death or serious bodily injury of any person; (2) who is not an organizer, leader, manager, or supervisor of others within a criminal organization; (3) who does not have significant ties to large-scale drug-trafficking organizations, gangs, or cartels; and (4) who does not have a significant criminal history. The potential impact of this directive on BOP's population is discussed later in this report.

[9] GAO, *Bureau of Prisons: Opportunities Exist to Enhance the Transparency of Annual Budget Justifications*, GAO-14-121 (Washington, D.C.: Dec. 6, 2013).

[10] BOP is appropriated funds through two accounts: Salaries and Expenses and Buildings and Facilities. We focused our review on the Salaries and Expenses account as it represents almost the entirety of BOP's budget.

[11] GAO, *Standards for Internal Control in the Federal Government*, GAO/AIMD-00.21.3.1 (Washington, D.C.: Nov. 1, 1999). Internal control is an integral component of an organization's management that provides reasonable assurance that the following objectives are being achieved: effectiveness and efficiency of operations, reliability of financial reporting, and compliance with applicable laws and regulations.

[12] The expert sources from which we requested or obtained analysis or information on sentencing issues were: the American Bar Association (ABA); the Association of State Correctional Administrators; the Brennan Center for Justice; the Council of State Governments/Justice Center; Families Against Mandatory Minimums; the Fraternal Order of Police; the Heritage Foundation; the National Association of Assistant U.S. Attorneys; the National Association of Former U.S. Attorneys; the Pew Charitable Trusts; "Right on Crime", a project of the Texas Public Policy Foundation in cooperation with the Justice Fellowship; the Sentencing Project; the Urban Institute; and the Vera Institute of Justice. We identified these expert entities through several means, including (1) asking officials at both the USSC and the Urban Institute who have previously worked on analyses and reports relevant to prison population data and criminal justice to identify entities they considered as expert in the field of sentencing reform and criminal justice, (2) conducting a literature search to identify publications issued by some of the entities on sentencing reform or corrections, and (3) identifying entities with known expertise and authoritativeness (e.g., the ABA) in the criminal justice field through literature searches.

[13] The USSC calculates the impact of sentencing changes in terms of bed year savings; 1 bed year is defined by the USSC as 12 months of prison time (e.g., one offender in prison for 1 year, or three offenders in prison for 4 months each, and so forth). Using the USSC estimates of saved bed years, we calculated savings that would result from sentence length reductions or from cost avoidance savings resulting from increases below what would otherwise occur if an option was not implemented, by multiplying bed years by the annual marginal cost for a prisoner. Marginal costs, calculated by BOP, cover such things as food, medical care, clothing, and utilities. For fiscal year 2014, the average annual marginal cost per offender is about $11,000. For some options that could affect the sentences of about 78,000 or more offenders, equal to the BOP July 2014 level of system- wide overcrowding, we also calculated per capita savings, as such sentence reductions could allow BOP to reduce its staff or close facilities.

[14] Texas was identified as a model for criminal justice system reforms in a joint January 2014 DOJ-Urban Institute report assessing the JRI initiative. See: Urban Institute- Department of Justice Bureau of Justice Assistance, *Justice Reinvestment Initiative State Assessment Report* (Washington, D.C.: January 2014).

[15] Of the 17 entities that acknowledged receipt of our request for comments, 3 did not provide substantive comments. Of these 3, 1 referred us to multiple articles published on criminal justice issues.

[16] An obligation is a definite commitment that creates a legal liability of an agency for the payment of goods or services received. An agency incurs an obligation, for example, when it places an order, signs a contract, awards a grant, purchases services, or takes other actions that require the government to make payments to the public or from one government account to another. See GAO, *A Glossary of Terms Used in the Federal Budget Process*, GAO-05-734SP (Washington, D.C.: September 2005). To report and monitor obligated funds throughout the bureau, BOP employs cost center accounting and designates managers for these cost centers. According to the Federal Accounting Standards Advisory Board, components of an organization must accumulate costs for each type of output they produce for various programs.

[17] Statement of Federal Financial Accounting Standards 4: *Managerial Cost Accounting Standards and Concepts. Federal Accounting Standards Advisory Board Handbook*, Version 12 (June 2013).

[18] In order to standardize the budgetary information received from federal agencies, the Office of Management and Budget (OMB) assigns object classifications according to the nature of the services or articles procured (e.g., Personnel Compensation; Supplies and Materials; Rent, Communications, and Utilities; etc.).

[19] According to BOP officials, privately operated secure contract facilities are low security and primarily house non-U.S. citizens convicted of crimes while in this country legally or illegally. Regarding the RRCs, BOP officials stated that they use an additional 49 RRCs through intergovernmental agreements for work release purposes. Home detention describes all circumstances under which an inmate is serving a portion of his or her sentence while residing in his or her home.

[20] National Institute of Corrections, a component of BOP, provides training, technical assistance, information services, and policy/program development assistance to federal, state, and local corrections agencies.

[21] Pub. L. No. 98-473, 98 Stat. 1987.

[22] Pub. L. No. 98-473, § 217, 98 Stat. 1987, 2017.

[23] 28 U.S.C. § 991(b)(1)(B).

[24] See *United States v. Booker*, 543 U.S. 220 (2005).

[25] See 18 U.S.C. § 3553(a).

[26] Some types of sentences are not counted in calculating criminal history points. These are: foreign sentences of imprisonment; sentences imposed by tribal courts; summary court martial sentences; sentences imposed for expunged, reversed, vacated, or invalidated convictions; sentences for certain petty offenses or minor misdemeanors. The Sentencing Guidelines list two classes of these minor misdemeanor or petty offenses that are not counted for criminal history purposes. One class consists of eight types of minor offenses—such as hunting and fishing violations or juvenile truancy— that are not counted regardless of the sentence imposed.

[27] 18 U.S.C. § 3553(e).

[28] 18 U.S.C. § 3553(f). For the safety valve exception, the court is to consider at sentencing (1) the defendant's criminal history; (2) whether the defendant used violence or credible threats of violence or possessed a firearm or other dangerous weapon in connection with the offense; (3) whether the offense resulted in death or serious bodily injury to any person; (4) whether the defendant was an organizer, leader, manager, or supervisor of others in the offense or was engaged in a continuing criminal enterprise; and (5) the defendant has truthfully provided to the government all information and evidence the defendant has concerning the offense or offenses that were part of the same course of conduct or of a common scheme or plan.

[29] Statement of Charles E. Samuels, Jr., Director of the Federal Bureau of Prisons, before the United States House Committee on Appropriations, Subcommittee on Commerce, Justice, Science and Related Agencies, April 10, 2014.

[30] BOP, *BOP Strategic Plan*, (Washington, D.C.: February 2014).

[31] The catalog contains specific dollar amounts for estimated savings by institution, but these figures are not verified by BOP's Central Office or other officials.

[32] BOP/PRD also reports frequent deficiencies and significant findings associated with operational effectiveness and compliance-related issues, such as correctional services and food safety. We determined these reported issues do not necessarily have a direct impact on operational efficiency and therefore were not included in the scope of our review.

[33] A deficiency generally refers to an internal control deficiency (e.g., an internal control is missing, needs improvement, or is not operated as designed). BOP officials stated that a deficiency is considered "frequent" if it arises multiple times, within a quarterly time period, in program reviews conducted at multiple institutions. A finding is an issue identified during the course of a review. BOP officials stated that findings are considered significant if the reported issue is associated with a high-cost program activity or an invaluable subject area such as quality of care. A deficiency generally refers to the ineffectiveness of an internal control activity. If the same finding or deficiency is reported across multiple reporting periods, it is considered a repeat problem.

[34] GAO

[35] GAO

[36] See 18 U.S.C. § 4102.

[37] See GAOor additional details on GCT. As authorized in statute, 18 U.S.C. § 3624(b), BOP may award "up to 54 days at the end of each year of the prisoner's term of imprisonment," or 54 days per year of sentence served. As applied by BOP, however, this actually results in 47 days earned per year of sentence imposed because inmates do not earn GCT credit for years they do not ultimately serve because of being released early. Calculation of the amount of time that BOP should award based on good conduct was contested in court. In *Barber v. Thomas*, 130 S. Ct. 2499 (2010), the Supreme Court upheld BOP's methodology against a challenge brought by inmate petitioners. As a result, BOP officials state that any change in the method of calculating GCT credits would require a change to the law. Therefore, for our purposes in this report, GCT is both a discretionary authority and one that is an option that could produce potential costs savings, provided the calculation method is changed. We include GCT in the list of discretionary authorities and as one of the sentencing guideline change options.

[38] 18 U.S.C. § 3621(e).

[39] 18 U.S.C. § 3624(c).

[40] DOJ, Office of the Inspector General: *The Department of Justice's International Prisoner Transfer Program*, I-2012-002 (Washington, D.C.: December 2011). The DOJ IG reported that, in addition to eligibility criteria constraints on using the program, other factors within BOP control also affected its use, such as incorrect determinations of inmate eligibility, language barriers hindering inmate understanding of the program, or delays in processing applications. The IG estimated that, for fiscal years 2005-2010, BOP delays in processing applications resulted in about $8 million in additional costs, or $1.33 million annually, on average, for each of those 6 years. The IG report stated that since 2001, Mexico's "significant restrictions" had resulted in few Mexican inmates being accepted for treaty transfer consideration. Data on BOP inmates by nationality are from BOP's SENTRY data system. The IG made several recommendations for BOP to address these findings, including ensuring that all staff involved in IPTP determinations are properly trained. BOP concurred with the IG's recommendations and stated that actions are under way to address them.

[41] Estimated cost avoidance based on a fiscal year 2013 marginal cost of $10,674 per offender.

[42] GAO

[43] DOJ, Office of the Inspector General: *The Federal Bureau of Prisons' Compassionate Release Pro*gram, I-2013-006 (Washington, D.C: April 2013). The IG made several recommendations for BOP to address these findings, including establishing time frames for processing requests at each step of the management review process. BOP generally concurred with the IG's recommendations and stated that actions are under way to address them.

[44] According to the revised program statement for Compassionate Release/Reduction in Sentence, the following were added: criteria regarding requests based on medical circumstances, nonmedical circumstances for elderly inmates, nonmedical circumstances in which there has been the death or incapacitation of the family member caregiver of an inmate's child, nonmedical circumstances in which the spouse or registered partner of an inmate has become incapacitated, and a list of factors that should be considered for all requests.

[45] Data were provided by BOP for calendar year releases. Cost avoidance savings were calculated by multiplying the BOP fiscal year 2013 marginal cost per offender ($10,674) by the number of releases. Costs as a percentage of BOP appropriations were calculated by dividing the cost savings by the cited BOP appropriations.

[46] RDAP participation is limited to prisoners with a verifiable substance use disorder within the 12 months prior to their arrest. They must also voluntarily apply for participation and be approved by BOP for the program. RRCs are run by private contractors and cost more than minimum security institutions, and about the same as low- or medium-security BOP prisons on an annual basis per offender. We reported daily costs per prisoner previously in GAOas follows: $70.79 for RRCs, $57.55 for minimum security, $69.53 for low security, and $71.91 for medium security.

[47] We did not include in cost savings the potential long-term savings that could result from reduced recidivism.

[48] GAOFor fiscal years 2009-2011, 15,302 RDAP participants completed the program and were eligible to receive a sentence reduction. However, of these participants, 19 percent received the maximum sentence reduction that corresponded to their sentence length.

[49] BOP did not provide an estimate of the savings from shortening the average sentence by 1.5 months. BOP stated that this funding level would mean that RDAP was operating at 100 percent of capacity; that is, all the available spaces would be taken.

[50] GAODuring an assessment for RRC placement, BOP policy requires prerelease RRC placement decisions be made on an individual basis and conducted in a manner consistent with certain statutory criteria. The criteria include (1) the resources of the facility contemplated, (2) the nature and circumstances of the offense, (3) the history and characteristics of the prisoner, (4) any statement by the court that imposed the sentence, and (5) any pertinent policy statement issued by the USSC. See 18 U.S.C. § 3621(b).

[51] A detainer is a document issued by a law enforcement entity, a jail, or correctional facility to seek custody of an individual for purposes of instituting legal proceedings.

[52] GAO

[53] This cost estimate is based on BOP RRC fiscal year 2013 average RRC cost of $26,645 per offender multiplied by the required 20,500 bed spaces.

[54] Pub. L. No. 111-220, 124 Stat. 2372. The Anti-Drug Abuse Act of 1986, Pub. L. No. 99-570, 100 Stat. 3207, included the federal criminal law distinction between "cocaine base" and other forms of cocaine. The thresholds triggering a 10-year prison penalty—5 kilograms of powder cocaine and 50 grams of cocaine base—created a 100-to-1 quantity ratio.

[55] Of these eight options, two related to the sentencing guidelines were approved by the USSC in April and July 2014; a third was directed by the Attorney General in August 2013. All three changes occurred during the course of this review. The two actions approved by the USSC would reduce lengths of prison terms for (1) most future federal drug offenders by amending the sentencing guidelines, and (2) currently incarcerated federal drug offenders by about 19 percent compared with current term lengths by amending a policy statement to give retroactive effect to the proposed amendment to the sentencing guidelines. However, under

28 U.S.C. § 994(p), Congress may modify or disapprove amendments to the sentencing guidelines. (The second action corresponds to the first and does not require separate congressional action.) The USSC retroactivity change would permit eligible offenders to ask courts to reduce their sentences beginning November 1, 2014. However, offenders whose requests are granted by the courts would be released no earlier than November 1, 2015. According to the USSC, sentences will be reduced retroactively only after consideration by a judge in each case. The third policy change went into effect in August 2013, when the Attorney General issued a memorandum to U.S. Attorneys informing prosecutors to decline to charge certain defendants in certain types of drug cases in such a manner as to trigger mandatory minimum sentences.

[56] The USSC calculated the potential savings in bed years; 1 bed year is defined by the USSC as 12 months' prison time (e.g., one offender in prison for 1 year, or three offenders in prison for 4 months each, and so forth.)

[57] USSC: *Analysis of the Impact of the 2014 Drug Guidelines Amendment If Made Retroactive* (Washington, D.C.: July 25, 2014). See this citation at http://www.ussc.gov.

[58] We calculated cost savings that would result from reductions in BOP population or from cost avoidance savings resulting from increases below what would otherwise occur if an option was not implemented, by multiplying USSC estimates of bed years saved by the annual marginal cost for a prisoner in BOP.

[59] DOJ reports that as of February 2014 BOP prisons were 32 percent overcrowded but medium- and high-security prisons were more overcrowded than low- and minimum- security institutions. Reducing overcrowding and costs would depend on which offenders were released, from where, and in what number. Note that a reduction in bed years does not necessarily translate into an immediate reduction in prison population.

[60] See option 6.

[61] We asked the USSC to estimate the number of offenders who would be eligible to be released or to have their sentence reduced (leading eventually to release), and to estimate the savings that would result from implementation of these eight options. Where estimates could be made by USSC, the savings were provided in bed years.

[62] BOP is appropriated funds through two accounts: Salaries and Expenses and Buildings and Facilities. We focused our review on the Salaries and Expenses account as it represents almost the entirety of BOP's budget.

[63] GAO, *Standards for Internal Control in the Federal Government*, GAO/AIMD-00.21.3.1 (Washington, D.C.: Nov. 1, 1999). Internal control is an integral component of an organization's management that provides reasonable assurance that the following objectives are being achieved: effectiveness and efficiency of operations, reliability of financial reporting, and compliance with applicable laws and regulations.

[64] The expert entities from which we requested or obtained analysis or information on sentencing issues were the American Bar Association (ABA); the Association of State Correctional Administrators; the Brennan Center for Justice; the Council of State Governments/Justice Center; Families Against Mandatory Minimums; the Fraternal Order of Police; the Heritage Foundation; the National Association of Assistant U.S. Attorneys; the National Association of Former U.S. Attorneys; the Pew Charitable Trusts; "Right on Crime," a project of the Texas Public Policy Foundation in cooperation with the Justice Fellowship; the Sentencing Project; the Urban Institute; and the Vera Institute of Justice.

[65] According to the USSC, the July 18, 2014, action amends a policy statement to provide for retroactive effect to the proposed amendment to the sentencing guidelines and as such, does not require submission to Congress.

[66] We calculated savings that would result from reductions in BOP population or cost avoidance savings resulting from increases below what would otherwise occur if an option was not implemented, by multiplying bed years saved by the annual marginal cost for a prisoner. BOP defines marginal costs as the cost of adding one offender for 1 year; these cover food, medical, clothing, and utilities. For fiscal year 2014, the average annual marginal cost per offender is about $11,000. For some options that could result in reduced sentences and earlier releases of about 78,000 or more offenders, we also calculated per capita savings, as such population reductions that could allow BOP to reduce its staff or close facilities.

[67] As of January 2014, there were 17 states that are or have been participants in DOJ's Justice Reinvestment Initiative (JRI) program. Of these 17, only 3—Louisiana, Ohio, and North Carolina—had had at least 1 year's experience implementing JRI-related programs. Texas is not a JRI participant but is cited as one of the models for JRI programs by DOJ.

[68] DOJ and the Urban Institute: *Justice Reinvestment Initiative State Assessment Report* (January 2014: Washington, D.C.) The DOJ Bureau of Justice Assistance funded the JRI, in a public-private partnership with the Pew Charitable Trusts, to provide technical assistance and financial support for system-wide criminal justice reform efforts. Under the JRI model, a bipartisan working group uses comprehensive data analyses to identify the drivers of the local corrections population and costs and foster support for a set of cost- effective policy options addressing those drivers.

[69] Of the 18 entities to which we sent a request for comments, 17 acknowledged receipt of our request. Of these 17, 3 did not provide substantive comments, leaving 14 that provided comments. Of the 3 that did not provide substantive comments, 1 referred us to multiple articles published on criminal justice issues.

[70] DOJ and the Urban Institute: *Justice Reinvestment Initiative State Assessment Report* (January 2014: Washington, D.C.) The Bureau of Justice Assistance (BJA) funded the JRI, in a public-private partnership with the Pew Charitable Trusts, to provide technical as- sistance and financial support for system-wide criminal justice

reform efforts. Under the JRI model, a bipartisan working group comprising key policymakers uses comprehensive data analyses to identify the drivers of the local corrections population and costs and foster support for a set of cost-effective policy options addressing those drivers.

[71] USSC guidelines are used to determine prison sentences based primarily on two factors: (1) the conduct associated with the offense (the offense conduct, which produces the offense level) and (2) the defendant's criminal history (the criminal history category). In general, criminal history points are calculated by adding 3 points for each prior sentence of imprisonment exceeding one year and one month; adding 2 points for each prior sentence of imprisonment of at least sixty days but not more than 13 months; adding 1 point for each prior sentence of less than sixty days, and so forth. This option would make more drug offenders eligible for sentencing by judges who would not be required to solely follow mandatory sentencing guidelines.

[72] *See, e.g.,* 21 U.S.C. §§ 841(b), 960(b) (2006) (establishing five-, ten-, and twenty-year minimum penalties in certain drug cases).

[73] Another approach would be for the President to reduce the sentence for all offenders eligible for such a change using his clemency powers. *See* U.S. CONST., art. II, § 2, c1. 2.

[74] A "bed year" is the cost to the BoP of incarcerating one inmate for one year. For example, one inmate who serves five years of imprisonment accounts for five bed years.

[75] The analysis was limited to data from fiscal year 1992 through September 30, 2013 (fiscal years 1 992 through 2013) because the Commission's data collection efforts prior to fiscal year 1992 were not as complete as in later years. For example, the Commission did not collect information on the type of drug involved in drug offenses prior to fiscal year 1992.

[76] *See* U.S. SENTENCING COMMISSION, MANDATORY MINIMUM PENALTIES IN THE FEDERAL CRIMINAL JUSTICE SYSTEM 154 (20 ll).

[77] *Jd.*

[78] *See* 18 U.S.C. § 3553(e); USSG §5K1.1.

[79] *See* 18 U.S.C. § 3553(t); USSG §5K3.1.

[80] *See* 2013 Sourcebook of Federal Sentencing Statistics, Table 30 (2014).

[81] *See* USSG §5G1.1 (which provides that the minimum guideline sentence may not be lower than any mandatory minimum penalty).

[82] *See* 2013 Sourcebook of Federal Sentencing Statistics, Table 30A (2014).

[83] Pub. L. No. 111- 220, 124 Stat. 2372 (2010) (hereinafter FSA].

[84] The new five year mandatory minimum threshold quantity of28 grams corresponds to approximately one ounce, which has been considered to be a threshold quantity for purposes of classifying the function of certain federal crack cocaine offenders. *See* UNITED STATES SENTENCING COMMISSION, REPORT TO THE CONGRESS: COCAINE AND FEDERAL SENTENCING POLICY 18 (MAY 2007) [hereinafter 2007 Commission Report].

[85] Because it now takes approximately 18 times more powder cocaine than crack cocaine to trigger the same statutory mandatory minimum penalties, some may refer to this penalty structure as an "18-to-1 drug quantity ratio."

[86] The FSA was enacted into law on August 3, 2010.

[87] *See* Dorsey v. United States, 567 U.S. ___, 132 S. Ct. 2321 (2012) (FSA's lower mandatory minimum penalties applied to offenders sentenced on and after August 3, 2010).

[88] USSG, 2011 Supp. to App. C, Amendment 748 (effective Nov. I, 2010).

[89] USSG, 2011 Supp. to App. C, Amendment 750 (effective Nov. I, 2011).

[90] Offenses involving 28 grams of crack cocaine were assigned a base offense level of26, and offenses involving 280 grams of crack cocaine were assigned a base offense level of 32. This approach is consistent with how the guidelines incorporate the statutory mandatory minimum penalties for all other drug offenses. The base offense level for some quantities of crack cocaine in the Drug Quantity Table did not change as a result of the FSA Guideline Amendment. Also, offenses involving quantities of less than 500 mg of crack cocaine were unaffected by the amendment and remained assigned to BOL 12.

[91] USSG, 2011 Supp. to App. C, Amendment 759 (effective Nov. I , 2011).

[92] *See generally* USSG, Preliminary Crack Retroactivity Data Report, Fair Sentencing Act (January 2014) (available at http://www.ussc.gov/Research_and_Statistics/Federal_Sentencing_Statistics/FSA_Amendment/index.cfm)

[93] A "bed year' is the cost to the BoP of incarcerating one inmate for one year. For example, one inmate who serves five years of imprisonment accounts for five bed years.

[94] While the 2012 *Guidelines Manual* was used for this analysis, the provisions of the 2013 Guidelines Manual that pertain to offenses under USSG §201.1 are unchanged.

[95] The analysis was limited to data from fiscal year 1992 through September 30, 2010 (fiscal years 1992 through 2010) because the Commission did not collect information on the type of drug involved in drug offenses prior to fiscal year 1992.

[96] For some of these offenders, the guideline range that applied at sentencing was derived from either the Career Offender (USSG §4B1.1) or Armed Career Criminal (USSG §4B1.4) provision. However, for the purpose of this analysis these offenders are considered to have been sentenced under the drug trafficking guideline as the court is required to calculate a guideline range for them under USSG §2D1.1 as well.

[97] Because many of the offenders currently incarcerated in the BoP for crack offenses were sentenced after August 3, 2010, the mandatory minimum penalty provisions applied by the courts in most of those cases were the lower penalties provided by the FSA. Some courts did continue to apply the pre-FSA minimum penalties to offenders sentenced after August 3, 2010 but who committed their crime prior to that date. However, the Supreme Court's opinion in *Dorsey* clarified that this practice was in error.

[98] U.S. SENTENCING COMMISSION, GUIDELINES MANUAL §2D1.1 (Unlawful Manufacturing, Importing, Exporting or Trafficking (Including Possession with Intent to Commit These Offenses); Attempt or Conspiracy) (2013) (hereinafter USSG); USSG §2D1.11 (Unlawfully Distributing, Importing, Exporting or Possessing a Listed Chemical; Attempt or Conspiracy).

[99] References in this memorandum to the "2014 drug guidelines amendment," "the amendment," or any similar references mean the amendment the Commission submitted to Congress on April 30,2014, that would modify the drug quantity tables in USSG §§2D1.J and 2D1.11.

[100] The analysis was limited to data from fiscal year 1992 and later because the Commission's data collection efforts prior to fiscal year 1992 were not as complete as in later years.

[101] Memorandum from the Office of Research and Data and the Office of General Counsel to Chair Saris, Commissioners, and Kenneth Cohen (May 27, 2014), *available at* www.ussc.gov.

[102] 18 U.S.C. § 3624(b).

[103] *Id.*

[104] Barber v. Thomas, 560 U.S. ___ (2010).

[105] Lanny Brewer, Assistant Attorney General, Criminal Division, U.S. Department of Justice, Remarks at the National District Attorneys Association Summer Conference (July 23, 2012) available at http://www.justice.gov/criminal/pr/speeches/2012/crm-speech

[106] A "bed year" is the cost to the BoP of incarcerating one inmate for one year. For example, one inmate who serves five years of imprisonment accounts for five bed years.

[107] The analysis was limited to data from fiscal year 1992 through September 30, 2013 (fiscal years 1992 through 2013) because the Commission's data collection efforts prior to fiscal year 1992 were not as complete as in later years. For example, the Commission did not collect information on the type of drug involved in drug offenses prior to fiscal year 1992.

[108] 18 U.S.C. § 3553(t); *see also* USSG §5Cl.2.

[109] *Id.*

[110] *See* USSG Ch.4, Pt.A, for a discussion on how the criminal history score is determined.

[111] Criminal history points are assessed by the court at the time of sentencing. *Id.*

[112] Offenders convicted of an offense for which the sentence imposed exceeded one year and one month are assessed three points under the sentencing guidelines. *See* USSG §4A1.1(a). Therefore, this Policy Option would expand safety valve relief to any offender who did not have any conviction that was assigned three points under the criminal history provisions of the guidelines.

[113] A "bed year" is the cost to the BoP of incarcerating one inmate for one year. For example, one inmate who serves five years of imprisonment accounts for five bed years.

[114] The analysis was limited to data from fiscal year 1992 through September 30, 2013 (fiscal years 1992 through 2013) because the Commission's data collection efforts prior to fiscal year 1992 were not as complete as in later years. For example, the Commission did not collect information on the type of drug involved in drug offenses prior to fiscal year 1992.

[115] *See* 28 U.S.C. § 994(o), which requires the Commission to periodically review and revise the sentencing guidelines.

[116] *See* 28 U.S.C. § 994(u), which requires that when the Commission "reduces the term of imprisonment recommended in the guidelines applicable to a particular offense or category of offenses, it shall specify in what circumstances and by what amount the sentences of prisoners serving terms of imprisonment for the offense may be reduced." The Commission does this through amendments to USSG §1B1.1O, which lists all of the amendments to the *Guidelines Manual* that may be retroactively applied.

[117] *See* 18 U.S.C.3582(c)(2), which authorizes the courts to resentence an incarcerated offender in light of the Commission's decision under 28 U.S.C. §§ 994(o) and (u) to retroactively apply an amendment to the *Guidelines Manual* if the sentencing range that applied at the time the offender was sentenced would be lower under the amended guideline.

[118] *See* U.S. SENTENCING COMMISSION, MANDATORY MINIMUM PENALTIES IN THE FEDERAL CRIMINAL JUSTICE SYSTEM 154 (2011).

[119] *Id.*

[120] *See* 18 U.S.C. § 3553(e); USSG §5K1.1.

[121] *See* 18 U.S.C. § 3553(f); USSG §5K3.1.

[122] USSG §2D1.1(b)(16).

[123] 18 U.S.C. § 3553(f); *see also* USSG §SC1 .2.

[124] *ld.*

[125] *See* USSG Ch.4, Pt.A, for a discussion on how the criminal history score is determined.

[126] Criminal history points are assessed by the court at the time of sentencing. *!d.*

[127] Offenders convicted of an offense for which the sentence imposed exceeded one year and one month are assessed three points under the sentencing guidelines. *See* USSG §4A1.1(a). Therefore, this Policy Option would expand safety valve relief to any offender who did not have any conviction that was assigned three points under the criminal history provisions of the guidelines.

[128] A "bed year" is the cost to the BoP of incarcerating one inmate for one year. For example, one inmate who serves five years of imprisonment accounts for five bed years.

[129] The analysis was limited to data from fiscal year 1992 through September 30, 20 13 (fiscal years 1992 through 2013) because the Commission's data collection efforts prior to fiscal year 1 992 were not as complete as in later years. For example, the Commission did not collect information on the type of drug involved in drug offenses prior to fiscal year 1 992.

[130] *See* 28 U.S.C. § 994(o), which requires the Commission to periodically review and revise the sentencing guidelines.

[131] *See* 28 U.S.C. § 994(u), which requires that when the Commission "reduces the term of imprisonment recommended in the guidelines applicable to a particular offense or category of offenses, it shall specify in what circumstances and by what amount the sentences of prisoners serving terms of imprisonment for the offense may be reduced." The Commission does this through amendments to USSG §181.10, which lists all of the amendments to the *Guidelines Manual* that may be retroactively applied.

[132] *See* 18 U.S.C. § 3582(c)(2), which authorizes the courts to resentence an incarcerated offender in light of the Commission's decision under 28 U.S.C. §§ 994(o) and (u) to retroactively apply an amendment to the *Guidelines Manual* if the sentencing range that applied at the time the offender was sentenced would be lower under the amended guideline.

[133] *See* U.S. SENTENCING COMMISSION, MANDATORY MINIMUM PENALTIES IN THE FEDERAL CRIMINAL JUSTICE SYSTEM 154 (2011).

[134] *Id.*

[135] *See* 18 U.S.C. § 3553(e); USSG §5K1.1.

[136] *See* 18 U.S.C. § 3553(f); USSG §5K3.1.

[137] USSG §2D1.1(b)(16).

In: The Federal Prison Population
Editor: Mason C. Darwin
ISBN: 978-1-63463-902-6

Chapter 2

THE FEDERAL PRISON POPULATION BUILDUP: OVERVIEW, POLICY CHANGES, ISSUES, AND OPTIONS*

Nathan James

SUMMARY

Since the early 1980s, there has been a historically unprecedented increase in the federal prison population. Some of the growth is attributable to changes in federal criminal justice policy during the previous three decades. An issue before Congress is whether policy makers consider the rate of growth in the federal prison population sustainable, and if not, what changes could be made to federal criminal justice policy to reduce the prison population while maintaining public safety. This report explores the issues related to the growing federal prison population.

The number of inmates under the Bureau of Prisons' (BOP's) jurisdiction has increased from approximately 25,000 in FY1980 to over 219,000 in FY2013. Since FY1980, the federal prison population has increased, on average, by approximately 5,900 inmates each year. Data show that a growing proportion of inmates are being incarcerated for immigration- and weapons-related offenses, but the largest portion of newly admitted inmates are being incarcerated for drug offenses. Data also show that approximately 7 in 10 inmates are sentenced for five years or less.

Changes in federal sentencing and correctional policy since the early 1980s have contributed to the rapid growth in the federal prison population. These changes include increasing the number of federal offenses subject to mandatory minimum sentences; changes to the federal criminal code that have made more crimes federal offenses; and eliminating parole.

There are several issues related to the growing federal prison population that might be of interest to policy makers:

- The increasing number of federal inmates, combined with the rising per capita cost of incarceration, has made it increasingly more expensive to operate and

* This is an edited, reformatted and augmented version of a Congressional Research Service publication, No. R42937, dated April 15, 2014.

maintain the federal prison system. The per capita cost of incarceration for all inmates increased from $21,603 in FY2000 to $29,291 in FY2013. During this same period of time, appropriations for the BOP increased from $3.668 billion to $6.445 billion.

- The federal prison system is increasingly overcrowded. Overall, the federal prison system was 36% over its rated capacity in FY2013, but high- and medium-security male facilities were operating at 52% and 45%, respectively, over rated capacity. At issue is whether overcrowding might lead to more inmate misconduct. The results of research on this topic have been mixed. One study found that overcrowding does not affect inmate misconduct; but the BOP, based on its own research, concluded that there is a significant positive relationship between the two.
- The inmate-to-staff ratio has increased from 4.1 inmates per staff member in FY2000 to 4.8 inmates per staff member in FY2013. The inmate to correctional officer ratio was the same in FY2013 as it was in FY2000 (9.9 inmates for each correctional officer), and the current inmate to correctional officer ratio is down from a high of 10.9 inmates per correctional officer in FY2005.
- The growing prison population is taking a toll on the infrastructure of the federal prison system. The BOP reports that it has a backlog of 159 modernization and repair projects with an approximate cost of $342 million. Past appropriations left the BOP in a position where it could expand bedspace to manage overcrowding but not reduce it. However, reductions in funding since FY2010 mean that the BOP will lack the funding to begin new prison construction in the near future. At the same time, it has become more expensive to expand the BOP's capacity.

Should Congress choose to consider policy options to address the issues resulting from the growth in the federal prison population, policy makers could choose options such as increasing the capacity of the federal prison system by building more prisons; investing in rehabilitative programming (e.g., substance abuse treatment or educational programs) as a way of keeping inmates constructively occupied and potentially reducing recidivism after inmates are released; or placing more inmates in private prisons.

Policy makers might also consider whether they want to revise some of the policy changes that have been made over the past three decades that have contributed to the steadily increasing number of offenders being incarcerated. For example, Congress could consider options such as (1) modifying mandatory minimum penalties, (2) expanding the use of Residential Reentry Centers, (3) placing more offenders on probation, (4) reinstating parole for federal inmates, (5) expanding the amount of good time credit an inmate can earn, and (6) repealing federal criminal statutes for some offenses.

INTRODUCTION

The Bureau of Prisons (BOP) is the largest correctional agency in the country in terms of the number of prisoners under its jurisdiction.[1] The BOP currently operates 119 correctional facilities in 35 states and Puerto Rico.[2] The BOP was established in 1930 to house federal inmates, professionalize the prison service, and ensure consistent and centralized administration of the federal prison system.[3]

Since the early 1980s, there has been a historically unprecedented increase in the number of inmates incarcerated in the federal prison system. The number of inmates under the BOP's jurisdiction has increased from approximately 25,000 in FY1980 to over 219,000 in FY2013.

In comparison, the federal prison population increased by approximately 12,000 inmates between 1930 and 1980. Since FY1980, the federal prison population has increased, on average, by approximately 5,900 inmates each fiscal year.

Some of the growth in the federal prison population is attributable to policy changes over the previous three decades, including

- increasing the number of federal offenses subject to mandatory minimum sentences,
- changes to the federal criminal code that have made more crimes federal offenses, and
- eliminating parole.

The BOP faces several challenges resulting from the increasing number of inmates placed under its supervision. The first is the increasing cost of operating the federal prison system. Data show that with each passing fiscal year it is increasingly more expensive to incarcerate an inmate in a federal prison, yet the BOP must operate the federal prison system within the annual appropriation approved by Congress. Second, the federal prison system is becoming more overcrowded, especially in high- and medium-security male prisons. Research conducted by the BOP suggests that there might be a link between higher levels of overcrowding and inmate misconduct. Third, the federal inmate population is increasing at a rate whereby the gap between the number of inmates and the number of staff and correctional officers is slowly starting to widen. Finally, the rising federal inmate population is starting to place a strain on the infrastructure of the federal prison system. The BOP has not been able to expand prison capacity at a rate that would allow it to close older prisons and it has also had to defer hundreds of millions of dollars in maintenance costs, which might result in either direct or indirect security problems.

There are a number of policy avenues lawmakers could consider should Congress choose to address the growth in the federal prison population. Several options—such as expanding the capacity of the federal prison system, continued investment in rehabilitative programs, and placing inmates in private prisons—either continue or expand current correctional policies. However, Congress might also consider changing some existing correctional or sentencing policies as a means of addressing some of the issues related to the growth of the federal prison population. Some of these options include placing some inmates in alternatives to incarceration, such as probation, or expanding early release options by allowing inmates to earn more good time credit or allowing inmates to be placed on parole once again. Congress could consider reducing the amount of time inmates are incarcerated in federal prisons by repealing mandatory minimum penalties for some offenses or reducing the length of the mandatory minimum sentence. Finally, policy makers could consider repealing federal criminal statutes for some offenses.

FEDERAL PRISON POPULATION

At the end of 1930, the BOP operated 14 facilities that held approximately 13,000 inmates.[4] By the end of 1940, the BOP had expanded to 24 facilities that held approximately 24,000 inmates.[5] The number of inmates in the federal prison system, with a few fluctuations, remained at approximately 24,000 for the next four decades.[6] Then, as shown in **Figure 1**, beginning in FY1980 the federal prison population started an unabated, three-decade increase. The total number of inmates under the BOP's jurisdiction increased from approximately 25,000 in FY1980 to over 219,000 in FY2013. Between FY1980 and FY2013, the federal prison population increased, on average, by approximately 5,900 inmates annually. The growth in the federal prison population was much higher between FY1990 and FY2009 compared to the period of FY1980 through FY1989. On average, the federal prison population increased by approximately 3,700 inmates per fiscal year between FY1980 and FY1989. In contrast, the average increase per fiscal year between FY1990 and FY1999 was approximately 7,600 inmates and between FY2000 and FY2009 it was approximately 7,500 inmates. The growth in the federal prison population for the first few years of the current decade has been erratic. The federal prison population only grew by nearly 1,500 inmates between FY2009 and FY2010, but in FY2011, it grew by more than 7,500 inmates, which is more in line with previous trends. The number of inmates under the BOP's jurisdiction continued to increase over the last two fiscal years, but at a much slower rate. The total number of inmates in federal prison increased by approximately 900 prisoners in FY2012 and approximately 600 inmates in FY2013, the lowest level of annual growth in the number of inmates in any fiscal year since FY1980.

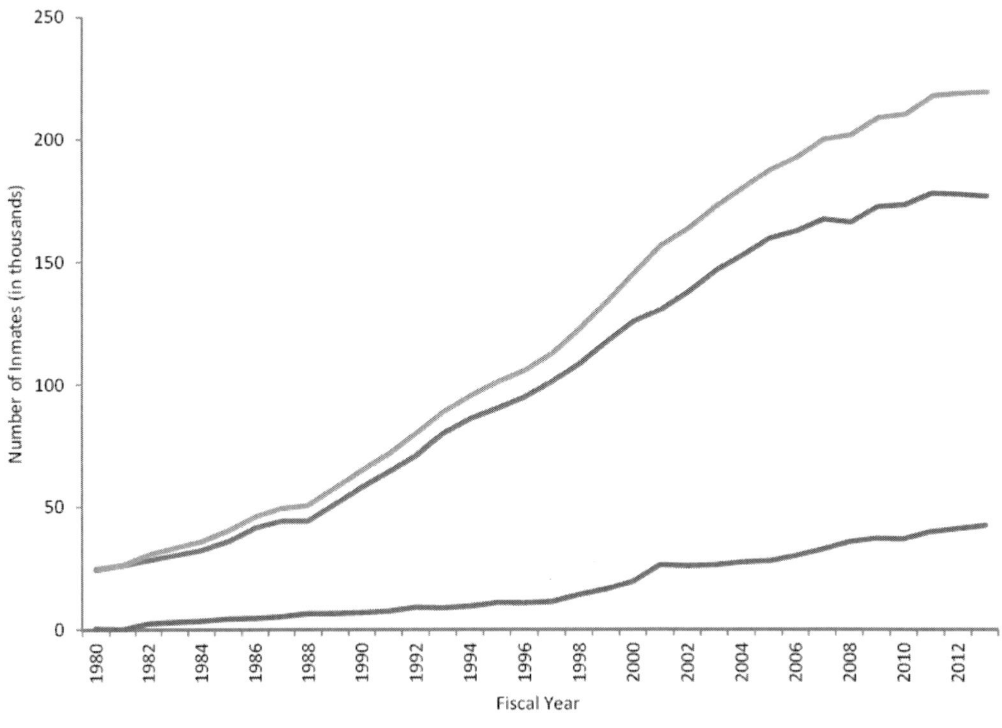

Institution (middle line)
Contract (lower line)
Total (upper line)
Source: Presentation of data provided by the U.S. Department of Justice, Bureau of Prisons.

Figure 1. Federal Prison Population, FY1980-FY2013; Number of inmates in thousands.

Recent trends in the federal prison population stand in contrast to overall incarceration trends. The Bureau of Justice Statistics (BJS) reports that the total number of inmates under the jurisdiction of state correctional authorities decreased each year between 2009 and 2012.[7] However, while the number of state inmates has decreased, the federal prison population has continued to increase, although growth over the past couple of fiscal years has been much slower than it was in the past.

The data in **Figure 1** also show that most of the federal prison population is incarcerated in a BOP facility, as opposed to a contract facility.[8] However, over the years the BOP has had to rely increasingly on contract facilities to help manage the federal prison population. In FY1980, less than 2% of federal inmates were housed in a contract facility. The number of federal inmates in contract facilities increased to nearly 11% in FY1990, approximately 14% in FY2000, and nearly 18% in FY2010.

The following discussion of some of the demographics of federal inmates uses data from the BJS rather than the BOP. BJS data on federal prisoners are only available for FY1998 through FY2011. Therefore, the BJS data cannot be used to show how these select demographics changed since the federal prison population started its sustained growth in the early 1980s. The proceeding discussion is intended to provide context for the discussion later in the report of potential policy options for addressing federal prison population growth.

Conviction Offense for Federal Inmates

As shown in **Figure 2**, in FY1998 approximately 18% of inmates entering the federal prison system were convicted for an immigration offense. There was a slight increase in the proportion of such inmates being sent to federal prison in both FY1999 and FY2000, but this trend was reversed by FY2002. However, in FY2003, the proportion of inmates entering the federal prison system for immigration offenses started an unabated increase. By FY2011, immigration offenders accounted for approximately 31% of all inmates entering the system that fiscal year. There was also a noticeable increase in the number of inmates entering the federal prison system for weapons-related convictions between FY1998 and FY2011, but it was not as pronounced as the increase in the number of inmates convicted for immigration offenses. Also, unlike the immigration offenders, the proportion of inmates entering federal prisons for weapons-related offenses has leveled off. One other noticeable trend is the decrease in the proportion of inmates being sent to federal prison for violent and property crimes. In FY1998, violent and property offenders comprised approximately 9% and 18%, respectively, of all inmates entering federal prison. By FY2011, these offenders accounted for approximately 4% and 10% of prison admissions. The proportion of offenders entering federal prison for public order offenses[9] remained relatively consistent between FY1998 and FY2011.

Despite the increase in the proportion of inmates entering the federal prison system for immigration offenses, drug offenders still constitute the largest portion of inmates entering federal prisons.

The proportion of inmates being sent to federal prison for drug offenses has decreased somewhat since FY1998 (when 41% of inmates entering federal prison were convicted for drug offenses).

In every fiscal year between FY1998 and FY2011, drug offenders constituted the largest proportion of prison admissions, though in FY2009-FY2011, immigration offenders were a close second. In FY2011, the vast majority of sentenced drug offenders, nearly 99%,[10] were sent to federal prison for trafficking offenses.[11]

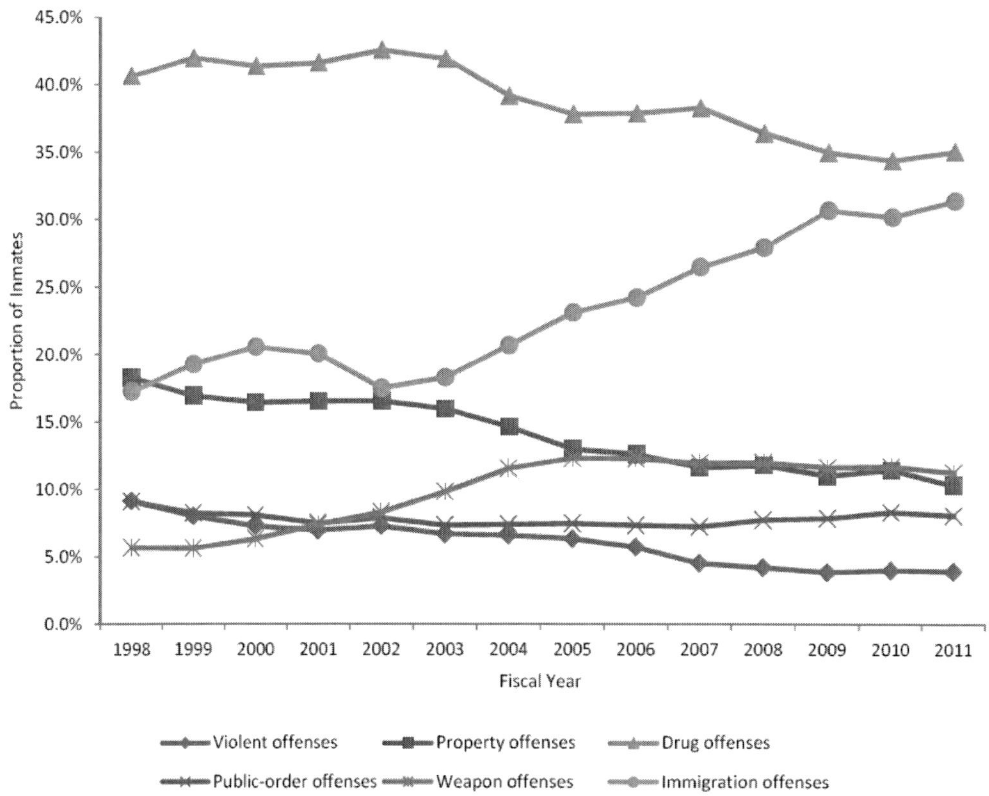

Source: Presentation of data from the U.S. Department of Justice, Bureau of Justice Statistics, Federal Criminal Case Processing Statistics.

Notes: Percentages were calculated excluding offenders whose conviction offense was classified as "unknown."

Figure 2. Conviction Offenses of Inmates Entering Federal Prison, FY1998-FY2011.

As shown in **Figure 3**, in FY1998, weapons and immigration offenders were 8% and 7%, respectively, of all federal inmates. By FY2011, weapons and immigration offenders comprised 15% and 13% of all federal inmates. By FY2011, approximately 8 out of every 10 inmates in federal prison were incarcerated for a drug, weapons, or immigration offense. While a growing proportion of federal inmates were incarcerated for drug, weapons, or immigration offenses, fewer inmates were incarcerated for violent offenses. In FY1998, nearly 12% of federal inmates were incarcerated for a violent offense; by FY2011, the proportion of federal inmates incarcerated for violent offenses decreased to 6%.

Length of Sentences for Federal Offenders

As shown in **Figure 4**, in any given fiscal year between FY1998 and FY2011, more than 7 in 10 inmates entering the federal prison system were sentenced to a term of incarceration that was five years or less. The data indicate three distinct trends in the sentencing of federal inmates. First, since FY1998 approximately 3 of every 10 inmates entering federal prisons were sentenced to a term of incarceration that was less than 1 year, though fewer inmates entered the federal prison system in FY2011 with a sentence of 1 year or less compared to FY1998. Second, since FY1998 there has been a slow, but steady, growth in the proportion of inmates sentenced to between 3 and 5 years of incarceration, and to a lesser extent, in the proportion of inmates sentenced to between 5 and 10 years of incarceration. Third, the number of inmates sentenced to more than 1 year but less than 3 years has been increasing since FY2004, and in FY2011 the proportion of inmates with a sentence in this range had reached the level it was at in FY2003.

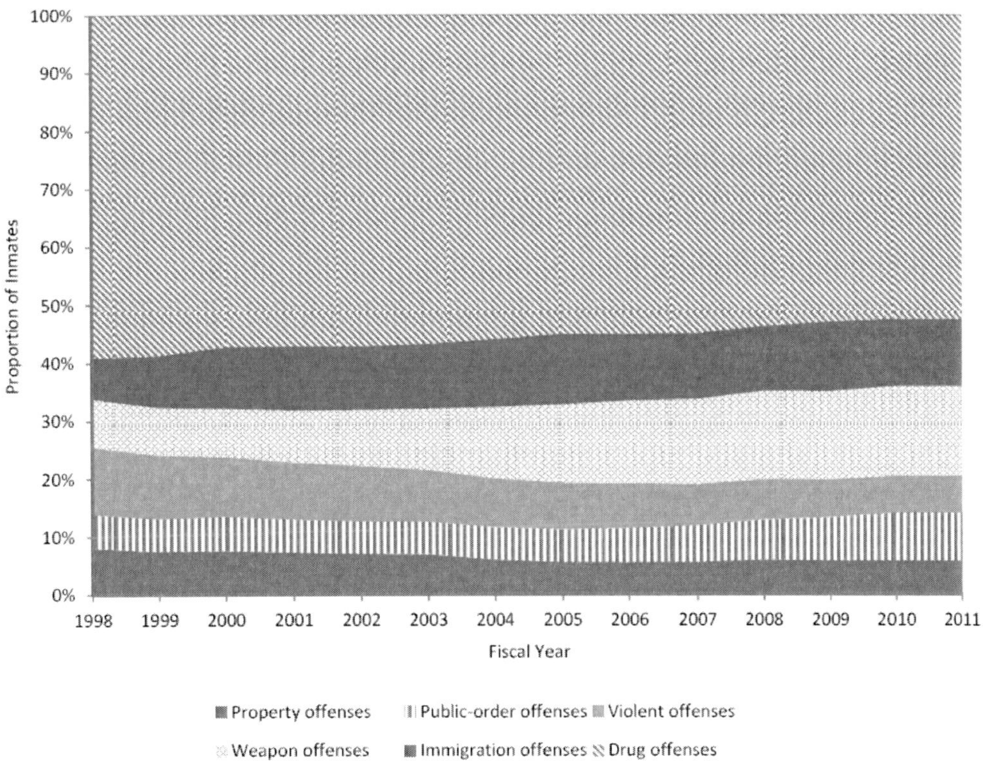

Source: Presentation of data from the U.S. Department of Justice, Bureau of Justice Statistics, Federal Criminal Case Processing Statistics.

Notes: Percentages were calculated excluding offenders whose sentence was classified as "unknown."

Figure 3. Inmates in Federal Prison at the End of the Fiscal Year, by Major Offense Type, FY1998-FY2011.

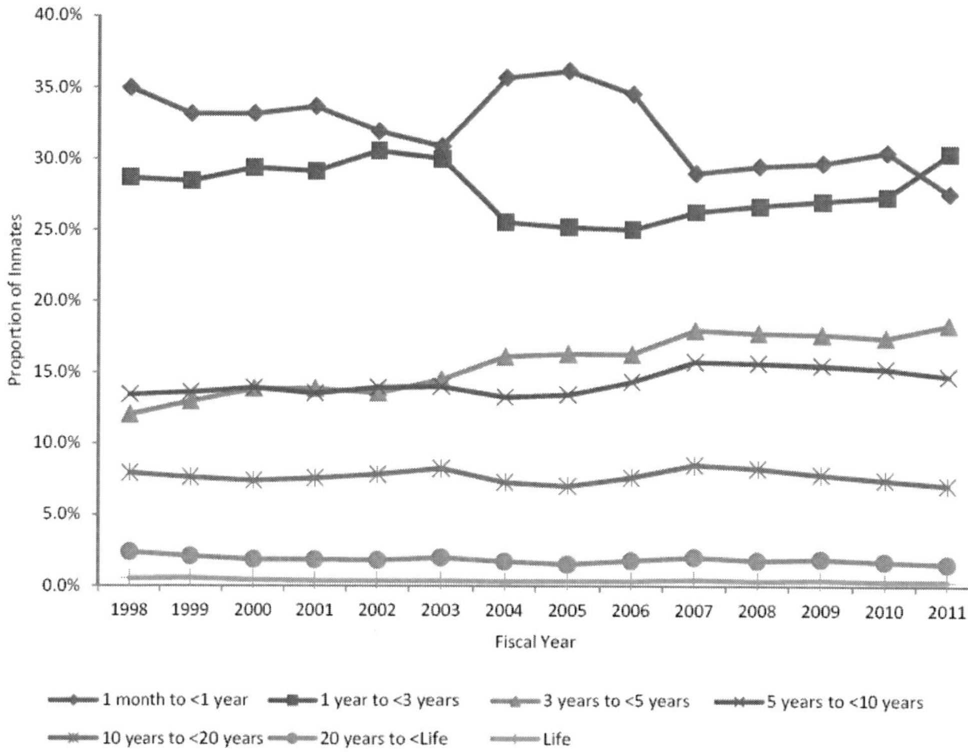

Source: Presentation of data from the U.S. Department of Justice, Bureau of Justice Statistics, Federal Criminal Case Processing Statistics.

Notes: Percentages were calculated excluding offenders whose sentence was classified as "unknown."

Figure 4. Length of Sentence for Inmates Entering Federal Prison, FY1998-FY2011.

POLICY CHANGES THAT CONTRIBUTED TO PRISON POPULATION GROWTH

A confluence of changes to federal sentencing and correctional policy since the early 1980s— including the expanded use of mandatory minimum penalties, the increased federalization of crime, and the abolition of parole for federal inmates—have contributed to the growing federal prison population. The expanded use of mandatory minimum penalties has resulted in offenders being sentenced to longer terms of imprisonment than they were 20 years ago. At the same time, the expanding federal criminal code, combined with greater enforcement of federal criminal statutes, has resulted in more people entering the federal criminal justice system. Thus, while more offenders are being arrested by federal law enforcement, tried in federal courts, and sentenced to incarceration in federal prisons for increasingly longer periods of time, the abolition of parole ensures that most inmates will serve all or nearly all of their sentences.

Mandatory Minimum Sentences

In a 2011 report, the United States Sentencing Commission (USSC) found that the enactment of a greater number of federal mandatory minimum sentences has, in part, contributed to the growing federal prison population. Mandatory minimum penalties have contributed to federal prison population growth because they have increased in number, have been applied to more offenses, required longer terms of imprisonment, and are used more frequently than they were 20 years ago.[12]

The number of mandatory minimum penalties in the federal code expanded as Congress made more offenses subject to such penalties. The USSC reported that the number of mandatory minimum penalties in the federal criminal code nearly doubled from 98 to 195 from 1991 to 2011.[13] Not only has there been an increase in the number of federal offenses that carry a mandatory minimum penalty, but offenders who are convicted of offenses with mandatory minimums are being sent to prison for longer periods. For example, the USSC found that, compared to FY1990 (43.6%), a larger proportion of defendants convicted of offenses that carried a mandatory minimum penalty in FY2010 (55.5%) were convicted of offenses that carried a mandatory minimum penalty of five years or more.[14]

While only offenders convicted for an offense carrying a mandatory minimum penalty are subject to those penalties, mandatory minimum penalties have, in effect, increased sentences for other offenders.[15] The USSC has incorporated many mandatory minimum penalties into the sentencing guidelines, which means that penalties for other offense categories under the guidelines had to increase in order to keep a sense of proportionality.[16] Research by the Urban Institute found that increases in expected time served contributed to half of the prison population growth between 1998 and 2010.[17] The increase in amount of time inmates were expected to serve was probably partially the result of inmates receiving longer sentences and partially the result of inmates being required to serve approximately 85% of their sentences after Congress eliminated parole for federal prisoners (this is discussed in greater detail in the "Eliminating Parole for Federal Inmates" section).

However, the increase in the federal prison population is not solely attributable to the increased use of mandatory minimum penalties. The USSC reported that the number of inmates in the federal prison system who were convicted of an offense that carried a mandatory minimum penalty increased 178%, from approximately 40,000 in FY1995 to nearly 112,000 in FY2010.[18]

Of these offenders, nearly 30,000 in FY1995 and approximately 80,000 in FY2010 were actually subject to a mandatory minimum penalty.[19] However, over the same time period there was a similar rate of growth in the number of inmates in federal prison who were not convicted of an offense that carried a mandatory minimum. In FY1995, nearly 32,000 inmates in federal prison were convicted of an offense that did not carry a mandatory minimum.[20] This increased 152%, to approximately 80,000 inmates, by FY2010.

Federalization of Crime

While the increase in the number of federal criminal statutes carrying a mandatory minimum sentence has contributed to the escalating federal prison population, the USSC also identified the federalization of crime[21] as another contributing factor to prison population growth. Over the past four decades the federalization of crime resulted in more people entering the federal criminal justice system as federal law enforcement agencies and the U.S. Attorneys Office started to enforce a broader array of federal offenses. The Urban Institute concluded that increased federal law enforcement activity contributed to about 13% of the growth in the federal prison population between 1998 and 2010, though the effects were not consistent across offense types and time.[22] For example, heightened immigration enforcement and increased investigation of weapons offenses contributed to approximately one-tenth of the population growth, but the growth in the prison population resulting from investigating more weapons offenses mainly occurred between 1998 and 2005.[23] However, decreased drug investigations reduced the federal prison population from what it might have been assuming that federal law enforcement priorities and practices had remained as they were in 1998.[24]

Eliminating Parole for Federal Inmates

The BOP has identified the abolition of parole for federal inmates as one cause of the growing federal prison population.[25] The Comprehensive Crime Control Act of 1984 (P.L. 98-473) abolished parole for federal inmates and modified how much good time credit an inmate could earn. Anyone sentenced to incarceration for a federal crime committed after November 1, 1987, is not eligible for parole. Abolishing parole in the federal correctional system means that the BOP has not only had to confine a growing number of inmates, but it also has to confine them until they serve all, or nearly all, of their sentences. The remainder of federal inmates will have to serve their entire sentence, minus any good time credit they might earn.[26]

Issues Related to Prison Population Growth

The growth of the federal prison population has given rise to several issues of interest to policy makers. These include

- the increasing cost of operating the federal prison system;
- overcrowding in federal prisons;
- an increasing inmate-to-staff ratio; and
- a growing need for capital investment in correctional facilities.

Analysis of these issues is provided below.

Cost of Operating the Federal Prison System

The burgeoning prison population has contributed to mounting operational expenditures for the federal prison system. Congress funds BOP's operations through two accounts: Salaries and Expenses (S&E) and Buildings and Facilities (B&F).[27] The S&E account (i.e., the operating budget) provides for the custody and care of federal inmates and for the daily maintenance and operations of correctional facilities, regional offices, and BOP's central office in Washington, DC. It also provides funding for the incarceration of federal inmates in state, local, and private facilities. The B&F account (i.e., the capital budget) provides funding for the construction of new facilities and the modernization, repair, and expansion of existing facilities.

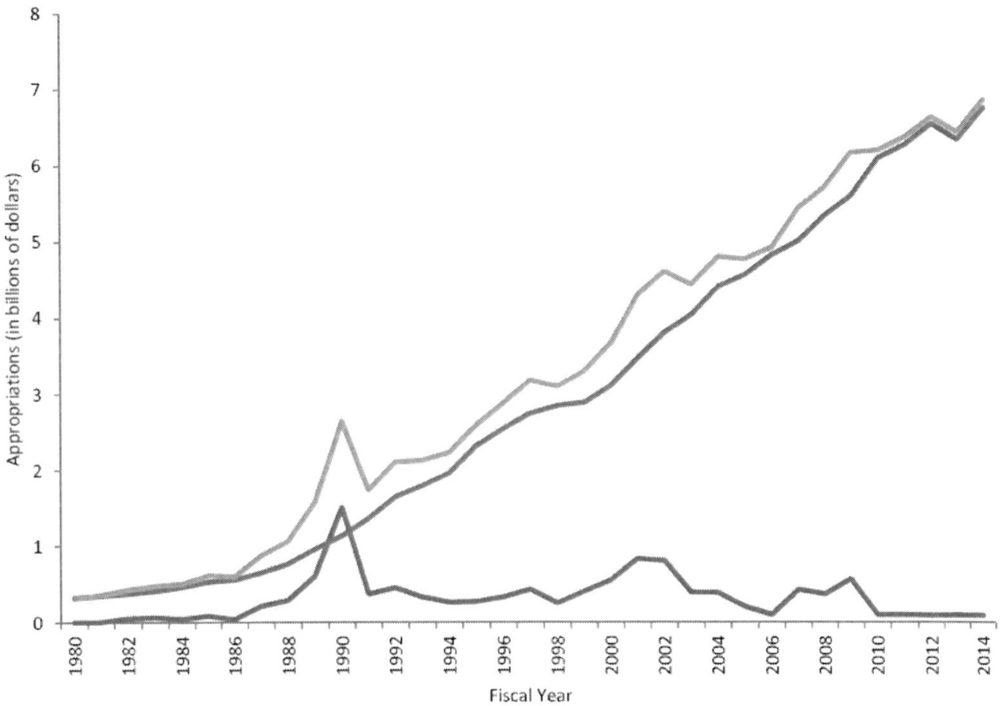

Salaries and Expenses (middle line)
Building and Facilities (lower line)
Total (upper line)
Source: Presentation of data provided by the U.S. Department of Justice, Bureau of Prisons.
Notes: Between FY1980 and FY1995, appropriations for the National Institute of Corrections (NIC) were provided in a separate account. After FY1995, the operating expenses for NIC are paid out of the BOP's S&E account. Therefore, to make appropriations for the S&E account as comparable as possible, appropriations for the NIC for FY1980-FY1995 were added to appropriations for the S&E account. Between FY1996 and FY2000, the BOP received an amount from the Violent Crime Reduction Trust Fund, which, according to the BOP, was used for substance abuse treatment. As such, these amounts were also added to the S&E account Appropriations include all supplemental and reprogrammed appropriations and rescissions to current year budget authority. The FY2013 enacted amount also includes the amount sequestered per the Budget Control Act of 2011 (P.L. 112- 25).

Figure 5. Appropriations for the BOP, FY1980-FY2014; Appropriations in billions of dollars.

As shown in **Figure 5**, the BOP's appropriations increased more than $6.544 billion from FY1980 ($330 million) to FY2014 ($6.874 billion). Between FY1980 and FY2014, the average annual increase in the BOP's appropriation was approximately $192 million. The data show that, by and large, growth in the BOP's appropriation is the result of ever-growing appropriations for the S&E account. This is not surprising considering the constant growth in the federal prison population and the fact that the S&E account provides funding for the care of federal inmates. Also, it has been argued that even though appropriations for the BOP's S&E account are discretionary, they are effectively mandatory because "[b]y law, the BOP must accept and provide for all [f]ederal inmates, including but not limited to inmate care, custodial staff, contract beds, food, and medical costs. The BOP cannot control the number of inmates sentenced to prison, and unlike other [f]ederal agencies, cannot limit assigned workloads and thereby control operating costs."[28] Appropriations for the B&F account have not grown as steadily as appropriations for the S&E account. This is, in part, explained by how funding for the B&F account is used; namely, Congress typically provides marked increases in this account only when there is a decision to expand prison capacity. For example, the noticeable spike in appropriations for the B&F account in FY1990 paved the way for an increase in BOP's prison capacity in the mid- to late 1990s.

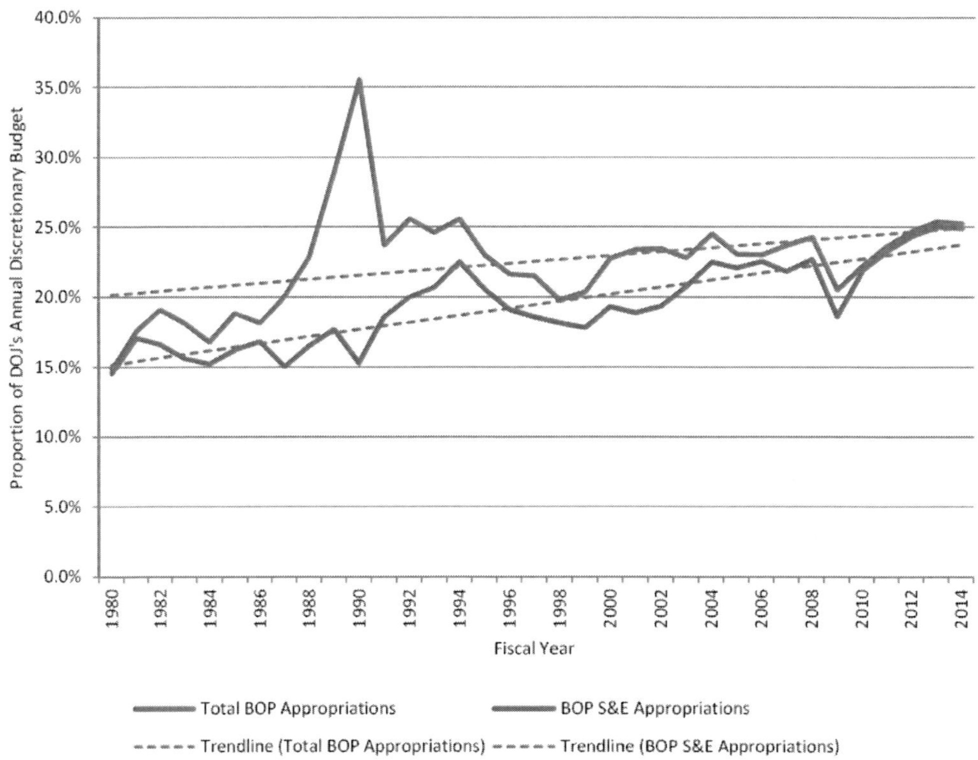

Source: The BOP's annual appropriation data was provided by the U.S. Department of Justice, Bureau of Prisons. Annual discretionary budget authority data for the Department of Justice for FY1980-FY2013 were taken from Table 5.4 from the FY2015 *Budget of the United States Government*.

Figure 6. The BOP's Appropriation as a Share of the DOJ's Discretionary Budget Authority, FY1980-FY2014.

The BOP's expanding budget is starting to consume a larger share of the DOJ's overall annual appropriation. **Figure 6** shows what proportion of the DOJ's annual discretionary budget was dedicated to the BOP. The BOP's overall budget is more susceptible to fluctuations due to changes in year-to-year appropriations for BOP's B&F account. The trend lines show that since FY1980 both the BOP's total budget and S&E account have, in general, encompassed a growing share of the DOJ annual appropriation. The noticeable spike in the BOP's share of the DOJ's annual appropriation in FY1990 was the result of Congress appropriating more than $1 billion for the B&F account. In addition, the decrease in the BOP's share of DOJ's appropriation observed in FY2009, a break in a general upward trend that started in FY2000, was the result of Congress appropriating an additional $4 billion for DOJ under the American Recovery and Reinvestment Act of 2009 (P.L. 111-5).

A comparison of the BOP's annual appropriations for its S&E and B&F accounts to the Administration's request for both accounts shows that Congress has been more likely to fund the Administration's request for prison construction and less likely to fully fund the Administration's request for the upkeep and care of the prison population (see **Figure 7**). The requested appropriation indicates what the BOP believed it would need to properly manage the growing prison population each fiscal year. The data suggest that in many fiscal years the BOP operated with a budget below what it felt was adequate given the growing number of inmates under its jurisdiction.

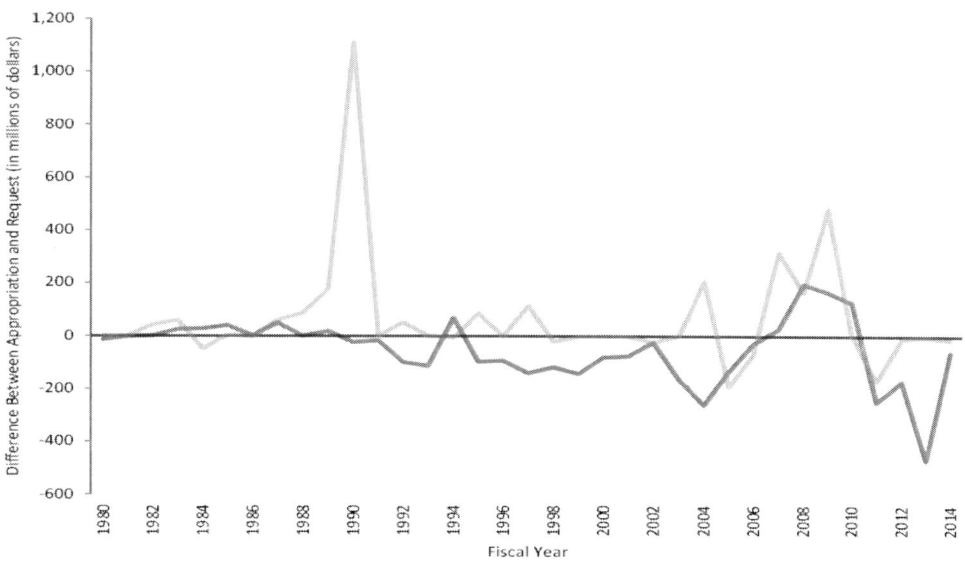

S&E (lower line)

B&F (upper line)

Source: Appropriated amounts were provided by the U.S. Department of Justice, Bureau of Prisons. The Administration's requested amounts were taken from the appendix to the *Budget of the United States Government*, for FY1980-FY2014.

Notes: Between FY1980 and FY1995, appropriations for the National Institute of Corrections (NIC) were provided in a separate account. After FY1995, the operating expenses for NIC are paid out of the BOP's S&E account. Therefore, to make appropriations for the S&E account as comparable as possible, appropriations for the NIC for FY1980-FY1995 were added to appropriations for the S&E account. Between FY1996 and FY2000, the BOP received an amount from the Violent Crime Reduction Trust Fund, which, according to the BOP, was used for substance abuse treatment. As such, these amounts were also added to the S&E account.

Figure 7. Difference Between Appropriations and the Administration's Request for the BOP's S&E and B&F Accounts; Amounts in millions of dollars.

The data presented in **Figure 7** show that between FY1980 and FY2014, Congress appropriated less than the Administration's request for the B&F account 16 times. Over the same time period Congress appropriated less than the Administration's request for the S&E account 22 times. In contrast to this general trend, however, the amount appropriated for the S&E account between FY2007 and FY2010 actually exceeded the Administration's request. The additional amounts, as noted by the House Committee on Appropriations, were to compensate for underfunding the BOP, which resulted in inadequate staffing levels and shortfalls in inmate programs.[29] Both the House and Senate Committee on Appropriations reported that they felt that the Administration's requests for the BOP were inadequate for several years, which did not allow the bureau to meet its basic operational needs.[30]

While it is not surprising that the BOP's annual appropriations would increase along with the prison population—after all, more inmates require more care and supervision, which requires additional funding—recent per capita expenditure data from the BOP indicate that it is getting more expensive each year to incarcerate an inmate in the federal system. As shown in **Table 1**, the overall per capita cost of incarcerating an inmate in the federal system has steadily increased from FY2000 to FY2013. Over this time period, the cost of incarceration rose from approximately $22,000 per inmate to more than $29,000 per inmate, an increase of 35.6%.

Table 1. Per Capita Cost of Incarceration in the Federal Prison System, FY2000-FY2013

Fiscal Year	All of BOP	Security Level				Federal Correctional Complexes[a]
		High	Medium	Low	Minimum	
2000	$21,603	$26,518	$21,417	$18,407	$17,452	$21,360
2001	22,175	26,135	21,806	18,846	17,788	20,543
2002	22,518	27,456	21,473	19,228	18,770	21,538
2003	23,180	26,461	21,946	19,480	18,136	21,948
2004	23,267	26,951	21,896	19,242	17,647	21,764
2005	23,431	26,377	21,718	19,193	17,478	22,458
2006	24,439	25,398	23,648	20,834	17,291	23,152
2007	24,923	26,109	23,492	21,922	17,812	22,804
2008	25,895	27,924	24,065	23,373	19,635	23,958
2009	27,251	32,119	25,442	24,087	20,772	25,750
2010	28,282	33,858	26,248	25,377	21,005	27,267
2011	28,894	34,629	26,852	26,853	21,286	27,516
2012	29,027	34,046	26,686	27,166	21,694	27,683
2013	29,291	33,887	27,278	27,386	21,960	28,330

Source: U.S. Department of Justice, Bureau of Prisons.

Notes: Per capita costs include support costs. The per capita cost of incarceration for all of BOP includes direct costs for federal detention centers, administrative security facilities, medical referral centers, privately operated institutions, residential reentry centers, and contracts with state and local institutions. It also includes support costs for federal detention centers, administrative security facilities, and medical referral centers.

a. Federal correctional complexes (FCC) contain two or more facilities with different security levels on the same grounds. For example, FCC Allenwood (PA) contains a high, medium, and low security facility.

However, the per capita cost of incarceration decreases as inmates are moved into lower-security level institutions. For example, in FY2013 it cost the BOP approximately $34,000 to house an inmate in a high-security facility. In comparison, it cost the BOP approximately $27,000 to house an inmate in either a medium- or low-security facility and nearly $22,000 to house an inmate in a minimum-security facility. This is partly because lower-security facilities do not require as many correctional officers; hence their operating expenditures are lower. In addition, the rated capacity for a facility decreases as the security level increases, meaning that higher-security facilities hold fewer inmates, which results in a higher per capita cost of incarceration for higher-security facilities. For example, even if the total operating expenditures for a high- and a low-security facility were the same for any given fiscal year, the per capita expenditure in the high-security facility would be greater because it held fewer inmates.

The BOP has identified rising utility, food, and medical care costs as three of the primary drivers of the increasing cost of the federal prison system.[31] The BOP's expenditures on utilities, food, and medical care have generally increased each fiscal year since FY2000.[32] As shown in **Figure 8**, on a per capita basis, nominal food costs increased 27% between FY2000-FY2013, nominal utility costs increased 68%, and nominal medical costs increased 83%. Nominal medical costs for the BOP are most likely increasing as the result of the general upward climb of health care costs in the United States, with annual increases in health care costs outstripping inflation.[33] The BOP reported that an increasing number of federal inmates require medical care, primarily as a result of the expanding inmate population. According to the BOP, conditions such as diabetes, hypertension, and infectious diseases have a slightly higher rate of incidence in the incarcerated population.[34] In addition, the federal prison population is aging—BJS data show that at the end of FY2011 approximately 15% of federal inmates were over the age of 50 and 4% were over the age of 60—and in general, older individuals require more medical care.

In addition to the rising nominal cost of utilities, food, and medical care, the nominal cost of providing rehabilitative programs for inmates has generally increased since FY2000 (see **Figure 9**). On a per capita basis, the BOP spends the most on education programs for inmates (not adjusted for inflation). In FY2013, the BOP spent nearly $250 more per inmate (not adjusted for inflation) for education programs than it did in FY2000, but the nominal per capita spending on education programs for FY2013 is down from a high of $847 per inmate in FY2011. The BOP had similar nominal per capita costs for substance abuse treatment programs and psychological services between FY2000 and FY2005. However, after FY2005, the nominal per capita costs for substance abuse treatment started to grow at a rate that exceeded that of psychological services. Between FY2000 and FY2013, nominal per capita spending on substance abuse treatment programs increased 114%. In comparison, nominal per capita spending on education programs increased 48% and nominal per capita spending on psychological services increased 29%.

The growing cost of providing education and substance abuse treatment programs might be the result of the BOP's need to expand access to programming in order to meet increasing demand. Under current law, the BOP is required to provide a functional literacy program for all mentally capable inmates who are not functionally literate and to offer literacy/General Equivalency Diploma (GED) programs for inmates who have not earned a high school diploma or its equivalent.[35] In addition, federal inmates are required to make satisfactory progress toward earning a high school diploma or a GED in order to earn their full allotment of good time credit.[36] The BOP reports that since these requirements went into effect, demand for literacy programs has increased.[37] Also, current law (18 U.S.C. §3621) requires BOP to provide, subject to appropriations, residential substance abuse treatment[38] and appropriate aftercare[39] for all eligible prisoners.[40] Prisoners who are convicted of nonviolent crimes and who successfully complete a residential substance abuse treatment program are eligible to have their sentence reduced by not more than one year.[41]

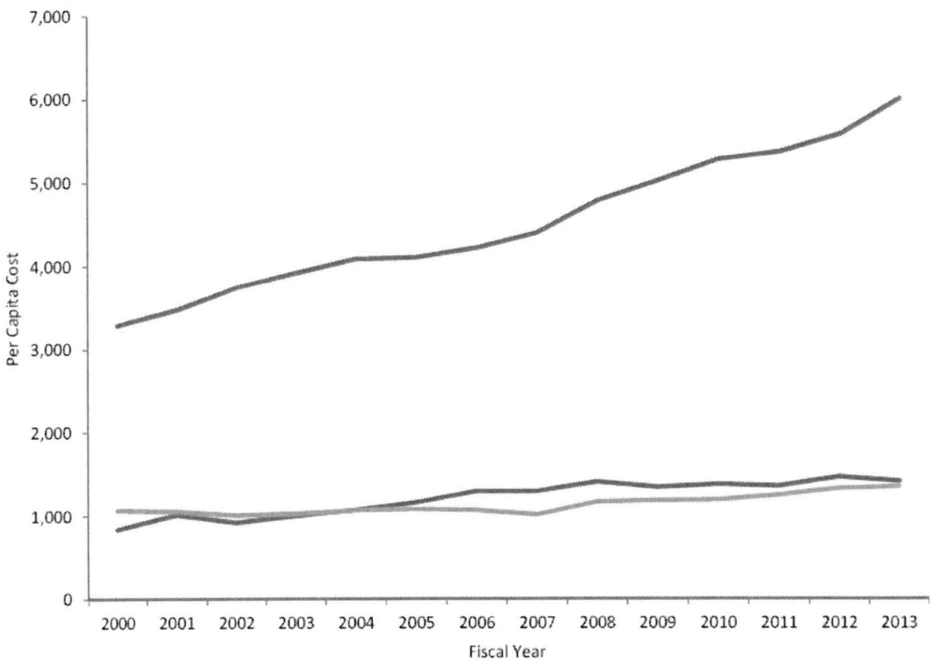

Medical (upper line)
Utilities (middle line)
Food (lower line)

Source: Based on a CRS analysis of data provided by the U.S. Department of Justice, Bureau of Prisons.

Notes: Per capita costs were calculated using figures on the number of inmates held in BOP facilities at the end of the fiscal year.

Figure 8. Per Capita Cost ($) of Medical Care, Utilities, and Food, FY2000-FY2013.

Obligations for psychology services include funding for most rehabilitative programming (e.g., mental health and sex offender treatment) other than education programs and substance abuse treatment. Per capita cost for psychology services increased starting in FY2007, which roughly coincides with provisions in the Adam Walsh Child Protection and Safety Act of 2006 (P.L. 109-248) requiring the BOP to provide sex offender treatment to all inmates who are in need of and suitable for it, and with the requirements in the Second Chance Act of 2007 (P.L. 110-199) that the BOP help prepare inmates for re-entry.

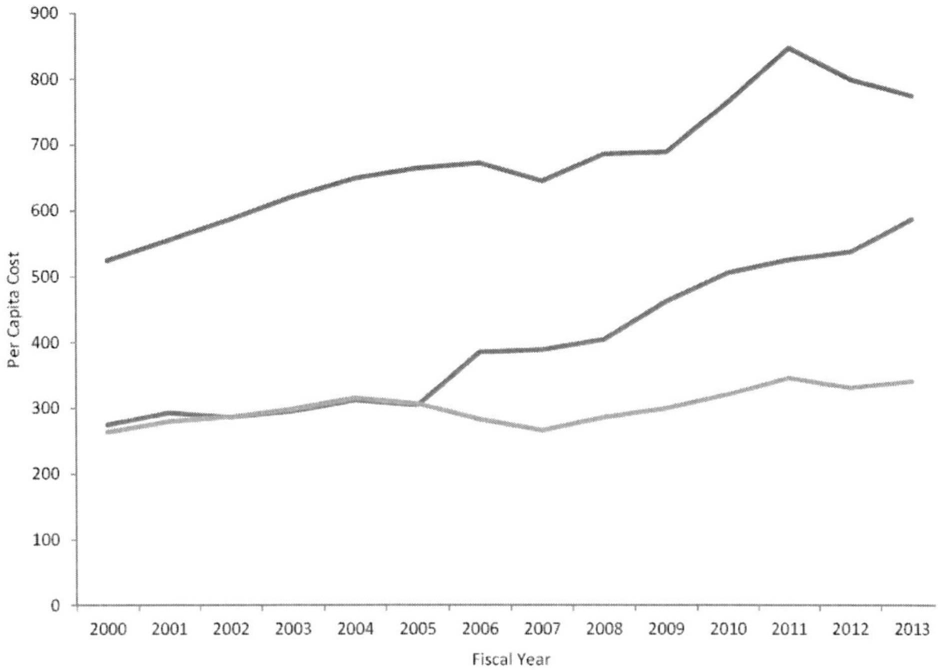

Substance abuse treatment (middle line)
Education (upper line)
Psychology services (lower line)
Source: Based on a CRS analysis of data provided by the U.S. Department of Justice, Bureau of Prisons.
Notes: Per capita costs were calculated using figures on the number of inmates held in BOP facilities at the end of the fiscal year.

Figure 9. Per Capita Cost ($) of Rehabilitative Programs, FY2000-FY2013.

The increasing cost of operating the federal prison system might be an issue for Congress as policy makers seek to find ways to reduce discretionary spending. The appropriations committees have already expressed concern that the continued growth in the federal prison population is not sustainable.[42] Unless there is a change in the upward trajectory in the number of inmates in the federal prison system, Congress will face a decision regarding appropriation of additional funds for the BOP. Assuming that growth in the budgetary requirements for the BOP exceeds the growth in the allocation for the Administration of Justice budget function under the annual budget resolution, policy makers might face a choice to reduce appropriations for other DOJ agencies or DOJ grant programs in order to fund the federal prison system.

Prison Overcrowding

The growth of the federal prison population has resulted in the BOP incarcerating more inmates than the federal prison system is rated to hold. Figure 10 shows that the level of overcrowding in the federal prison system has changed over the years. Overcrowding reflects the difference between how many inmates the federal prison system is "rated" to hold and how many inmates the system actually holds.[43] For example, if the overcrowding level is 35%, this means that the number of inmates held in the federal system is 35% above the number of inmates the system is rated to hold. Between FY1991 and FY1997, the federal prison system's capacity nearly doubled (a 95.2% increase) while the institutional population increased by 57.0% over this same time period. The BOP was able to reduce prison overcrowding between FY1991 and FY1997 by adding more bedspace, but it also changed the way it calculated rated capacity for each of its facilities. Prior to FY1991, the BOP calculated its capacity based on single cell occupancy (i.e., one inmate per cell). But starting in FY1991, the BOP allowed for double bunking (i.e., two inmates to one cell) in its facilities, which resulted in an increase in its rated capacity, which in turn resulted in a decrease in overcrowding.

Source: FY1981-FY2013 crowding levels were provided by the U.S. Department of Justice, Bureau of Prisons.

Notes: Overcrowding rates for FY1981-FY1990 are not directly comparable to crowding rates after FY1990 because the BOP changed the way that it calculated its capacity.

Figure 10. Overcrowding in the Federal Prison System, FY1981-FY2013.

Data show that overcrowding in BOP facilities started to increase after FY1997, and it peaked in FY2004 when overcrowding was at 41%. The BOP's prison capacity expanded 30.7% between FY1997 and FY2004 while the prison population grew by 50.9%. Overcrowding remained around 35% between FY2005 and FY2010 after a steady growth between FY1997 and FY2004. However, prison overcrowding increased to 39% by the end of FY2011, the highest level since FY2004. Prison overcrowding decreased slightly in FY2012

(38%) and FY2013 (36%), due to a decrease in the institutional prison population (between FY2011 and FY2013 there were 1,085 fewer inmates held in BOP facilities), an increase in the number of beds (the BOP added 1,931 beds between FY2011 and FY2013), and greater use of contract bedspace (there were 2,615 more inmates in contract facilities in FY2013 than there were in FY2011).

Data from the BOP indicate that while federal prisons have been operating at 30% or more over rated capacity for more than a decade, the overcrowding problem is worse in high- and medium-security male facilities (see **Table 2**). Medium-security male facilities were operating at well over 50% of rated capacity for the early part of the previous decade. Overcrowding in medium-security facilities was brought down in the latter part of the previous decade because the BOP opened several additional facilities, but medium security overcrowding levels generally increased between FY2006 and FY2011, but overcrowding has decreased slightly over the past two fiscal years. For the earlier part of the previous decade, overcrowding in high security male facilities, in general, was not as bad as it was in medium security facilities. However, since FY2006, high security facilities have been more crowded than medium and low security facilities and above the average overcrowding within the federal prison system in general. Since FY2006, overcrowding in high security male facilities has been near or above 50%.

Table 2. Overcrowding in All BOP facilities and Low-, Medium-, and High-Security Male Facilities, FY1995-FY2013

Fiscal Year	All Facilities	Male Low	Male Medium	Male High
1995	25%	33%	52%	40%
1996	24%	31%	42%	65%
1997	22%	23%	37%	52%
1998	26%	27%	48%	56%
1999	31%	37%	51%	51%
2000	32%	42%	50%	54%
2001	32%	38%	58%	42%
2002	33%	39%	58%	41%
2003	39%	39%	59%	58%
2004	41%	45%	62%	49%
2005	34%	43%	42%	35%
2006	36%	41%	37%	53%
2007	37%	35%	42%	53%
2008	36%	35%	44%	50%
2009	37%	40%	47%	49%
2010	37%	37%	43%	53%
2011	39%	37%	51%	55%
2012	38%	40%	47%	51%
2013	36%	39%	45%	52%

Source: U.S. Department of Justice, Bureau of Prisons.

Notes: All BOP facilities include minimum security male facilities and secure female facilities, in addition to low, medium, and high security male facilities.

The BOP has attempted to address prison overcrowding by placing a growing proportion of federal inmates in contract facilities. While this has undoubtedly helped control prison overcrowding to some degree, it is also drawing resources away from BOP's other operations. **Figure 11** shows how growth in funding for the Contract Confinement[44] decision unit compares to growth in the Inmate Care and Programs[45] and Institutional Security and Administration[46] decision units and the S&E account overall. **Figure 11** shows that in most fiscal years since FY1999, growth in funding for contract confinement exceeded that of the S&E account overall. Increased funding for contract confinement has come at the cost of slower growth for the Inmate Care and Programs and Institutional Security and Administration decision units, especially the latter, which in most fiscal years grew at a rate below either the S&E account or the Inmate Care and Programs decision unit, or both.

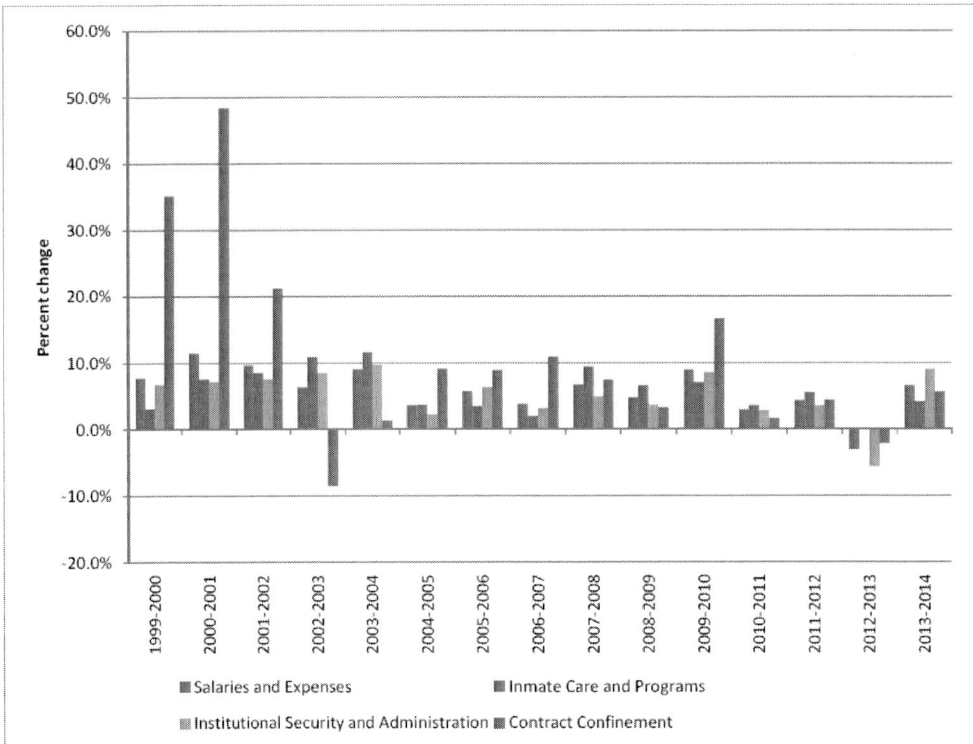

Source: FY1999-FY2014 amounts provided by the U.S. Department of Justice, Bureau of Prisons.
Notes: Figure does not include funding for the Management and Administration decision unit.

Figure 11. Growth in Funding for Contract Confinement, Inmate Care and Programs, Institutional Security and Administration, and Overall Salaries and Expenses.

Continued increases in prison overcrowding could be an issue for Congress given concerns about a potential link between prison overcrowding and increases in assaults and other inmate misconduct. Research on the link between prison overcrowding and inmate misconduct has been inconsistent, with some research showing a positive association between the two, other research showing no relationship, and some research even suggesting that there is a negative relationship between overcrowding and misconduct (i.e., as overcrowding increases, misconduct decreases).[47] A group of researchers conducted a meta-analysis that sought to synthesize the results of research on the overcrowding-misconduct link. Their research, which was based on 16 studies that provided 120 estimates of the correlation between overcrowding and inmate misconduct, concluded that, overall, overcrowding did not substantially influence inmate misconduct.[48]

Based on its own research, in which it collected data from 73 all-male low-, medium-, and high-security federal prisons from July 1996 to December 2004, the BOP concluded that there is a significant positive relationship between overcrowding and misconduct. The analysis conducted by the BOP included statistical methods to control for stable traits within each prison and to test the effect of other variables that prior research indicated were related to inmate misconduct. The BOP estimated that for every one percentage point increase in a prison's overcrowding (measured as the ratio of the number of inmates to the prison's rated capacity), the prison's annual serious assault rate increased by 4.1 assaults per 5,000 inmates.[49]

Why do the results of the BOP's analysis disagree with the results of the meta-analysis described above? One possible explanation is the relatively long period over which the BOP collected data for its study. Research has shown that the prevalence of misconduct increased with the length of the study.[50] As such, the results of the BOP's analysis might suggest a link between overcrowding and misconduct because it included more data points than the studies included in the meta-analysis. Also, it has been argued that because of differences between federal and state prisons, the results of research that tests the link between overcrowding and misconduct in the federal prison system might not be directly comparable to similar analyses using state-level data.[51] If this is the case, the results of the meta-analysis may not be directly comparable to the results of the BOP's study because most of the studies included in the meta-analysis used state-level data.

A Government Accountability Office (GAO) report on prison crowding highlights some of the problems overcrowding can cause in BOP facilities and how those problems might contribute to inmate misconduct. The GAO reported that in order to manage the growing inmate population, the BOP has had to triple or quadruple bunk some inmates and in other instances the BOP has had to convert common areas, such as a television room, into temporary housing space, which can result in inmates with a higher propensity for violence spending more time with other inmates.[52] In addition, due to prison crowding, inmates may experience crowded bathroom facilities, reduced shower times, shortened meal times, longer waits for food service, and limited recreational activities.[53] The increasing number of inmates housed in BOP facilities might decrease the availability of program opportunities, resulting in inmate idleness and waiting lists for rehabilitative programs like education, vocation training, substance abuse treatment, and faith-based reentry programs.[54]

The reduction in rehabilitation opportunities can affect the BOP's ability to manage the prison population. As mentioned above, inmates who successfully complete a residential substance abuse treatment program can have up to one year taken off of their sentence. However, the BOP reported long wait lists for admission to a residential substance abuse treatment program, which limited the BOP's ability to admit inmates early enough to allow them to earn the maximum reduction in their sentences.[55] Also, under current law, in order for inmates to earn their full allotment of good time credit per year, one of the conditions is that the inmate is making satisfactory progress on completing a GED (assuming the inmate does not have a GED or a high school diploma).[56] Overcrowding can also decrease the number of meaningful work opportunities available to inmates. Within any given prison there are only so many jobs related to operating and maintaining the prison for inmates to participate in, and with recent changes to how executive branch agencies procure goods produced by the Federal Prison Industries (FPI), there are fewer opportunities for an inmate to work in an FPI factory.[57]

Inmate-to-Staff Ratio

Another issue related to the growth of the federal prison population is increasing inmate-to-staff ratios. **Table 3** shows both the inmate-to-staff ratio and the inmate-to-correctional officer ratio for the federal prison system since FY2000.[58] The inmate-to-staff ratio has held steady (approximately five inmates to every BOP staff member) since FY2005, but this is higher than the inmate-to-staff ratio in FY2000 (approximately four inmates to every BOP staff member). The inmate-to-correctional officer ratio has been approximately twice the inmate-to-staff ratio. The ratio of inmates to correctional officers was approximately 10 to 1 in FY2013, the same as it was in FY2000. However, the inmate-to-correctional officer ratio was nearly 11 to 1 in FY2004 and FY2005. The inmate-to-correctional officer ratio has remained fairly steady even though the BOP has increased the number of correctional officers by 2% or more in 9 of the past 13 fiscal years. Data presented in **Figure 12** also indicate that the slight decrease in the inmate-to-staff and the inmate-to-correctional officer ratio observed in FY2012 and FY2013 might be the result of a decrease in the number of inmates held in BOP facilities. To put these figures in perspective, the Bureau of Justice Statistics reports that in 2005, the inmate-to-staff ratio for all state correctional agencies was 3.3 to 1 and the ratio of inmates to correctional officers was 4.9 to 1.[59] The inmate-to-staff and inmate-to-correctional officer ratios for the five largest state correctional systems (in terms of inmate population) in 2005 were, respectively,

- California: 3.6 to 1 and 6.1 to 1,
- Texas: 4.3 to 1 and 5.9 to 1,
- Florida: 3.8 to 1 and 4.9 to 1,
- New York: 2 to 1 and 3 to 1, and
- Georgia: 3.6 to 1 and 5.4 to 1.[60]

While it might appear somewhat surprising that the BOP would have an inmate-to-correctional officer ratio that was twice the ratio of inmates to staff—especially since the data presented above indicate that state correctional agencies have inmate-to-correctional officer ratios that are much closer to inmate-to-staff ratios—the BOP trains all of its staff as correctional officers, which means that the bureau does not need as many correctional officers to maintain the same level of security as other correctional agencies. For example, in many state prisons it would not be uncommon for a correctional officer to be stationed in a classroom while an instructor was teaching a class. However, since all staff in BOP facilities have been trained as correctional officers, the BOP does not place a correctional officer in classrooms during instructional periods.

Table 3. Inmate-to-Staff and Inmate-to-Correctional Officer Ratios for the Federal Prison System

	Number of Inmates per...	
Fiscal Year	All BOP Staff	Correctional Officers
2000	4.1	9.9
2001	4.1	9.7
2002	4.3	10.1
2003	4.5	10.5
2004	4.7	10.8
2005	4.9	10.9
2006	4.9	10.6
2007	4.9	10.6
2008	4.9	10.4
2009	4.9	10.6
2010	4.8	9.8
2011	4.9	10.2
2012	4.8	10.0
2013	4.8	9.9

Source: Based on a CRS analysis of data provided by the U.S. Department of Justice, Bureau of Prisons.
Notes: Ratios were calculated using figures on the number of inmates held in BOP facilities at the end of the fiscal year.

A review of BOP staffing levels by the GAO suggests that federal prison facilities might be understaffed. The GAO cites a DOJ study from August 2010 that concluded that nearly all BOP facilities had fewer correctional officers on staff than needed.[61] The GAO noted that with the exception of hiring staff when a new facility opens, the number of staff positions has generally not increased as the prison population has increased, which is reflected by the slow, but relatively steady, increase in the inmate-to-staff ratio (the GAO reported that the inmate-to-staff ratio in FY1997 was 3.6:1).[62] The GAO reported that staffing in BOP facilities is, on average, less than 90% of authorized levels. The fact that the inmate-to-staff ratio has increased while the inmate-tocorrectional officer ratio has remained fairly steady might be the result of the way that wardens make staffing decisions. The BOP funds staffing levels to the extent possible after the costs of caring for the inmate population (e.g., food, clothing, and medical care) are met. A warden might choose to use his or her allotted funding to fill more correctional officers positions while leaving more support staff positions unfilled. The overall inmate-to-staff ratio, which includes staff in the BOP's central office and regional offices, might mask staffing issues experienced by individual facilities. The GAO reported that the BOP calculates a ratio of inmates to institutional staff. From FY2006 to FY2011, the inmate to total institutional staff ratio for all facilities and for all male facilities was approximately 5.2:1. Also, the overall inmate-to-staff and inmate-to-correctional officer ratios do not reflect the fact that those ratios can vary based on the type of institution, the time of day, and the day of the week.[63] For example, the inmate-to-correctional officer ratio might be higher in low-security facilities compared to medium- and high-security facilities (though, arguably, this should be expected because lower security inmates should require less supervision). In addition, the inmate-to-correctional officer ratio might be lower during the night shift than during the day shifts.

The GAO also reported that staffing levels might be affected by some identified recruitment challenges the BOP faces. For example, some BOP officials reported that they have had problems with finding enough qualified candidates.[64] Furthermore, officials have reported problems with hiring professional staff (e.g., psychologists or medical staff) because BOP salaries were less than those paid for similar work in the surrounding community.[65]

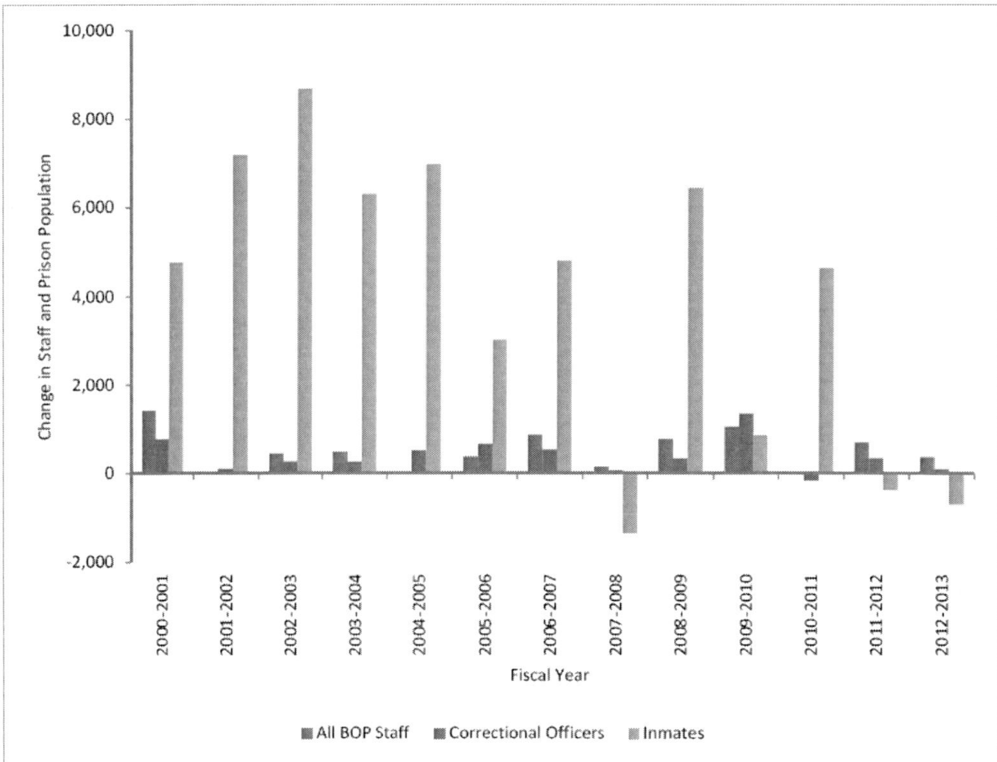

Source: Based on a CRS analysis of data provided by the U.S. Department of Justice, Bureau of Prisons.

Notes: Changes in the inmate population is only for inmates incarcerated in BOP facilities, not the total inmate population which would include inmates held in private facilities.

Figure 12. Change in BOP Staff, Correctional Officers, and Institutional Inmate Population.

The data also show that in order to bring down either the inmate-to-staff ratio or the inmate-tocorrectional officer ratio, there would have to be a significant increase in the BOP's S&E appropriation relative to the growth in the size of the federal prison population.[66]

Inmate-to-staff ratios might be an issue for Congress because it could mean that BOP facilities are less secure. In the research conducted by the BOP that evaluated causes of inmate misconduct (discussed above), the BOP estimated that a one-inmate increase in a prison's inmate-to-staff ratio increased the prison's annual serious assault rate by 4.5 assaults per 5,000 inmates.[67] In addition, more inmates per staff member could mean less access to rehabilitative programming because higher inmate-to-staff ratios could mean that BOP would not have the resources to meet the increasing demand for education, substance abuse treatment, and other rehabilitative programs. Through the Second Chance Act of 2007 (P.L. 110-199), Congress has required the BOP to help prepare inmates for re-entry, and rehabilitative programming could be a key component of the BOP's efforts to prepare inmates for post-release life. Therefore, if the BOP does not have the resources to hire staff at a rate commensurate with the rate of increase in the federal prison population, the BOP might not be able to fully prepare inmates for their transition back to the community.

Prison Construction and Maintenance

Funds for new prison construction and expansion and the modernization and repair of existing facilities come from BOP's Buildings and Facilities (B&F) account. Appropriations for the B&F account have fluctuated over the past 32 fiscal years. Congress made a substantial investment in prison construction and expansion from FY1989-FY1992, with an appropriation of nearly $3 billion for the B&F account. There was another spike in appropriations for the B&F account between FY1999 and FY2004, when Congress appropriated approximately $3.4 billion. A comparison of the history of appropriations for the B&F account and historical overcrowding levels in BOP facilities shows that there is a lag between Congress appropriating funding for additional bedspace and a reduction in prison overcrowding. This is because it can take several years for the BOP to identify a location for a new prison, award the contracts for construction of the facility, complete construction, and bring the prison "online" by hiring new employees to staff the facility.

Data provided by the BOP indicate that it is becoming more expensive to expand federal prison capacity. The data presented in **Figure 13** represent the total cost of each prison the BOP has built since 1994 divided by the rated capacity of the facility; this provides an indication of how much it has cost the BOP to expand its rated capacity by one inmate over the past 20 years. The data show that, in general, the per inmate cost of expanding the system's rated capacity increased.

The growing prison population and related overcrowding is contributing to the deterioration of the BOP's facilities. As discussed above, the B&F account, in addition to providing funding for prison construction, also provides funding for the maintenance of the BOP's prison facilities. The BOP currently operates 119 prison facilities, and approximately one-third of those facilities are more than 50 years old.[68] Moreover, failure to perform adequate maintenance on existing facilities can result in larger capital investment in future years as prisons and utility systems deteriorate and, according to the BOP, can cause direct and/or indirect security problems.[69] According to the BOP, some prisons are experiencing "extensive wear and tear, as well as premature deterioration" because the facilities are holding more inmates than they were originally designed to hold.[70] The BOP reports that it has a backlog of 185 major (projects that cost $300,000 or more) modernization and repair (M&R) projects with an approximate cost of $370 million.[71] The amount required to work through the current backlog of M&R projects is more than what Congress has appropriated for M&R projects going back to FY1999 (see **Table A-2**). The estimate only reflects "major" projects (repairs costing $300,000 or more) that have been approved by the BOP's administration for funding when appropriations are available. As such, the $342 million estimate probably does not capture the full extent of all needed repairs.

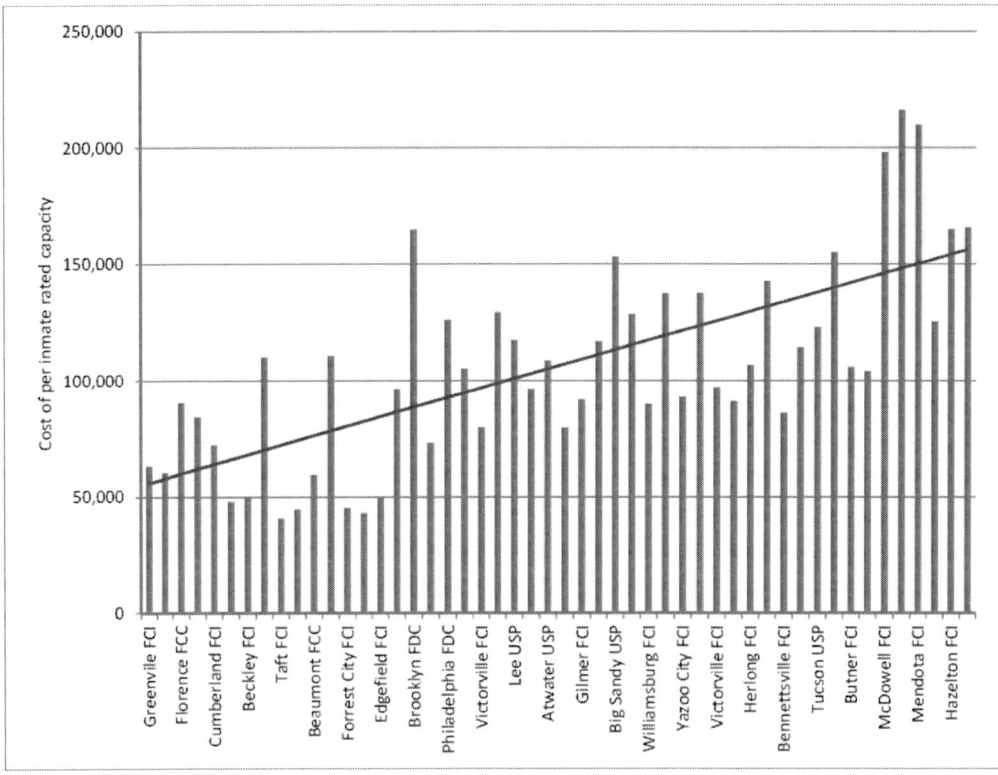

Source: Based on a CRS analysis of data provided by the U.S. Department of Justice, Bureau of Prisons.

Notes: Each bar in Figure 13 represents the total cost of building a new prison divided by the number of beds in the completed prison. The data are presented in chronological order based on when the prison was opened and accepting inmates.

Figure 13. The Cost of Expanding Rated Prison Capacity by One Inmate.

Appropriations for the B&F account have enabled the BOP to expand bedspace at a rate where it can manage overcrowding but not reduce it in any significant manner. The BOP has seen a slight decrease in overcrowding in recent fiscal years, but that is partly the result of a decrease in the number of inmates held in BOP facilities rather than a significant expansion in bedspace. However, recent reductions in funding for the New Construction decision unit under the B&F account mean that the BOP will lack the funding to begin any new prison construction in the near future, which could result in increased overcrowding in the federal prison system if the federal prison population does not continue to decrease (see **Table A-2**).

The current state of expansion in prison capacity means that the BOP cannot close older prisons. It is likely that more money will have to be spent to properly maintain a prison the longer it is in operation, especially when it is housing more inmates than it was rated to hold. In addition to having lower maintenance costs, newer prisons also have the advantage of updated designs and technology upgrades that allow for fewer correctional officers to safely monitor more inmates.

SELECT POLICY OPTIONS

The analyses presented above show that the growth in the federal prison population over the past three decades has resulted in an increasingly expensive federal prison system that is overcrowded and aging and where facilities might not be staffed at an optimal level. Congress could choose to address the mounting number of federal inmates either in the context of existing correctional policies or by changing the current policies. Specific policy options under these two courses are discussed in more detail below.

Continuing or Expanding Current Correctional Policies

Under the umbrella of continuing existing policies, Congress could consider addressing issues related to the burgeoning federal prison population by (1) expanding the capacity of the federal prison system, (2) continuing to invest in rehabilitative programming, (3) placing more inmates in private correctional facilities, or some combination of the three.

Expanding the Capacity of the Federal Prison System

Arguably one of the most straightforward approaches for managing the steadily increasing number of federal inmates is to expand the capacity of the federal prison system. Congress could choose to mitigate some issues related to federal prison population growth by appropriating more funding so the BOP could expand prison capacity to alleviate overcrowding, update and properly maintain existing facilities, and hire additional staff. While a large-scale expansion of the federal prison system might help reduce overcrowding, it takes several years for a prison to be built and be ready to accept inmates, so if Congress chooses to appropriate funding for an expansion of the BOP's infrastructure, it could be several years before overcrowding is reduced. Even if the federal prison population stabilized at the current level, the BOP would have to add over 47,000 additional beds in order to eliminate overcrowding. The BOP projects the federal prison population to increase to nearly 234,400 inmates by FY2019.[72] These projections are based on what has happened in the past, and as discussed above, the federal prison population has been increasing for more than 30 years. Should Congress choose to invest in a wide-scale expansion of prison capacity, and the prison population decreases in the future, the surplus bedspace could allow the BOP to close some of its older facilities, which, in general, require more maintenance and need higher inmate-to-staff ratios to safely operate.

Critics contend that expanding the capacity of the federal prison system does not address the continued growth of the federal prison population. Also, this policy option would not resolve the issue of the rising cost of the federal prison system; in fact, it could exacerbate it. However, alternatives that would reduce the federal prison population would most likely involve prosecuting fewer people in federal courts, providing ways for inmates to be released before they served a significant proportion of their sentences, putting more inmates into diversionary programs, or placing more offenders on some form of community supervision. If Congress does not wish to take any of these steps, a large-scale expansion of the federal prison system might be the sole way to manage the effects of an increasing prison population. Some may argue that in order to protect public safety Congress should appropriate the funding necessary to expand the federal prison system rather than adopt policy changes that would reduce the prison population through early releases, alternatives to incarceration, or fewer prosecutions.

Investing in Rehabilitative Programs

A review of the literature on rehabilitative programs (e.g., academic and vocational education, cognitive-behavioral programs, and both community- and prison-based drug treatment) suggests that there are enough scientifically sound evaluations to conclude that they are effective at reducing recidivism, which could potentially help stem growth in the federal prison population in the future.[73] The BOP offers a variety of rehabilitation programs such as academic and vocational education, work programs through the Federal Prison Industries (FPI), substance abuse treatment, and cognitive-behavioral programs that focus on promoting pro-social behavior.[74] One possible option for reducing the federal prison population would be to ensure that the BOP has the resources it needs to provide rehabilitative services to inmates.

At a time when some policy makers are considering reducing discretionary funding for federal agencies, there might be some effort to restrain the growth of the BOP's appropriations, including for rehabilitative services. The BOP has to administer the federal prison system within the funds appropriated for it by Congress. As shown in **Figure 9**, the per capita cost of providing rehabilitative programming for inmates has been increasing. If the BOP does not have sufficient resources, it might not be able to provide rehabilitative programming to all inmates who need it. The federal prison population has continued to grow, and unless there is a change in the trend over the past 30-plus years, it would appear likely that there will be a growing need for and cost of rehabilitative programming in the federal prison system.

It could be argued that in order to reduce the growing cost of operating the federal prison system, the BOP should reduce funding for rehabilitative programming and invest solely in providing for the subsistence of inmates and maintaining a level of staffing that is adequate to ensure that federal prisons are secure. However, reducing programming opportunities might result in more inmate idleness, which might result in more inmate misconduct. Moreover, as noted above, the BOP is authorized to reduce an inmate's sentence by up to one year for successfully completing a residential substance abuse treatment program; therefore, reducing programming opportunities could hamper one of the few avenues the BOP has for releasing inmates early. It is also possible that BOP might be able to realize some long-term cost savings by successfully rehabilitating inmates. For example, research by the Washington State Institute for Public Policy (WSIPP) suggests that effective rehabilitation programs can result in cost savings.[75]

As policy makers consider the appropriate level of funding for the BOP in light of concerns about the federal deficit and potential freezes or reductions in non-defense discretionary spending, they could consider whether it is prudent to increase resources for the BOP's rehabilitative programs in the near term in order to realize potential long-term benefits. As outlined above, the BOP's appropriations have increased along with the federal prison population. Yet, current funding may be inadequate for the BOP to provide more rehabilitative opportunities to federal inmates. The size of the effect that decreased recidivism among federal offenders would have on the BOP's budget would depend on how many new inmates the BOP incarcerates. If new commitments exceed the number of inmates released who do not return to prison then the demand for prisons, personnel, and inmate programs and services would continue to grow, although possibly at a slower rate. If the number of new commitments is less than the number of inmates released who do not return to prison then the demand for prisons, personnel, and inmate programs and services would decrease. However, even if the growth of the federal prison population slows, the demand for increased BOP appropriations may continue.

Placing More Inmates in Private Prisons

The BOP has placed an increasing share of federal inmates in contract facilities as a way of managing the growth in the federal prison population. Congress might also consider whether *more* federal inmates should be housed in private facilities as a means of reducing crowding in federal prisons and potentially reducing the cost of operating the federal prison system. The number of inmates under the BOP's jurisdiction held in contract facilities has steadily increased since the early 1980s, and the BOP expects the trend to continue into the later part of this decade. However, the growth in the number of inmates held in contract facilities is mostly the result of more inmates being placed in Residential Reentry Centers (RRCs) at the end of their sentences. Most BOP inmates held in private correctional facilities are low-level, non-citizen offenders. The debate about whether to house inmates in privately operated correctional facilities has been framed by two overarching questions: (1) can private facilities incarcerate inmates at a lower cost and (2) can private facilities provide services that are equal or superior to the services provided in public institutions?

The BOP attempted to answer these questions, at the behest of Congress, by operating the Taft Correctional Institution (TCI) as a private facility as a part of a privatization demonstration project.[76] The BOP awarded a contract to the Geo Group (formerly Wackenhut Corrections Corporation) to operate the facility from 1997 to 2007.[77] The BOP, through the National Institute of Justice, funded an evaluation of TCI and three similar BOP facilities,[78] which was conducted by Abt Associates, Inc. In addition, the BOP's Office of Research, in conjunction with the Center for Naval Analyses (CNA) Corporation, conducted its own evaluation of TCI and the similar facilities. Both the Abt and BOP evaluations found that TCI was cheaper to operate on a per diem basis than the three comparable facilities, but the two evaluations offer different conclusions as to how much was saved by operating TCI as a private institution. The Abt analysis concluded that the average per diem cost of incarceration for the three BOP-operated facilities in FY1999 was 18.9% greater than the per diem cost of incarceration for TCI; in FY2000 it was 20.0% greater; in FY2001 it was 17.5% greater; and in FY2002 it was 14.8% greater.[79] In comparison, the BOP analysis concluded that the average per diem cost of incarceration for the three BOP-operated facilities in FY1999 was 4.0% greater than the per diem cost of incarceration for TCI; in FY2000 it was 5.4% greater; in FY2001 it was 0.3% greater; and in FY2002 it was 2.2% greater.[80] The two primary reasons for the different conclusions are economies of scale[81] realized by TCI and differences in how per diem rates were calculated.[82] TCI had on average 300 more inmates each year than the three BOP-operated prisons, which means that TCI was able to take advantage of economies of scale that decreased average costs. In the BOP analysis, the researchers adjusted for these economies of scale by estimating what expenditures would have been for the BOP facilities if they had prison populations similar to TCI. In addition, the Abt analysis assumed that the BOP would not provide many resources to support TCI's operations, resulting in a large amount of savings from reduced indirect overhead costs. The BOP analysis assumed that the BOP would continue to incur some overhead expenses related to overseeing TCI. As such, the BOP included a 10%-12% overhead rate in its analysis.

Both analyses found that TCI had an assault rate that was lower than what would have been expected based on the composition of its inmate populations, but so did two of the other three BOP-operated facilities in the study (the other BOP-operated facility had an assault rate that was similar to what would have been expected). However, random drug testing showed that inmates in TCI were more likely to use drugs than inmates in other BOP facilities. TCI also had two escapes from inside the facility's secure perimeter over a roughly four-year period. In comparison, the BOP had three escapes from a secure prison during the same time period, even though the BOP was operating over 100 facilities at the time.

Research that reviewed the results of state and local efforts to privatize correctional systems generally found that it is questionable whether privatization can deliver lower costs and whether services provided by private prisons are comparable to services provided by public prisons.[83]

One of the first studies to quantitatively summarize the results of several evaluations of prison privatization efforts found that regardless of whether the prison was privately or publicly operated, the economies of scale, the prison's age, and the prison's security level were the most significant determinants of the daily per diem cost.[84] The researchers concluded that "[a]lthough specific privatization policy alternatives may result in modest cost savings ... relinquishing the responsibility of managing prisons to the private sphere is unlikely to alleviate much of the financial burden on state correctional budgets."[85] Their conclusions are echoed by a review of the literature on privatization. In this analysis, the researchers concluded "that prison privatization provides neither a clear advantage nor disadvantage compared with publicly managed prisons. Neither cost savings nor improvements in quality of confinement are guaranteed through privatization."[86] However, even though both studies limited their analyses to the most methodologically sound evaluations, these evaluations are still limited to the same issues described above, namely, what costs are considered when the evaluators calculated whether privatization could lower correctional costs. As discussed above, these assumptions can have a considerable effect on the results of the evaluation.

Placing more inmates in private facilities could help alleviate overcrowding in federal prisons without the need to invest in a large-scale expansion of federal prison bedspace. Expanding capacity through contracting for additional bedspace rather than building new prisons could give Congress the flexibility to reduce capacity if the federal prison population decreased in the future.

However, research suggests that moving federal prisoners into private prisons might not help to control the rising costs of the federal prison system. Also, medium and high security facilities are the most crowded, and the BOP is less inclined to place medium and high security inmates in private facilities. Congress might also consider whether it wants to place a greater portion of the federal prison population in the custody of private operators when the BOP has less direct oversight over the day-to-day operations of private facilities.

Changing Existing Correctional and Sentencing Policies to Reduce the Prison Population

Policy makers might also consider whether they want to revise some of the changes that have been made to federal criminal justice policy over the past three decades. A confluence of these changes has resulted in an increasing number of offenders being sent to federal prisons. Should Congress decide to change federal criminal justice policy to try to reduce the number of inmates held in federal prisons, policy makers might start by considering which offenders are incarcerated and the length of their sentences.

Changes to Mandatory Minimum Penalties

As discussed earlier, the USSC concluded that, in part, mandatory minimum penalties have contributed to the growing federal prison population. It might be argued that some or all mandatory minimum penalties should be repealed as a way to manage the growth of the federal prison population. Allowing defendants to be sentenced using the federal sentencing guidelines could allow for more individualized sentencing, thereby allowing the court to mete out punishment using an array of variables that reflect a more nuanced analysis of a defendant's culpability. Opponents of widespread use of mandatory minimum penalties contend that they are a blunt instrument with which to determine a proper sentence. The USSC reported that "certain mandatory minimum provisions apply too broadly, are set too high, or both, to warrant the prescribed minimum penalty for the full range of offenders who could be prosecuted under the particular criminal statute."[87] Also, to the extent that mandatory minimum penalties have contributed to sentence inflation as a result of the USSC incorporating them into the federal sentencing guidelines, repealing some mandatory minimum penalties might reduce the amount of time inmates serve in federal prison.

However, proponents of the continued use of mandatory minimum penalties contend that after the Supreme Court's ruling in *United States v. Booker*[88] and its progeny (e.g., *Gall v. United States*[89] and *Kimbrough v. United States*),[90] which rendered the sentencing guidelines effectively advisory, Congress has a responsibility to set minimum penalties for some offenses as a way to limit judicial discretion, thereby preventing unwanted sentencing disparities. It has been argued that mandatory minimum penalties promote uniformity and fairness for defendants, transparent and predictable outcomes, and a higher level of truth and integrity in sentencing.[91] Also, should Congress choose to repeal some or all mandatory minimum penalties, policy makers would relinquish their ability to control the amount of time inmates serve for certain offenses.

Even if Congress chooses not to repeal any mandatory minimum sentences, policy makers could review current mandatory minimum penalties to ensure that they are (1) not excessively severe, (2) narrowly tailored to apply only to those offenders who warrant such punishment, and (3) applied consistently.[92]

Alternatives to Incarceration

During the 1980s many states instituted a series of alternatives to incarceration as a way to respond to an increasing number of convicted offenders and wide-scale prison overcrowding.[93] Prior to this, sentencing options were limited to incarceration or probation. However, there was growing sentiment that some crimes were too severe to be punished by placing the offender on probation, but those same crimes were not severe enough to warrant incarceration. Therefore, states started to develop a series of alternative sentences that fell somewhere between probation and incarceration. These alternatives included house arrest, electronic monitoring, intensive supervision, boot camps, split sentences, day reporting centers, fines, and community service.[94] The programs provide graduated sanctions that might be more appropriate than either probation or incarceration, and provided a higher level of offender restraint and accountability than traditional probation. Some also provide higher levels of treatment or services for problems such as substance abuse, low education levels, and unemployment.

A majority of the evaluations of intensive supervision and electronic monitoring programs found that there was no significant difference in recidivism rates between offenders sentenced to alternatives to incarceration and offenders in control groups.[95] This means that increasing surveillance and control of offenders' activities does not decrease their criminal activities. Ironically, while these programs were created as a means of reducing the number of incarcerated individuals, the increased surveillance might increase the probability that violations of the terms of probation will be detected, which could increase the number of inmates as probationers are often incarcerated for technical violations. One shortcoming of the research is that since most intensive supervision programs increase the probability of detection, there is no way to tell if the underlying level of criminality changed between the treatment and control groups, that is, the increased probability of detection might mean that offenders in the control group are simply more likely to be caught when they commit crimes, even though offenders in the control group commit crime at the same, or even higher, rate. Also, the research tended to focus on whether the restraining aspects of the program could reduce recidivism. Some evaluations found that inmates who received treatment while participating in an intensive supervision program were less likely to be arrested.[96]

Placing More Inmates on Probation

Congress could consider whether there are alternative ways to properly manage offenders convicted of committing relatively minor crimes without sending them to prison. Data from BJS show that in FY2011 over half of inmates entering federal prison were sentenced to three years or less. Given the relatively short sentences these inmates received, it is likely that they were sentenced for relatively minor offenses. One policy option Congress could consider is amending penalties for some offenses to allow more defendants to be placed on probation rather than being sentenced to a period of incarceration. However, the *Booker* decision that rendered the federal sentencing guidelines advisory might influence any debate Congress would have over who would be placed on probation. The sentencing guidelines placed substantial restrictions on when courts could sentence defendants to probation. Under Section 5B1.1 of the sentencing guidelines, defendants can only be placed on probation if their sentence under the guidelines is equal to or less than 15 months. Nonetheless, after the Supreme Court's ruling in *Booker*, federal judges are not required to impose a sentence within the range calculated under the sentencing guidelines. Therefore, judges can impose probation for offenders unless (1) the defendant has been convicted of a class A or B felony,[97] (2) probation is statutorily precluded as a sentencing option, or (3) the defendant is sentenced to a term of imprisonment for the same or different offense that is not a petty offense.[98]

Data from the Administrative Office of the U.S. Courts suggest that in the post-*Booker* era courts have not chosen to sentence outside the guideline range to place more offenders on probation. Since the mid-1970s, a dwindling proportion of defendants sentenced for federal offenses were placed on probation (see **Figure 14**). The decrease in the proportion of sentenced defendants placed on probation coincides with the implementation of the federal sentencing guidelines. The data also show that the proportion of defendants that were placed on probation has further decreased since the *Booker* decision. Approximately 14% of defendants in FY2004 received probation; by FY2012, about 11% of defendants were placed on probation.

Data show that the risk of recidivism for probationers is the highest in the first year after being placed on probation.[99] It has been argued that surveillance and services should be front-loaded (i.e., more intensive at the beginning of a term of probation) to try to mitigate recidivism and other negative consequences that might occur during the first year that an offender is serving on probation.

A common argument from advocates of decreasing the use of incarceration is that it is cheaper to supervise an offender in the community than it is to incarcerate that individual. The Administrative Office of the U.S. Courts reports that the average annual cost of probation supervision was $3,347 per probationer in 2012.[100] In comparison, the average annual cost of incarceration for FY2012 was $29,027 per inmate. However, some of the lower cost of probation relative to incarceration might be the result of fewer and lower-risk offenders being placed on probation. It is possible that the annual cost of probation would increase if Congress expanded the number of people placed on probation and implemented some of the changes discussed below.

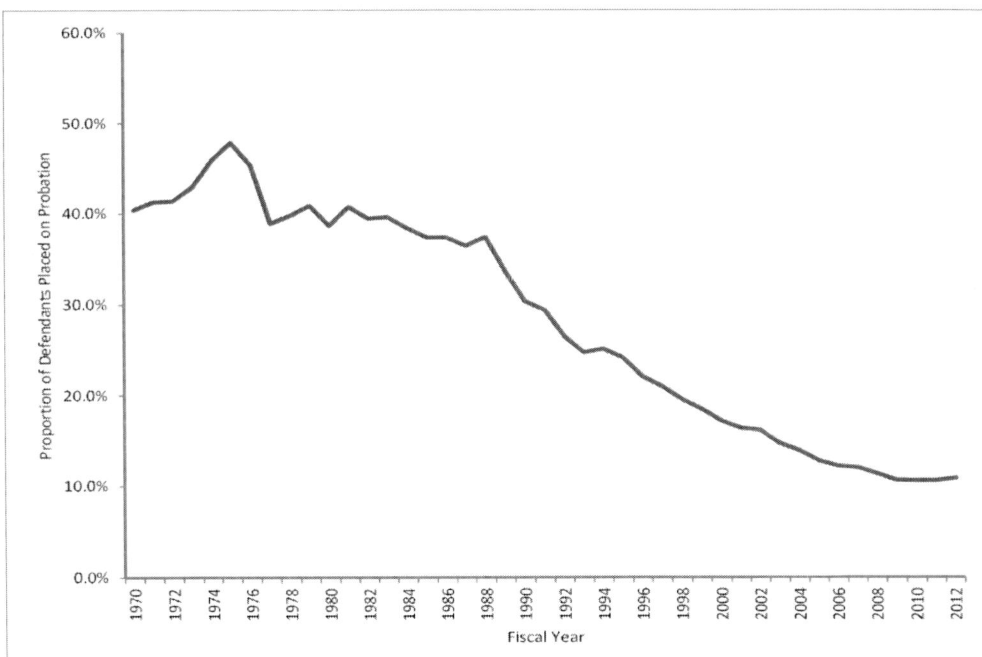

Source: FY1970-FY1996 data were taken from *Sourcebook of Criminal Justice Statistics, 1996*, Table 5.27. Data for FY1997-FY2012 were taken from *Judicial Business of the U.S. Courts* for each respective fiscal year.

Figure 14. Proportion of Sentenced Defendants in Federal Courts Placed on Probation.

Should Congress choose to expand probation as a sentencing option for more offenses, research suggests that probation programs that use a validated risk assessment tool to sort offenders into high- and low-risk groups and focus resources and supervision on higher-risk offenders might be more effective at reducing recidivism.[101] Research also suggests that probation programs that offer a mix of evidence-based treatment that is delivered to offenders who are the most likely to benefit from it along with surveillance are more effective at reducing recidivism than surveillance-only probation.[102] As one expert noted, "'[t]reatment' alone is not enough, nor is 'surveillance' by itself adequate. Programs that can increase offender-to-officer contact *and* [emphasis original] provide treatment have reduced recidivism."[103]

Researchers have found that participants in probation programs that subject probationers with substance abuse issues to frequent random drug testing and that require probationers who violate the terms of their probation to serve intermediate sanctions, such as a short stay in jail, are less likely to recidivate than those who were on regular probation.[104] Another option Congress might consider is allowing probationers who strictly adhere to their conditions of probation to be released early. Research has shown that an earned discharge strategy can reduce recidivism.[105]

Expanding the Use of Residential Reentry Centers

Congress could also consider extending the BOP's authority to place inmates with short sentences who are deemed to be low security risks directly into Residential Reentry Centers (RRCs, i.e., halfway houses).

A *New York Times* (*Times*) investigation of halfway houses in New Jersey might raise some questions among policy makers about whether placing some federal inmates in RRCs rather than federal prisons is a viable policy option. Like the BOP, the New Jersey Department of Corrections contracts with private halfway houses to give inmates the opportunity to reestablish themselves in society before being released from custody. The *Times* investigation found that approximately 5,100 inmates have escaped since 2005 and that some inmates have committed new offenses after they escaped.[106] However, many escaped inmates were captured or returned within hours or days.[107] The *Times* also uncovered instances of lax security because counselors were either poorly trained, outnumbered, or feared for their safety; inmate-on-inmate violence; and questionably delivered rehabilitative services.[108]

The Department of Justice's Office of the Inspector General (OIG) completed an audit of six RRCs[109] that the BOP had contracts with to determine whether the RRCs' operations were conducted in compliance with the BOP's requirements and whether the BOP effectively administers and monitors RRC contracts.[110]

The OIG's audit included a review of the files of 177 inmates who were transferred to one of the six RRCs between FY2008 and FY2010. The OIG concluded that the RRCs adequately met most Statement of Work (SOW)[111] requirements; however, the six RRCs did not fully comply with conditions related to substance abuse testing, escapes, and authorized inmate absences. Specifically, the OIG found that 30% of the inmates with histories of substance abuse did not have documentation showing that they were given required drug tests.[112] The OIG found that from FY2008 to FY2010, approximately 3% of the inmates transferred to the six RRCs included in the audit escaped.[113]

In addition, the OIG found that 92 of the 177 inmates included in the audit had 434 authorized absences where they returned to the RRC more than one hour late, and no disciplinary action was taken or documented for 65 of the 71 inmates who returned more than one hour late with no reason for their tardiness.[114] The OIG also concluded that the BOP's monitoring procedures were sufficient to identify most RRC deficiencies related to compliance with the SOW and that corrective actions were implemented.

The *Times* investigation of halfway houses in New Jersey and the OIG's audit of RRCs might raise some potential issues for Congress. The *Times* report suggests that several of the problems experienced in the halfway houses that were the subject of its investigation resulted from the New Jersey Department of Corrections and local sheriffs' departments using halfway houses as a means of reducing prison and jail overcrowding, which resulted in inmates with violent histories and/or who were convicted for violent offenses being placed in halfway houses. These inmates were then supervised by employees with little training, who were not correctional officers and who, in some instances, feared the inmates because they were substantially outnumbered.

This suggests that if Congress wanted to use RRCs as a way of reducing overcrowding in federal prisons that placement in RRCs should be limited to low-level, non-violent offenders. The *Times* article includes accounts from staff who reported fearing for their safety while patrolling the halfway houses at night because of lax security and high inmate-to-staff ratios. This might mean that should RRCs be used as a way to reduce the number of inmates held in federal prisons, the BOP will need to ensure that RRCs have properly trained and adequate staff and that the RRCs have satisfactory security measures in place. The findings from the OIG audit suggest that the BOP might need to increase its oversight of the RRCs it contracts with. This could mean that the BOP would need additional staff and an increase in its travel budget so BOP staff could make more frequent visits to RRCs.

If policy makers were concerned about whether RRCs are a valid alternative to placing some offenders in federal prison, Congress could choose to provide funding for a program that would allow the federal government to contract with local jails to provide short-term bedspace. One possible example is the Cooperative Agreement Program (CAP) whereby the U.S. Marshals Service (USMS) provided capital investment funding to local jails in exchange for guaranteed bedspace for federal detainees.[115] While the CAP was limited to securing bedspace for people in the custody of the USMS (i.e., people who have not yet been convicted of a crime), it is possible that the program could be expanded to allow the federal government to expand local jail capacity in order to secure bedspace for some lower-level federal inmates who are serving short sentences. It is likely that jails would be more secure than RRCs. In addition, jails are staffed by correctional officers, who might be better prepared to supervise federal inmates.

Allowing the BOP to confine more low-level inmates in RRCs would mean fewer inmates would be placed into already overcrowded facilities while still receiving a punishment for criminal behavior and supervision of their actions for a given period of time. However, FY2013 data published by the BOP show that per capita expenditures for RRCs ($26,612) were higher than the per capita cost of confining a prisoner in a minimum security prison ($21,960), and only slightly lower than the cost of confining an inmate in a low security prison ($27,386), so placing more low-level inmates in RRCs might not generate a substantial amount of savings.[116]

Congress could also consider whether to require courts to place certain offenders in RRCs for violating the terms of their supervised release rather than returning them to prison. As mentioned, the BOP might not save a significant amount of money by placing a greater number of inmates in RRCs, but by placing more of these short-term inmates in RRCs the BOP would have additional bedspace.

In addition, the BOP would not have to invest time and money into re-processing the offender through the prison system.[117] This is not to suggest that all inmates who have their supervised release revoked would be suitable for RRC placement. Indeed, inmates who are arrested and/or convicted for serious offenses would most likely need to be placed in a secure facility. However, offenders who have their supervised release revoked for technical violations (e.g., repeatedly failing drug tests) might be suitable for placement in a less secure environment that still allows for monitoring of their actions.

All of the alternatives to incarceration discussed above place the offender in the community, which means there is some level of risk that the offender could commit new offenses, because even though the offender would be supervised, the level of supervision would most likely provide a lower level of control over the individual's actions than would be provided by correctional officers in a secure environment.

Early Release Measures

One possible way to reduce the growth of the federal prison population would be to expand the early release measures for federal inmates. There are several options Congress could consider if policy makers wanted to expand early release options for federal inmates, including (1) reinstating parole, (2) expanding good time credits, and (3) expanding the conditions under which courts could reduce sentences pursuant to 18 U.S.C. Section 3582(c)(1)(A).

Reinstating Parole

One option Congress might consider is whether to reinstate parole in the federal system. As discussed above, inmates sentenced for an offense in a federal court committed after November 1, 1987, are not eligible to be released on parole. Parole is one way correctional authorities can release inmates who are deemed to be at a low risk for recidivism and place them in community supervision for the remainder of their sentences.

Should Congress consider reinstating parole for federal inmates, there are several salient issues that policy makers might think about. First, how would a parole system work within the current determinate sentencing structure used in federal courts? Traditionally, discretionary parole has been combined with an indeterminate sentencing structure (i.e., a system whereby the court could impose a sentence for a crime within a range prescribed in law).

Indeterminate sentences allow the court to tailor sentences to each defendant, but this gave rise to concerns about whether some sentences were arbitrary and unfair. For example, two defendants who were convicted for similar crimes might receive different sentences depending on which judge happened to be presiding over their case. When combined with a parole board's discretion over when, if ever, someone would be granted parole, two defendants who were convicted of similar crimes could end up serving significantly different amounts of time in prison.

Congress sought to limit the discretion of the federal judiciary and the executive branch when it eliminated parole and replaced indeterminate sentencing with the sentencing guidelines. Parole might not be irreconcilable with a determinate sentencing structure. Courts could continue to use sentencing guidelines as a guidepost for determining a defendant's sentence and each inmate could then be eligible for parole after serving a certain portion of his or her sentence.

However, should Congress allow federal inmates to be eligible for parole, it would grant the executive branch, through the U.S. Parole Commission (hereinafter, "commission"), some measure of control over determining how much time an inmate serves in prison. Congress might choose to limit some of the commission's discretion by setting a higher threshold for determining what portion of an inmate's sentence must be served before he or she is eligible to be placed on parole.[118]

Should Congress choose to reinstate parole for federal inmates, another key question would be whether eligibility would be made retroactive to inmates who were sentenced for federal crimes after November 1, 1987. As discussed above, approximately 3% of inmates currently incarcerated in federal facilities are still eligible for parole, which means that at the end of FY2011 there were nearly 204,600 inmates in federal prison who were not eligible for parole. Making eligibility for parole retroactive could potentially reduce the federal prison population in a shorter amount of time than it would if only newly convicted inmates were eligible for parole consideration. Data from the BOP indicate that nearly three-quarters of inmates have served at least 25% of their sentence, meaning that if Congress reinstated the old parole eligibility rules, a majority of federal inmates would be eligible for parole consideration.[119] It would appear likely that the commission and the U.S. Probation and Pretrial Services office would need increased resources in order to properly manage what would likely be a significant increase in their caseloads.

There might be some concern about whether allowing federal inmates to be released on parole would pose a threat to public safety. Concerns about recidivism are not unfounded. Research published by the Bureau of Justice Statistics found that over two-thirds (67.5%) of inmates released in 1994 were rearrested within three years and nearly half (46.9%) were convicted for a new crime.[120] While the data are dated, this remains one of the most comprehensive studies on recidivism. Concerns about offenders committing new crimes while on parole have led some jurisdictions to implement intensive supervision programs where parolees are subject to more rigorous conditions of release and more frequent contacts with a parole officer. While intensive supervision programs might in theory reduce the likelihood that parolees commit new offenses while in the community, the body of research on intensive supervision programs suggests that these programs do not reduce recidivism.[121] Depending on how recidivism is defined, intensive supervision programs may actually increase "recidivism" because they are more likely to detect technical violations of the conditions of release.[122] This can create a paradox for policy makers: parole might be considered as a means of reducing the prison population, but it might actually increase the number of inmates in prisons as more return to prison for violating the conditions of parole. Should Congress choose to reinstate parole, policy makers might consider evidence-based measures so that parole helps as many inmates successfully transition back into the community as possible. The options Congress could consider are similar to those outlined above for successful probation programs, namely

- using a validated risk assessment tool to sort parolees into high- and low-risk groups;
- ensuring that parolees with a demonstrated need for rehabilitative programming have access to evidence-based, appropriately delivered programs;
- requiring parolees who violate their conditions of release to serve intermediate sanctions rather than returning them to prison; and
- allowing parolees who strictly adhere to the conditions of their parole to be released early.

Also, like probationers, data indicate that parolees are at the highest risk for recidivism during their first year of parole.[123] This suggests that in order to decrease the risk of recidivism services should be more intensive during the parolee's first year on release. Some research suggests that intensive supervision programs can reduce recidivism when they are combined with treatment and rehabilitative programming.[124]

Expanding Good Time Credits

Another potential policy option Congress could consider as a means to slow the growth of, or possibly reduce, the federal prison population is to expand the BOP's authority to grant good time credit to inmates. As outlined above, Congress abolished parole for federal inmates in the 1980s, which means that inmates cannot be released before serving their entire sentence, minus any good time credit, even if the inmate's risk of recidivism is low. Under current law, the BOP can grant up to 54 days of good time credit per year to inmates serving a sentence of more than one year, assuming the inmate has demonstrated "exemplary compliance with institutional disciplinary regulations" and is making satisfactory progress on completing a GED (assuming the inmate does not have a GED or a high school diploma).[125]

In addition to the amount of good time credit an inmate can earn, the BOP is allowed to reduce a non-violent inmate's sentence by up to one year if the inmate participates in residential substance abuse treatment.[126] It has been argued that teaming good time credit with a program that places inmates with objectively assessed needs and risks in evidence-based programs to address those needs and risks can reduce recidivism and cut prison costs.[127] Congress could consider allowing the BOP to award good time credit for inmates who have a need for and successfully complete rehabilitative programs other than residential drug abuse treatment.

However, expanding good time credit for participation in rehabilitative programming would likely require Congress, at least in the short term, to expand funding for rehabilitative programs and inmate skills and needs assessments. While expanding current good time credit policies might help reduce prison overcrowding, there might be some concern that the BOP would effectively be reducing inmates' sentences without the sentencing court's approval. Additional good time credit would also allow inmates to be released before serving a significant (85%) portion of their sentence, a key rationale for why parole was eliminated in the first place. In addition, some may feel that regardless of an inmate's efforts to rehabilitate himself or herself or the risk he or she would pose to society when released, the inmate was sent to prison as a punishment for a crime, hence the inmate should serve his or her full sentence.

Sentence Reduction

In addition to allowing the BOP to grant more good time credit to inmates, Congress could also consider whether to amend the conditions under which courts can reduce an inmate's sentence. Under current law (18 U.S.C. §3582(c)(1)(A)), the BOP can petition the court to reduce an inmate's sentence if the court finds that "extraordinary and compelling reasons warrant such a reduction"; or the inmate is at least 70 years of age, has served at least 30 years of his or her sentence, and a determination has been made by the Director of the BOP that the inmate is not a danger to the safety of any other person or the community. Congress required the USSC, when issuing a policy statement regarding sentence modification under 18 U.S.C. Section 3582(c)(1)(A), to "describe what should be considered extraordinary and compelling reasons for sentence reduction, including the criteria to be applied and a list of specific examples."[128] Under Section 1B1.13 of the U.S. Sentencing Guidelines, the USSC deemed the following circumstances to be "extraordinary and compelling reasons" for a sentence reduction:

- The inmate is suffering from a terminal illness.
- The inmate is suffering from a permanent physical or medical condition, or is experiencing deteriorating physical or mental health because of the aging process, that substantially diminishes the ability of the defendant to provide self-care within the environment of a correctional facility and for which conventional treatment promises no substantial improvement.
- The death or incapacitation of the inmate's only family member capable of caring for the inmate's minor child or minor children.
- As determined by the Director of the BOP, there exists in the inmate's case an extraordinary and compelling reason other than, or in combination with, the reasons described above.

Pursuant to 28 U.S.C. Section 944(t), rehabilitation of an inmate is not, by itself, an extraordinary and compelling reason for granting a sentence reduction. If the court grants a sentence reduction under 18 U.S.C. Section 3582(c)(1)(A), the court is also allowed to impose a term of probation or supervised release, with or without conditions, for a period up to the amount of time that was remaining on the inmate's sentence.

One of the critiques of this program is that it relies on the BOP to petition the court for a review of an inmate's sentence. One commentator argues that the BOP narrowly interprets when inmates should be allowed to apply for a sentence reduction, effectively limiting applications to cases where the inmate is terminally ill and near death.[129] The policy statement governing the program states that consideration for a sentence reduction under 18 U.S.C. Section 3582(c)(1)(A) is limited to "particularly extraordinary or compelling circumstances which could not reasonably have been foreseen by the court at the time of sentencing."[130] In August 2013, the BOP revised its compassionate release policy statement to broaden the circumstances under which it will consider a sentence reduction request to include the following:

- terminal and non-terminal (e.g., the inmate has a serious physical or mental impairment) medical circumstances;
- circumstances for elderly inmates;

- circumstances in which there has been the death or incapacitation of the family member caregiver of an inmate's child; and
- circumstances in which the spouse or registered partner of an inmate has become incapacitated.[131]

Before submitting a compassionate release request to the court, the BOP will continue to consider whether an inmate's release would pose a danger to the safety of anyone in the community.[132] The BOP made changes to its compassionate release policy as a part of the DOJ's "Smart on Crime" initiative.[133] Changes to the compassionate release policy were also made in response to an Office of the Inspector General's report that uncovered problems with how the BOP administered the program and critiques from external advocacy groups.[134]

Notwithstanding the changes the BOP recently made to its compassionate release policy, Congress could consider modifications to the requirements for sentence reduction under 18 U.S.C. Section 3582(c)(1)(A) to allow more inmates to have their sentences reduced. For example, Congress could consider allowing courts to consider rehabilitation—either as an extraordinary and compelling reason on its own, or in consort with other reasons—when making determinations about sentence reductions. Expanding the authority of courts to grant a sentence reduction could allow inmates deemed to be a low threat to public safety to be placed in the community earlier, thereby freeing up bedspace in federal prisons.

An inmate granted a sentence reduction could still be required to serve a term of supervised release, which would allow federal probation officers to monitor the inmate after he or she is released, a possible advantage over allowing inmates to be released early by increasing good conduct time. However, it is likely that the judicial branch would require additional resources in order to process more applications for sentence reductions under the program and properly monitor inmates whose sentences were reduced but who were placed on supervised release.

Also, there might be a question as to whether this would turn the courts into de facto parole boards. Congress eliminated parole in the federal system, in part, over concerns that inmates were incarcerated for less than an appropriate amount of time and disparities in decisions over who received parole. Under this possible system, inmates could be released before serving a majority of their sentences, but Congress could address this concern by not allowing inmates to be eligible for a sentence reduction until they have served a certain portion of their entire sentence.

A potentially more difficult issue for Congress to address is how judges would make decisions if granted broader authority to reduce sentences under the program. It is possible that an inmate's opportunity to receive a sentence reduction would depend on which judge ruled on the inmate's petition. This concern mirrors some of the concerns that existed about how much sway parole boards held over who was granted parole.

Congress could also consider amending the requirements under 18 U.S.C. Section 3582(c)(1)(A) so that inmates could be released before turning 70. Research indicates that most offenders "age-out" of crime; that is, the older offenders get, the less likely they are to commit new crimes.[135]

It appears likely that more elderly inmates could safely be released from confinement and placed on home confinement for the remainder of their sentences.[136] However, the data show that granting early release to elderly offenders would only have a minimal effect on prison overcrowding.

In FY2011 approximately 15% of federal inmates were over the age of 50 and 4% were over the age of 60.[137] In addition, while elderly inmates might pose a reduced threat to public safety, there is likely to be some sentiment that any offender, regardless of age and safety risk, should serve his or her entire sentence.

Modifying the "Safety Valve" Provision

There are other potential amendments to the criminal code Congress could consider if policy makers wanted to potentially reduce the size of the federal prison population. For example, Congress could consider expanding the "safety valve" provision under 18 U.S.C. Section 3553(f). The safety valve provision allows judges to impose a sentence without regard to the mandatory minimum sentences for certain drug offenses[138] if the following conditions are met:

- The defendant does not have more than one criminal history point, as determined under the sentencing guidelines.
- The defendant did not use violence or credible threats of violence or possess a firearm or other dangerous weapon (or induce another participant to do so) in connection with the offense.
- The offense did not result in death or serious bodily injury to any person.
- The defendant was not an organizer, leader, manager, or supervisor of others in the offense, as determined by the sentencing guidelines, and was not engaged in a continuing criminal enterprise.
- No later than the time of the sentencing hearing, the defendant has truthfully provided to the government all information and evidence the defendant has concerning the offense or offenses that were part of the same course of conduct or of a common scheme or plan, but the fact that the defendant has no relevant or useful or other information to provide or that the government is already aware of the information shall not preclude a determination by the court that the defendant has not complied with the requirements of the provision.

Currently, the safety valve provision cannot be applied to defendants facing a mandatory minimum sentence for an offense that is not drug-related. The safety valve provision was enacted after Congress became concerned that the mandatory minimum sentencing provisions could result in equally severe penalties for both the more and the less culpable offenders.[139] Congress could consider expanding the provision so that it would apply to defendants facing mandatory minimum sentences for offenses other than drug crimes. This option would allow Congress to retain mandatory minimum penalties that can still be applied to more serious offenders while allowing judges to sentence less serious offenders to shorter periods of incarceration.

One idea put forth is to amend current law so that judges could apply the safety valve in instances where the recommended sentencing guideline range is below the mandatory minimum penalty and where the defendant's offense did not result in death or serious bodily injury to anyone and the defendant has provided the government with all information and evidence available to the defendant.[140] Under the proposal, the defendant could not be sentenced to less than the minimum of the sentencing range calculated under the sentencing guidelines.

Many of the conditions placed on the current safety valve provision would remain (e.g., not using violence or possessing a weapon and not being an organizer or leader in the offense), but rather than being a bar from being eligible for the safety valve, they would be factors for the court to consider when deciding whether to sentence a defendant below the mandatory minimum penalty. Judges would be required to state for the record why they chose to impose a sentence below the mandatory minimum penalty, and those decisions would be subject to appellate review.

However, as noted above, the USSC has incorporated many mandatory minimum sentences into the sentencing guidelines. Therefore, in some instances the guideline sentence might be equal to or exceed the mandatory minimum penalty, which would render the proposed safety valve provision moot. One possible solution to this conundrum would be to allow the USSC to give due consideration to mandatory minimum penalties when formulating the sentencing guidelines, but not requiring the USSC to make the guidelines consistent with mandatory minimum penalties.[141]

Repealing Federal Criminal Statutes for Some Offenses

One of the highlighted reasons for the growth in the federal prison population was the "federalization" of offenses that were traditionally under the sole jurisdiction of state authorities. Policy makers could consider revising the U.S. Code so that federal law enforcement focuses on crimes where states do not have jurisdiction over the offenses or where the federal government is best suited to investigate and prosecute the offenders (e.g., the offense involves multiple individuals acting together to commit crimes across several states).

Some crimes will always be federal offenses. For example, the federal government will always be responsible for prosecuting individuals who commit immigration-related offenses because immigration laws are solely the jurisdiction of the federal government. However, over the years the federal government has become more involved in investigating, prosecuting, and incarcerating people who commit drug offenses and offenses where a convicted felon is found to be in possession of a firearm. In many instances, states have criminal penalties for individuals who commit these types of crimes. For example, in his testimony before the House Subcommittee on Crime, Terrorism, and Homeland Security at a hearing on the unintended consequences of mandatory minimum penalties, Eric Sterling, the President of the Criminal Justice Policy Foundation, argued

> [f]ederal drug cases should focus exclusively on the international organizations that use their profits from the manufacture and distribution of cocaine, opium and heroin, methamphetamine, and cannabis to finance assassinations, terrorism, wholesale corruption and bribery, organized crime generally, and the destabilization of our allies...Every state in the U.S. has a great capacity to investigate, prosecute and punish the high-level local drug traffickers that operate within their jurisdiction. State and local police and prosecutors outnumber federal agents and prosecutors. State prisons far exceed the capacity of federal prisons...Almost none of the crack [cocaine] dealers that

> proliferate in countless U.S. neighborhoods warrant federal prosecution. There are neighborhood criminals and their crimes are state crimes. If a state's law does not adequately punish a crack [cocaine] dealer, *that is the state's problem. Inadequate state laws do not warrant wasting very scarce, powerful federal resources even on serious neighborhood criminals* [emphasis original].[142]

Scaling back the scope of the federal criminal code could help reduce the size of the federal prison population in the future by reducing the number of people prosecuted and sentenced to incarceration in federal courts.

However, this policy option could increase the burden on state criminal justice systems since they would be responsible for prosecuting and incarcerating offenders who are no longer tried in federal courts. By year-end 2012, according to the BJS, 21 state correctional systems were at or above their highest capacity, and another 14 state correctional systems were between 90% and 99% of their highest capacity.[143] Since nearly three-quarters of states have prison systems that are operating at 90% of capacity or higher, it would appear that if the federal government chooses not to prosecute some offenses, thereby leaving states with the responsibility to do so, it would require states to either expand their prison capacities or possibly decline to prosecute some offenses.

Also, it is possible that an expansion of state correctional systems could have a significant effect on state finances. The Vera Institute of Justice reported that state correctional spending has nearly quadrupled over the past two decades, which makes it the fasting-growing budget item after Medicaid.[144] The National Association of State Budget Officers reported that in FY2013, correctional expenditures accounted for 6.8% of all state general fund expenditures, though this was down from 7.3% of general fund expenditures in FY2011.[145]

In FY2013, Michigan dedicated the largest portion of its general fund to correctional expenditures (22.5%), while Minnesota dedicated the least (2.3%).[146] Since states typically cannot run a budget deficit, any expansion in correctional expenditures would have to be paid for with cuts to other state services, increased taxes, or issuing bonds.

CONCLUSION

There are almost 195,000 more inmates incarcerated in federal prisons currently than there were in FY1980, a 790% increase in the federal prison population. The growth in the federal prison population is the result of several changes to the federal criminal justice system, including expanding the use of mandatory minimum penalties; the federal government taking jurisdiction in more criminal cases; and eliminating parole for federal inmates.

The analyses presented in this report show that the BOP faces several challenges resulting from the increasing number of inmates in the federal prison system. First, it is increasingly expensive to operate the federal prison system. Second, the federal prison system is becoming more overcrowded, especially in high- and medium-security male prisons. Third, the cost of caring for more inmates has left the BOP in a position where it might not be able to hire an adequate number of staff.

Finally, the steady influx of inmates combined with dwindling levels of funding for prison construction and maintenance has placed a strain on the federal prison system's infrastructure.

If Congress moves forward with a debate about prison and sentencing reform, policy makers might also consider whether incarcerating more offenders would continue to generate a significant deterrent effect.

Research suggests that while incarceration did contribute to lower violent crime rates in the 1990s, there are declining marginal returns associated with ever-increasing levels of incarceration.[147]

The diminishing level of return resulting from higher levels of incarceration might be explained by the fact that higher levels of incarceration are likely to include more offenders who are either at the end of their criminal careers or who were at a low risk of committing crimes at a high rate (so-called "career criminals").[148]

Another possible reason for diminishing marginal returns might be that more of the individuals incarcerated over the past three decades have been incarcerated for crimes where there is a high level of replacement.[149] For example, if a serial rapist is incarcerated, not only is there the potential to prevent future sexual assaults that would have been committed by the offender, but it is also probable that no one else will take that offender's place. However, if a drug dealer is incarcerated, it is possible that someone will step in to take that person's place; therefore, no further crimes may be averted by incarcerating the individual.

The unprecedented increase in the federal prison population over the past three decades was not the result of a singular policy change; likewise, it would appear that, should Congress choose to address prison population growth, it would require a multi-faceted approach to reduce the number of federal inmates in any substantive manner. Congress might consider options—such as expanding the capacity of the federal prison system, continued investment in rehabilitative programs, and placing inmates in private prisons—that would either continue or expand current correctional policies.

However, Congress might also consider changing or reversing some of the policies that have been put into place over the years which contributed to the increasing number of federal prison inmates. Some of these options include placing some inmates in alternatives to incarceration, such as probation, or expanding early release options by allowing inmates to earn more good time credit or allowing inmates to be placed on parole once again.

Congress could consider reducing the amount of time inmates are incarcerated in federal prisons by limiting the number of crimes subject to mandatory minimum penalties or reducing the length of the mandatory minimum sentence. Finally, policy makers could consider allowing states to investigate and prosecute offenses that have become subject to federal jurisdiction over the past three decades.

APPENDIX. SELECT BOP DATA

Table A-1. Appropriations for the BOP by Account; Number of Inmates Under the BOP's Jurisdiction; and the Number and Capacity of and Overcrowding in BOP Facilities

Appropriations amounts are in thousands of dollars

Fiscal Year	Appropriations			Prison Population			Prison Facilities		
	Salaries and Expenses	Buildings and Facilities	Total	Institution	Contract	Total	Number	Capacity	Over-crowding
1980	$323,884	$5,960	$329,844	24,268	372	24,640	41	—	—
1981	351,759	10,020	361,779	26,195	118	26,313	43	23,648[a]	11%[a]
1982	378,016	56,481	434,497	28,133	2,398	30,531	43	24,072[a]	17%[a]
1983	412,133	66,667	478,800	30,214	3,002	33,216	43	23,936[a]	26%[a]
1984	464,850	47,711	512,561	32,317	3,478	35,795	43	24,874[a]	30%[a]
1985	536,932	86,043	622,975	36,001	4,329	40,330	46	25,532[a]	41%[a]
1986	561,480	44,082	605,562	41,506	4,549	46,055	47	27,785[a]	49%[a]
1987	656,941	219,249	876,190	44,194	5,184	49,378	47	27,854[a]	59%[a]
1988	772,013	297,076	1,069,089	44,142	6,371	50,513	52	28,143[a]	57%[a]
1989	962,016	612,914	1,574,930	51,153	6,609	57,762	58	31,727[a]	61%[a]
1990	1,138,778	1,511,953	2,650,731	58,021	6,915	64,936	64	34,239[a]	69%[a]
1991	1,363,645	374,358	1,738,003	64,131	7,377	71,508	68	42,531	51%
1992	1,649,121	462,090	2,111,211	70,670	9,008	79,678	69	48,527	46%
1993	1,793,470	339,225	2,132,695	79,799	8,766	88,565	72	57,610	39%
1994	1,962,605	269,543	2,232,148	85,850	9,312	95,162	75	64,751	33%
1995	2,319,722	276,301	2,596,023	90,159	10,799	100,958	83	72,039	25%
1996	2,546,893[b]	334,728	2,881,621	94,695	10,748	105,443	86	76,442	24%
1997	2,748,427[c]	435,200	3,183,627	101,091	11,198	112,289	91	83,022	22%
1998	2,847,777[d]	255,133	3,102,910	108,207	14,109	122,316	92	86,051	26%
1999	2,888,853[e]	410,997	3,299,850	117,295	16,394	133,689	94	89,581	31%
2000	3,111,073[f]	556,780	3,667,853	125,560	19,565	145,125	97	94,927	32%
2001	3,469,739	833,822	4,303,561	130,327	26,245	156,572	100	98,425	32%

Table A-1. (Continued)

	Appropriations			Prison Population			Prison Facilities		
Fiscal Year	Salaries and Expenses	Buildings and Facilities	Total	Institution	Contract	Total	Number	Capacity	Over-crowding
2002	3,805,118	807,808	4,612,926	137,527	25,909	163,436	102	103,262	33%
2003	4,044,788	396,632	4,441,420	146,212	26,287	172,499	103	105,193	39%
2004	4,414,313	393,515	4,807,828	152,518	27,377	179,895	109	108,537	41%
2005	4,571,385	205,076	4,776,461	159,501	27,893	187,394	116	118,652	34%
2006	4,830,160	99,961	4,930,121	162,514	30,070	192,584	114[g]	119,510	36%
2007	5,012,433	432,425	5,444,858	167,323	32,697	200,020	114	122,189	37%
2008	5,346,740	372,720	5,719,460	165,964	35,704	201,668	114	122,366	36%
2009	5,600,792	575,807	6,176,599	172,423	36,336	208,759	115	125,778	37%
2010	6,106,231	99,155	6,205,386	173,289	36,938	210,227	116	126,713	37%
2011	6,282,410	98,957	6,381,367	177,934	39,834	217,768	117	127,795	39%
2012	6,551,281	90,000	6,641,281	177,556	41,131	218,687	118	128,359	38%
2013	6,349,248	95,356	6,444,604	176,849	42,449	219,298	119	129,726	36%
2014	6,769,000	90,000	6,859,000	—	—	—	—	—	—

Source: U.S. Department of Justice, Bureau of Prisons.

Notes: The BOP did not provide capacity and overcrowding data for FY1980. Appropriation amounts in Table A-1 include all supplemental and reprogrammed appropriations and any rescissions of enacted budget authority, but they *do not* include rescissions of *unobligated balances*. From FY1980 to FY1995, funding for the National Institute of Corrections (NIC) was included in a separate account. Since FY1996, funding for the NIC has been included in the S&E account. Funding for the NIC for FY1980-FY1995 was added to the S&E account to make funding for the S&E account comparable across fiscal years. The FY2013 enacted amount includes the amount sequestered per the Budget Control Act of 2011 (P.L. 112-25).

[a] Capacity and overcrowding were calculated based on single cell occupancy

[b] Includes $13.5 million appropriated from the Violent Crime Reduction Trust Fund.

[c] Includes $25.2 million appropriated from the Violent Crime Reduction Trust Fund.

[d] Includes $26.1 million appropriated from the Violent Crime Reduction Trust Fund.

[e] Includes $26.5 million appropriated from the Violent Crime Reduction Trust Fund.

[f] Includes $22.5 million appropriated from the Violent Crime Reduction Trust Fund.

[g] In FY2006, the BOP closed four stand-alone prison camps and activated two new prisons.

Table A-2. Appropriations for the BOP, by Decision Unit, FY1999-FY2014 Appropriations in thousands of dollars

	Salaries and Expenses				Buildings and Facilities	
Fiscal Year	Inmate Care and Programs	Institution Security and Administration	Contract Confinement	Management and Administration	New Construction	Modernization and Repair
1999	$1,090,148	$1,401,349	$255,062	$142,249	$322,963	$88,034
2000	1,123,856	1,494,809	344,773	147,635	441,003	115,777
2001	1,208,480	1,601,518	511,579	148,162	710,816	123,006
2002	1,311,335	1,722,567	620,145	151,071	675,040	132,768
2003	1,454,481	1,868,538	567,365	154,404	262,956	133,676
2004	1,624,308	2,050,417	574,473	165,115	177,620	164,000
2005	1,682,656	2,094,917	627,135	166,677	25,372	179,704
2006	1,740,011	2,227,223	683,031	179,895	48,115	51,846
2007	1,774,048	2,297,055	757,851	183,479	368,875	63,550
2008	1,942,077	2,409,112	814,529	181,022	302,720	70,000
2009	2,070,002	2,495,196	840,933	194,661	465,180	110,627
2010	2,215,992	2,708,651	981,112	200,476	25,386	73,769
2011	2,294,174	2,783,664	996,772	207,800	25,335	73,622
2012	2,421,272	2,880,290	1,040,213	209,506	23,035	66,695
2013	2,424,620	2,717,938	1,017,297	189,393	23,649	71,707
2014	2,525,039	2,966,364	1,074,808	202,789	22,852	67,148

Source: U.S. Department of Justice, Bureau of Prisons.

Notes: Amounts in Table A-2 include all supplemental and reprogrammed appropriations and any rescissions of enacted budget authority, but they *do not* include rescissions of *unobligated balances*. The FY2013 enacted amount includes the amount sequestered per the Budget Control Act of 2011 (P.L. 112-25).

End Notes

[1] E. Ann Carson and Daniela Golinelli, *Prisoners in 2012: Trends in Admissions and Releases, 1991-2012*, U.S. Department of Justice, Office of Justice Programs, Bureau of Justice Statistics, NCJ 243920, Washington, DC, December 2013, p. 39.

[2] Data provided by the U.S. Department of Justice, Bureau of Prisons.

[3] U.S. Department of Justice, Bureau of Prisons, *About the Bureau of Prisons*, p. 1, hereinafter "*About the Bureau of Prisons*."

[4] U.S. Department of Justice, Bureau of Prisons, *Historical Information*, http://www.bop.gov/about/history

[5] Ibid.

[6] Ibid.

[7] The number of inmates under the jurisdiction of state correctional authorities in 2009 was 1,407,369; in 2010 it was 1,404,032; in 2011 it was 1,382,421; and in 2012 it was 1,353,198. E. Ann Carson and Daniela Golinelli, *Prisoners in 2012—Advanced Counts*, U.S. Department of Justice, Office of Justice Programs, Bureau of Justice Statistics, NCJ 242467, Washington, DC, July 2013, p. 2.

[8] Contract facilities include bedspace the BOP contracts for in privately operated prisons, Residential Reentry Centers (i.e., halfway houses), and state and local correctional facilities.

[9] Public order offenses include tax law violations; bribery; perjury; national defense; escape; racketeering and extortion; gambling; liquor; mailing or transporting of obscene materials; traffic; migratory birds; conspiracy, aiding and abetting, and jurisdictional offenses; violations of regulatory laws and regulations in agriculture, antitrust, labor law, food and drug, motor carrier, and other regulatory offenses.

[10] Data downloaded from U.S. Department of Justice, Office of Justice Programs, Bureau of Justice Statistics, *Federal Criminal Case Processing Statistics*, http://bjs.ojp.usdoj.gov/fjsrc/index.cfm.

[11] "Trafficking offenses" include an offense where an offender knowingly and intentionally imported or exported any controlled substance in schedule I, II, III, IV, or V (as defined by 21 U.S.C. §812). It includes manufacturing, distributing, dispensing, selling, or possessing with intent to manufacture, distribute, or sell a controlled substance or a counterfeit substance; exporting any controlled substance in schedules I-V; manufacturing or distributing a controlled substance in schedule I or II for purposes of unlawful importation; or making or distributing any punch, die, plate, stone, or any other thing designed to reproduce the label upon any drug or container, or removing or obliterating the label or symbol of any drug or container. It also includes knowingly opening, maintaining or managing any place for the purpose of manufacturing, distributing, or using any controlled substance (for example, 19 U.S.C. §1590; 21 U.S.C. §§333(e), 825(a)-(d), 830(a), 841(a)-(b) (d)(e)(g), 842(a), 843(a)(b), 845, 846, 848, 854, 856, 858, 859(a)(b), 860(a), 861(c)(f), 952(a)(b), 953(a)(e), 957, 959, 960(a)(b)(d), 961, 962, and 963; and 46A U.S.C. §§1903(g) and (j)). U.S. Department of Justice, Office of Justice Programs, Bureau of Justice Statistics, *Compendium of Federal Justice Statistics, 2004*, NCJ 213476, Washington, DC, December 2006, p. 119, http://www.bjs.gov/content/pub/pdf/ cfjs04.pdf.

[12] U.S. Sentencing Commission, *Report to Congress: Mandatory Minimum Penalties in the Federal Criminal Justice System*, Washington, DC, October 2011, p. 63, hereinafter "*Mandatory Minimum Penalties in the Federal Criminal Justice System*."

[13] Ibid., pp. 71-72.

[14] Ibid., p. 76.

[15] Erik Luna and Paul G. Cassell, "Mandatory Minimalism," *Cardozo Law Review*, vol. 32, no. 1 (September 2010), pp. 16-17; James E. Felman, on behalf of the American Bar Association, statement before the United States Sentencing Commission in the Hearing on Mandatory Minimums, May 27, 2010, p. 9, hereinafter "Felman testimony."

[16] Ibid.

[17] Kamala Mallik-Kane, Barbara Parthasarathy, and William Adams, *Examining Growth in the Federal Prison Population, 1998 to 2010*, The Urban Institute, Washington, DC, September 2012, p. 10, hereinafter "*Examining Growth in the Federal Prison Population*."

[18] The USSC limited its analysis of the number of inmates in federal prisons who were convicted of or subject to a mandatory minimum penalty to FY1995-FY2010 because the commission's analysis relied on combining USSC data with BOP data and there were limitations with the data prior to FY1995. *Mandatory Minimum Penalties in the Federal Criminal Justice System*, p. 81.

[19] Even though a defendant might be convicted for an offense that carries a mandatory minimum penalty there are mechanisms whereby the court may impose a term of imprisonment that is below the mandatory minimum (i.e., the defendant can be convicted for an offense carrying a mandatory minimum penalty, but the defendant

is not subject to a mandatory minimum penalty when sentenced). For example, under 18 U.S.C. §3553(e), the court "[u]pon motion of the Government...shall have the authority to impose a sentence below a level established by statute as a minimum sentence so as to reflect a defendant's substantial assistance in the investigation or prosecution of another person who has committed an offense." Section 3553(e) also requires the sentence to be imposed in accordance with the federal sentencing guidelines.

[20] *Mandatory Minimum Penalties in the Federal Criminal Justice System*, p. 82.

[21] The USSC defined "federalization of crime" as the transformation of traditional state and local criminal offenses into federal crimes. Ibid., p. 63.

[22] *Examining Growth in the Federal Prison Population*, p. 10.

[23] Ibid.

[24] Ibid., p. 11.

[25] U.S. Department of Justice, Bureau of Prisons, *Historical Information*, http://www.bop.gov/about/history

[26] Each prisoner serving a term of imprisonment of more than one year, but not prisoners serving a life sentence, can receive a good time credit of up to 54 days per year to count toward serving the sentence. The amount of the credit is subject to the determination of the BOP. 18 U.S.C. §3624(b).

[27] For a more in-depth analysis of the BOP's appropriations, see CRS Report R42486, *The Bureau of Prisons (BOP): Operations and Budget*, by Nathan James.

[28] U.S. Congress, Senate Committee on Appropriations, Subcommittee on Commerce, Justice, Science, and Related Agencies, *Departments of Commerce and Justice, and Science, and Related Agencies Appropriations Bill, 2013*, report to accompany S. 2323, 112th Cong., 2nd sess., April 19, 2012, S.Rept. 112-158 (Washington: GPO, 2012), p. 64.

[29] U.S. Congress, House Committee on Appropriations, *Omnibus Appropriations Act, 2009*, committee print, 111th Cong., 1st sess., March 2009 (Washington: GPO, 2009), p. 274.

[30] Ibid. See also, U.S. Congress, House Committee on Appropriations, *Departments of Transportation and Housing and Urban Development, and Related Agencies Appropriations Act, 2010*, Conference Report to Accompany H.R. 3288, 111th Cong., 1st sess., December 8, 2009, H.Rept. 111-366 (Washington: GPO, 2009), p. 671; U.S. Congress, Senate Committee on Appropriations, Subcommittee on Commerce, Justice, Science, and Related Agencies, *Departments of Commerce and Justice, and Science, and Related Agencies Appropriations Bill, 2013*, report to accompany S. 2323, 112th Cong., 2nd sess., April 19, 2012, S.Rept. 112-158 (Washington: GPO, 2012), p. 65.

[31] U.S. Department of Justice, Bureau of Prisons, *FY2015 Performance Budget, Congressional Submission, Salaries and Expenses*, pp. 25, 29, and 45; hereinafter, "BOP's FY2015 S&E Budget Justification."

[32] Data provided by the Bureau of Prisons.

[33] Alex Nussbaum, "Health Care Costs Rise Faster Than U.S. Inflation Rate," *Bloomberg*, May 21, 2012 (article on file with author).

[34] BOP's FY2015 S&E Budget Justification, p. 23.

[35] See 18 U.S.C. §3624(f)(1) and 18 U.S.C. §3624(b)(3).

[36] Each prisoner serving a term of imprisonment of more than one year, but not prisoners serving a life sentence, can receive a good time credit of up to 54 days per year to count toward serving the sentence. The amount of the credit is subject to the determination of BOP. 18 U.S.C. §3624(b).

[37] BOP's FY2015 S&E Budget Justification, p. 30.

[38] "Residential substance abuse treatment" is defined as a course of individual and group activities and treatment, lasting at least six months, in residential treatment facilities set apart from the general prison population (which may include pharmacotherapies, where appropriate) that may extend beyond the six-month period. 18 U.S.C. §3621(e)(5)(A).

[39] "Aftercare" is defined as placement, case management, and monitoring in a community-based substance abuse treatment program when the prisoner leaves the custody of BOP. 18 U.S.C. §3621(e)(5)(C).

[40] An "eligible prisoner" is defined as a prisoner who is determined by BOP to have a substance abuse problem and to be willing to participate in a residential substance abuse treatment program. 18 U.S.C. §3621(e)(5)(B).

[41] The following categories of inmates are not eligible for early release: (1) Immigration and Customs Enforcement detainees; (2) pretrial inmates; (3) contractual boarders (for example, District of Columbia, state, or military inmates); (4) inmates who have a prior felony or misdemeanor conviction for homicide, forcible rape, robbery, or aggravated assault, or child sexual abuse offenses; (5) inmates who are not eligible for participation in a community-based program as determined by the institution's warden on the basis of his or her professional discretion; or (6) inmates whose current offense is a felony. 28 C.F.R. §550.55.

[42] In the conference report for the Consolidated and Further Continuing Appropriations Act, 2012 (i.e., the "minibus," P.L. 112-55), the conferees expressed concern that "the current upward trend in the prison inmate population is unsustainable and, if left unchecked, will eventually engulf the [Department of Justice's] budgetary resources." U.S. Congress, House of Representatives, *Agriculture, Rural Development, Food and Drug Administration, and the Related Agencies Programs for the Fiscal Year Ending September 30, 2012, and for Other Purposes*, Conference Report to Accompany H.R. 2112, 112th Cong., 1st sess., November 14, 2011, H.Rept. 112-284 (Washington, DC: GPO, 2011), p. 241.

[43] Rated capacity, as calculated by the BOP, assumes some level of double bunking (i.e., two inmates to a cell) across the federal prison system. The amount of double bunking allowed depends on the facility's security level (i.e., minimum, low, medium, or high). The BOP calculates each facility's rated capacity using the following formulas: minimum and low security institutions at 100 percent double bunking; medium security institutions at 50 percent double bunking and; high security institutions at 25 percent double bunking. For example, if a high security facility had 500 cells, the facility's rated capacity would be 625 inmates. The rated capacity is intended to reflect the number of prisoners that the institution can house safely and securely with adequate access to services and rehabilitative programs.

[44] This decision unit provides for the costs associated with the confinement of federal inmates in contract facilities, which include private prisons, residential re-entry centers, state and local facilities, and home confinement. It provides funding for the management and oversight of contract confinement functions. The decision unit also provided funding for the National Institute of Corrections.

[45] This decision unit covers the cost of inmate food, medical supplies, institutional and release clothing, welfare services, transportation, gratuities, staff salaries, and operational costs of functions directly related to providing inmate care. It provides funding for inmate programs, including education and vocational training, psychological services, religious programs, and drug treatment. All of the drug treatment programs discussed above are funded from this decision unit. The decision unit also covers costs associated with regional and central office administration and support related to providing inmate care.

[46] This decision unit covers costs associated with the maintenance of facilities and institution security. It funds institution maintenance, motor pool operations, powerhouse operations, institution security and other administrative functions. The decision unit also covers costs associated with regional and central office administrative and management support functions such as research and evaluation, systems support, financial management, budget functions, safety, and legal counsel.

[47] Travis W. Franklin, Courtney A. Franklin, and Travis C. Pratt, "Examining the Empirical Relationship Between Prison Crowding and Inmate Misconduct: A Meta-analysis of Conflicting Research Results," *Journal of Criminal Justice*, vol. 34, no. 4 (July-August 2006), p. 401, hereinafter "Examining the Empirical Relationship Between Prison Crowding and Inmate Misconduct."

[48] Ibid., pp. 407-408.

[49] U.S. Department of Justice, Bureau of Prisons, *The Effects of Changing Crowding and Staffing Levels in Federal Prisons on Inmate Violence Rates, Executive Summary*, October 2005, hereinafter "*The Effects of Changing Crowding and Staffing Levels in Federal Prisons on Inmate Violence Rates*."

[50] John Wooldredge, Timothy Griffin, and Travis Pratt, "Considering Hierarchical Models for Research on Inmate Behavior: Predicting Misconduct with Multilevel Data," *Justice Quarterly*, vol. 18, no. 1 (March 2001), p. 212.

[51] Benjamin Steiner and John Wooldredge, "Rethinking the Link Between Institutional Crowding and Inmate Misconduct," *The Prison Journal*, vol. 89, no. 2 (June 2009), pp. 227-228.

[52] U.S. Government Accountability Office, *Bureau of Prisons: Growing Inmate Crowding Negatively Affects Inmates, Staff, and Infrastructure*, GAO-12-742, September 2012, p. 18, hereinafter "GAO prison crowding report."

[53] Ibid., p. 19.

[54] Ibid., pp. 19-20.

[55] Ibid., pp. 20-21.

[56] 18 U.S.C. §3624(b)(1).

[57] For more information on changes in how executive branch agencies procure goods produced by the FPI and the number of inmates working in FPI factories, see CRS Report RL32380, *Federal Prison Industries: Overview and Legislative History*, by Nathan James.

[58] "Staff" includes all employees of a facility whereas "correctional officers" only include employees whose primary duties are to supervise inmates.

[59] James J. Stephen, *Census of State and Federal Correctional Facilities, 2005*, U.S. Department of Justice, Office of Justice Programs, Bureau of Justice Statistics, NCJ 222182, Washington , DC, October 2008, p. 5.
[60] Ibid., p. 22.
[61] GAO prison crowding report, p. 23.
[62] Ibid., p. 22.
[63] Ibid. pp. 23-24.
[64] Ibid., p. 22.
[65] Ibid.
[66] For more information on how the BOP's appropriations are split between decision units and what funding under those decision units is used for, see CRS Report R42486, *The Bureau of Prisons (BOP): Operations and Budget*, by Nathan James.
[67] *The Effects of Changing Crowding and Staffing Levels in Federal Prisons on Inmate Violence Rates.*
[68] U.S. Department of Justice, Bureau of Prisons, *FY2015 Performance Budget, Congressional Submission, Buildings and Facilities*, p. 9.
[69] Ibid., pp. 9-10.
[70] Ibid., pp. 23-24.
[71] Ibid., p. 26.
[72] BOP's FY2015 S&E Budget Justification, p. 3.
[73] Doris Layton MacKenzie, *What Works in Corrections: Reducing the Criminal Activities of Offenders and Delinquents* (New York: Cambridge University Press, 2006), pp. 331-333, hereinafter, "*What Works in Corrections*."
[74] For more information on the BOP's rehabilitative programs see CRS Report R41525, *Federal Prison Inmates: Rehabilitative Needs and Program Participation*, by Nathan James.
[75] Steve Aos, Marna Miller, and Elizabeth Drake, *Evidence-based Public Policy Options to Reduce Future Prison Construction, Criminal Justice Costs, and Crime Rates*, Washington State Institute for Public Policy, Olympia, WA, October 2006.
[76] The conference report (H.Rept. 104-863) for the Omnibus Consolidated Appropriations Act, 1997 (P.L. 104-208) incorporates, by reference, language from the Senate report (S.Rept. 104-353) to accompany the Senate committee-reported version of H.R. 3814 (104th Congress), that requires the BOP to undertake "a 5-year prison privatization demonstration project" involving the facility that the BOP built in Taft, CA.
[77] The Taft Correctional Institution is still operating as a private facility. After the contract with the Geo Group expired in 2007, the contract was recompeted and it was awarded to Management and Training Corporation.
[78] The three similar facilities included in the evaluation were FCI Yazoo City, FCI Elkton, and FCI Forrest City.
[79] Gerry Gaes, "Cost, Performance Studies Look at Prison Privatization," *NIJ Journal* , no. 259 (March 2008), p. 33.
[80] Ibid.
[81] "Economies of scale" generally refers to the increase in efficiency of production that accompanies expanded production. In economic terms, this means that the average cost of the good produced decreases and production increases because fixed costs are shared over an increased number of goods. In terms of the BOP evaluation of TCI, "economies of scale" would refer to the decreased per prisoner costs resulting from spreading the prison's operating costs over a greater number of inmates.
[82] Ibid., p. 34.
[83] Travis C. Pratt and Jeff Maahs, "Are Private Prisons More Cost-effective Than Public Prisons? A Meta-analysis of Evaluation Research Studies," *Crime and Delinquency*, vol. 45, no. 3 (July 1999), pp. 358-371; Dina Perrone and Travis C. Pratt, "Comparing the Quality of Confinement and Cost-effectiveness of Public Versus Private Prisons: What We Know, Why We Do Not Know More, and Where to Go From Here," *The Prison Journal*, vol. 83, no. 3 (September 2003), pp. 301-322; Brad W. Lundahl, Chelsea Kunz, and Cyndi Brownell, et al., "A Meta-analysis of Cost and Quality of Confinement Indicators," *Research on Social Work Practice*, vol. 19, no. 4 (July 2009), pp. 383-394.
[84] Travis C. Pratt and Jeff Maahs, "Are Private Prisons More Cost-effective Than Public Prisons? A Meta-analysis of Evaluation Research Studies," *Crime and Delinquency*, vol. 45, no. 3 (July 1999), p. 367.
[85] Ibid., pp. 367-368.
[86] Brad W. Lundahl, Chelsea Kunz, and Cyndi Brownell, et al., "A Meta-analysis of Cost and Quality of Confinement Indicators," *Research on Social Work Practice*, vol. 19, no. 4 (July 2009), p. 392.
[87] *Mandatory Minimum Penalties in the Federal Criminal Justice System*, p. 345.
[88] 543 U.S. 220 (2005).
[89] 552 U.S. 38 (2007).

[90] 552 U.S. 85 (2007).

[91] Erik Luna and Paul G. Cassell, "Mandatory Minimalism," *Cardozo Law Review*, vol. 32, no. 1 (September 2010), p. 11.

[92] *Mandatory Minimum Penalties in the Federal Criminal Justice System*, p. 368.

[93] *What Works in Corrections*, p. 304.

[94] Ibid.

[95] Ibid., p. 306.

[96] Ibid., p. 318.

[97] A class A felony is an offense where the maximum term of imprisonment authorized is life imprisonment or death. A class B felony is an offense where the maximum term of imprisonment authorized is 25 years or more. 18 U.S.C. §3559(a).

[98] 18 U.S.C. §3561(a).

[99] Ibid., p. 519.

[100] Administrative Office of the U.S. Courts, "Supervision Costs Significantly Less than Incarceration in Federal System," July 18, 2013 (document on file with author).

[101] Joan Petersilia, "Community Corrections: Probation, Parole, and Prisoner Reentry," in *Crime and Public Policy*, ed. James Q. Wilson and Joan Petersilia (New York: Oxford University Press, 2011), pp. 521-522, hereinafter, "Community Corrections: Probation, Parole, and Prisoner Reentry."

[102] Ibid., p. 522.

[103] Ibid.

[104] Kevin McEvoy, "HOPE: A Swift and Certain Process for Probationers," *NIJ Journal*, no. 269 (March 2012), p. 17.

[105] Community Corrections: Probation, Parole, and Prisoner Reentry, p. 524.

[106] Sam Dolnick, "As Escapees Stream Out, a Penal Business Thrives," *New York Times*, June 17, 2012, p. A1.

[107] Ibid., p. A16.

[108] Sam Dolnick, "Poorly Staffed, a Halfway House in New Jersey is Mired in Chaos," *New York Times*, June 18, 2012; Sam Dolnick, "At Penal Unit, A Volatile Mix Fuels a Murder," *New York Times*, June 19, 2012.

[109] The RRCs were located in Denver, CO; Leavenworth, KS; El Paso, TX; Boston, MA; Washington, DC; and Kansas City, MO.

[110] U.S. Department of Justice, Office of the Inspector General, *Audit of the Federal Bureau of Prisons' Contracting for and Management of Residential Reentry Centers*, Audit Report 12-20, Washington, DC, March 2012, p. 5.

[111] The Statement of Work (SOW) for RRCs is the primary document that outlines all of the BOP's requirements for contractors operating RRCs. The SOW requires RRCs to develop individualized program plans for each inmate that focus on, when applicable, reestablishing relationships with family, obtaining and maintaining employment, obtaining drug and alcohol abuse treatment, and finding housing. At the same time each RRC must: (1) be able to locate and verify the whereabouts of inmates at all times; (2) establish an surveillance program to deter and detect the illegal introduction of drugs and alcohol into the facility; (3) effectively discipline inmates; and (4) prepare and maintain required documentation. Ibid., p. 3.

[112] RRCs are required to randomly test at least 5% of all inmates for drugs and alcohol monthly, with a minimum of one inmate tested per month. In addition, an inmate with a known history of drug abuse, or who is suspected of illegal drug use, must be tested no less than four times per month. RRCs are also required to give inmates a breathalyzer test every time they return from an unsupervised activity. Ibid., pp. 7-8.

[113] The OIG notes that there are three types of escapes: regular, technical new, and technical old. "Regular" escapes most closely fit the definition of what most would consider an escape. A regular escape is when an inmate fails to remain in RRC custody by (1) not reporting to the facility for admission at the scheduled time; (2) not remaining at the approved place of employment, training, or treatment during the hours specified by the terms of the employment, training, or treatment program; (3) not returning to the facility at the time prescribed; (4) not returning from an authorized furlough or pass at the time and place stipulated; (5) not abiding by conditions of employment, or curfew conditions of home confinement; or (6) leaving the facility without the permission of RRC staff. "Technical new" escapes occur when an inmate fails to remain in the RRC's custody by being arrested for a new charge. "Technical old" escapes occur when an inmate fails to remain in the RRC's custody by being arrested for an outstanding warrant while residing at a RRC. Of the escapes reported in the OIG's report, 75.3% were regular escapes, 12.7% were technical new escapes, and 11.9% were technical old escapes. Ibid. p. 15.

[114] RRCs can only authorize an inmate to leave for approved activities, including job searches, employment, religious services, and visitations with family and friends. Other than for employment or programming

activities, such as drug abuse counseling, an inmate must generally be at the RRC facility from 9:00 p.m. to 6:00 a.m., unless the director has granted an exemption. RRCs are allowed to grant passes or furloughs to release inmates overnight or to travel distances of more than 100 miles. Ibid., pp. 18-19.

[115] Funding for this program was discontinued after FY2004.

[116] Data provided by the U.S. Department of Justice, Bureau of Prisons.

[117] For more information on how inmates are processed through the federal prison system, see CRS Report R42486, *The Bureau of Prisons (BOP): Operations and Budget*, by Nathan James.

[118] Federal inmates who are eligible for parole (i.e., inmates sentenced before November 1, 1987) can be released after serving one-third of their sentences (if sentenced to a term of incarceration greater than one year) or after 10 years if sentenced to life or a term or incarceration over 30 years. However, the sentencing court could designate a minimum term of imprisonment the defendant would have to serve before being eligible for parole. The minimum term of imprisonment designated by the court could be less, but not more, than one-third of the sentence imposed. The sentencing court could also fix the maximum sentence to be served, at which point the inmate could be released on parole. 18 U.S.C. §§4205(a) and 4205(b), as it was in effect before being repealed by §218(a) of P.L. 98-473.

[119] Data provided by the U.S. Department of Justice, Bureau of Prisons.

[120] Patrick A. Langan and David J. Levin, United States Department of Justice, Bureau of Justice Statistics, *Recidivism of Prisoners Released in 1994*, Report NCJ193427, June 2002. For a summary of this study and other studies on recidivism, see CRS Report RL34287, *Offender Reentry: Correctional Statistics, Reintegration into the Community, and Recidivism*, by Nathan James.

[121] Doris Layton MacKenzie, *What Works in Corrections: Reducing the Criminal Activities of Offenders and Delinquents* (New York: Cambridge University Press, 2006), p. 310.

[122] Ibid.

[123] Community Corrections: Probation, Parole, and Prisoner Reentry, p. 524.

[124] Doris Layton MacKenzie, *What Works in Corrections: Reducing the Criminal Activities of Offenders and Delinquents* (New York: Cambridge University Press, 2006), p. 318.

[125] 18 U.S.C. §3624(b)(1).

[126] 18 U.S.C. §3621(e)(2)(B).

[127] Dora Schriro, "Is Good Time a Good Idea? A Practitioner's Perspective," *The Federal Sentencing Reporter*, vol. 21, no. 3 (February 2009), p. 181.

[128] 28 U.S.C. §994(t).

[129] Stephen R. Sady, "Second Look Resentencing under 18 U.S.C. §3582(c) as an Example of Bureau of Prisons Policies That Result in Overincarceration," *Federal Sentencing Reporter*, vol. 21, no. 3 (February 2009), p. 167.

[130] U.S. Department of Justice, Bureau of Prisons, *Compassionate Release/Reduction in Sentence: Procedures for Implementation of 18 U.S.C. §§ 3582(c)(1)(A) and 4205(g)*, Program Statement 5050.49, p. 1.

[131] Rafael Lemaitre, *Real #DrugPolicyReform: DOJ's New Criteria on Compassionate Release Requests*, Executive Office of the President, Office of National Drug Control Policy, August 12, 2013 (document on file with the author).

[132] Ibid.

[133] The DOJ's "Smart on Crime" initiative is a "comprehensive review of the criminal justice system aimed at ensuring federal laws are enforced more fairly, and federal resources are used more efficiently, by focusing on top law enforcement priorities." Ibid.

[134] Ibid.

[135] Lindsey Devers, *Desistance and Developmental Life Course Theories: Research Summary*, U.S. Department of Justice, Office of Justice Programs, Bureau of Justice Assistance, Washington, DC, November 9, 2011, p. 7.

[136] Under §231(g) of the Second Chance Act of 2007 (P.L. 110-199), the BOP was directed to conduct a pilot program in FY2009 and FY2010 whereby eligible inmates would be placed on home confinement for the remainder of their sentences. Inmates eligible to participate in the pilot program were 65 or older; non-violent or non-sex offenders; not serving a life sentence; severed the greater of 10 years or 75% of their sentences; did not have a history of escape or escape attempts; and were determined to not be at risk for recidivism. The Government Accountability Office (GAO) reported that of the 855 inmates who applied for the pilot program, 71 (8.3%) were determined by the BOP to have met the criteria for the program and were eventually placed on home confinement. The GAO noted that as of June 2012, none of the inmates placed on home confinement had recidivated or violated the terms of release. However, the BOP reported that it did not save any money by placing elderly inmates on home confinement; in fact, the BOP reported that it cost approximately $540,000

more to place the inmates on home confinement. The GAO contends that the BOP's conclusions might not be a reliable indicator of the potential cost of the program should it be continued or expanded. First, while the BOP knows what it paid RRCs to monitor inmates placed on home confinement, the BOP does not know the exact cost of home confinement. The BOP negotiates with RRCs to provide supervision of inmates placed on home confinement. RRCs are paid a per diem rate to house an inmate and they are paid 50% of the per diem rate to supervise an inmate placed on home confinement. However, the BOP does not require RRC contractors to separate the cost of home confinement services and RRCs bedspace, so the BOP does not actually know the cost of home confinement. Second, some of the costs of the pilot program would have been incurred regardless because the BOP is currently authorized to place all of the inmates in the program on home confinement for up to six months. Government Accountability Office, *Federal Bureau of Prisons: Methods for Estimating Incarceration and Community Corrections Costs and Results of the Elderly Offender Pilot*, GAO-12-807R, Washington, DC, July 27, 2012.

[137] Data from the U.S. Department of Justice, Office of Justice Programs, Bureau of Justice Statistics, *Federal Criminal Case Processing Statistics*, http://www.bjs.gov/fjsrc/.

[138] These offenses are trafficking in various controlled substances (21 U.S.C. §841), possession of certain controlled substances (21 U.S.C. §844), attempt or conspiracy to violate controlled substance provisions carrying mandatory minimum sentences (21 U.S.C. §846), smuggling controlled substances in violation of 21 U.S.C. §§952, 953, 955, 957, or 959 (21 U.S.C. §960), and attempt or conspiracy to violate the controlled substance import/export provisions (21 U.S.C. §963).

[139] CRS Report R41326, *Federal Mandatory Minimum Sentences: The Safety Valve and Substantial Assistance Exceptions*, by Charles Doyle. See also U.S. Congress, House Committee on the Judiciary, *Mandatory Minimum Sentencing Reform Act of 1994*, to accompany H.R. 3979, 103rd Cong., 2nd sess., March 24, 1994, H.Rept. 103-460 (Washington: GPO, 1994), p. 2.

[140] Paul G. Cassell and Erik Luna, "Sense and Sensibility in Mandatory Minimum Sentencing," *Federal Sentencing Reporter*, vol. 23, no. 3 (February 2011), p. 222.

[141] Ibid., p. 225.

[142] Statement of Eric E. Sterling, President of the Criminal Justice Policy Foundation, U.S. Congress, House Committee on the Judiciary, Subcommittee on Crime, Terrorism, and Homeland Security, *Mandatory Minimums and Unintended Consequences*, Hearing on H.R. 2934, H.R. 834 and H.R. 1466, 111th Cong., 1st sess., July 14, 2009, H.Hrg. 111-48 (Washington: GPO, 2010), pp. 114-115.

[143] E. Ann Carson and Daniela Golinelli, *Prisoners in 2012: Trends in Admissions and Releases, 1991-2012*, U.S. Department of Justice, Office of Justice Programs, Bureau of Justice Statistics, NCJ 243920, Washington, DC, December 2013, p. 42.

[144] Christian Henrichson and Ruth Delaney, *The Price of Prisons: What Incarceration Costs Taxpayers*, Vera Institute of Justice, New York, NT, January 2012, p. 2.

[145] National Association of State Budget Officers, *State Expenditure Report: Examining Fiscal 2011-2013 State Spending*, Washington, DC, 2013, p. 56.

[146] Ibid.

[147] Anne Morrison Piehl and Bert Useem, "Prisons," in *Crime and Public Policy*, ed. Joan Petersilia and James Q. Wilson, 2nd ed. (New York: Oxford University Press, 2011), p. 542.

[148] Doris Layton MacKenzie, "Reducing the Criminal Activities of Known Offenders and Delinquents: Crime Prevention in the Courts and Corrections," in *Evidence-based Crime Prevention*, ed. Lawrence W. Sherman, David P. Farrington, Brandon C. Welsh and Doris Layton MacKenzie (New York: Routledge, 2002), p. 337.

[149] Bert Useem and Anne Morrison Piehl, *Prison State: The Challenge of Mass Incarceration* (New York: Cambridge University Press, 2008), p. 74.

In: The Federal Prison Population
Editor: Mason C. Darwin

ISBN: 978-1-63463-902-6

Chapter 3

THE BUREAU OF PRISONS (BOP): OPERATIONS AND BUDGET*

Nathan James

SUMMARY

The Bureau of Prisons (BOP) was established in 1930 to house federal inmates, professionalize the prison service, and ensure consistent and centralized administration of the federal prison system. The BOP is the largest correctional agency in the country, in terms of the number of prisoners under its jurisdiction. The BOP must confine any offender convicted and sentenced to a term of imprisonment in a federal court.

All BOP correctional facilities are classified according to one of five different security levels: minimum, low, medium, high, or administrative. An inmate's designation to a particular institution is based primarily on the level of security and supervision the inmate requires; the level of security and staff supervision the institution is able to provide; and the inmate's program needs. All inmates undergo a comprehensive intake screening when they are admitted to a BOP facility. The BOP provides health care for all inmates either through each prison's ambulatory care clinics or by contracting for services through local hospitals. The BOP also provides mental health treatment to inmates who demonstrate a need for it through staff psychologists. The BOP has an established inmate disciplinary system, whereby sanctions are imposed on inmates for committing prohibited acts. An inmate is allowed to request a review of his or her conditions of confinement through the BOP's Administrative Remedy Program. Inmates have access to a variety of rehabilitational programs including education programs, substance abuse treatment, vocational education, and work opportunities. In order to help aid an inmate's transition back into the community, inmates can be placed in a Residential Reentry Center (i.e., a halfway house) for a period of time before their sentence expires.

Changes in federal criminal justice policy since the early 1980s have resulted in a continued increase in the federal prison population. The number of inmates under the BOP's jurisdiction has increased nearly eight-fold (790%) from approximately 24,600

* This is an edited, reformatted and augmented version of a Congressional Research Service publication R42486, prepared for Members and Committees of Congress, dated March 4, 2014.

inmates in FY1980 to nearly 219,300 inmates in FY2013. Since FY1980, the federal prison population has increased, on average, by approximately 5,900 inmates each year.

The burgeoning federal prison population has led Congress to increase appropriations for the BOP's operations and infrastructure. In FY1980, Congress appropriated $330.0 *million* for the BOP. By FY2014, the total appropriation for the BOP reached $6.859 *billion*. The additional funding for the BOP was necessary to cover the costs of providing services to a growing prison population, expanding prison capacity, and hiring additional staff to manage the expanding federal prison system.

The annual growth in the federal prison population has outstripped the BOP's prison capacity, resulting in overcrowding in the federal prison system. Congress could choose to mitigate some of the issues related to federal prison population growth by appropriating more funding so the BOP could hire additional staff and expand prison capacity to alleviate overcrowding. On the other hand, Congress could also consider ways to reduce the number of inmates held in federal prison by considering alternatives to incarceration, such as increasing good time credit for inmates who participate in certain rehabilitative programs, placing more low-level offenders on community supervision in lieu of incarceration, or reducing mandatory minimum penalties for some offenses.

INTRODUCTION

The Bureau of Prisons (BOP) is the largest correctional agency in the country, in terms of the number of prisoners under its jurisdiction.[1] The BOP must confine any offender convicted and sentenced to a term of imprisonment in a federal court.

Changes in federal criminal justice policy since the early 1980s—enforcing a growing number of federal crimes, replacing indeterminate sentencing with a determinate sentencing structure through sentencing guidelines, and increasing the number of federal offenses subject to mandatory minimum sentences—have led to continued rapid growth in the federal prison population. The number of inmates under the BOP's jurisdiction has increased from approximately 24,600 inmates in FY1980 to nearly 219,300 inmates in FY2013. Since FY1980, the federal prison population has increased, on average, by approximately 5,900 inmates each year.

The burgeoning federal prison population has led Congress to increase appropriations for the BOP's operations and infrastructure. In FY1980, Congress appropriated $330.0 *million* for the BOP; by FY2014, the total appropriation for the BOP reached $6.859 *billion* (see *Figure 1*). Even after adjusting for inflation, the BOP's budget increased by nearly $173.2 million per year between FY1980 and FY2014.[2]

The annual growth in the federal prison population has outstripped the BOP's current capacity, resulting in overcrowding in the federal prison system. The BOP reports that at the end of FY2013, the federal prison system was operating at 36% over rated capacity.[3] Congress could choose to mitigate some issues related to federal prison population growth by appropriating more funding so the BOP could hire additional staff and expand prison capacity to alleviate overcrowding. On the other hand, Congress could also consider ways to reduce the number of inmates held in federal prison by considering alternatives to incarceration, such as increasing good time credit for inmates who participate in certain rehabilitative programs, placing more low-level offenders on community supervision in lieu of incarceration, or reducing mandatory minimum penalties for some offenses.

This report provides an overview of how the BOP manages the growing federal prison population and examines the BOP's appropriations since FY1980.

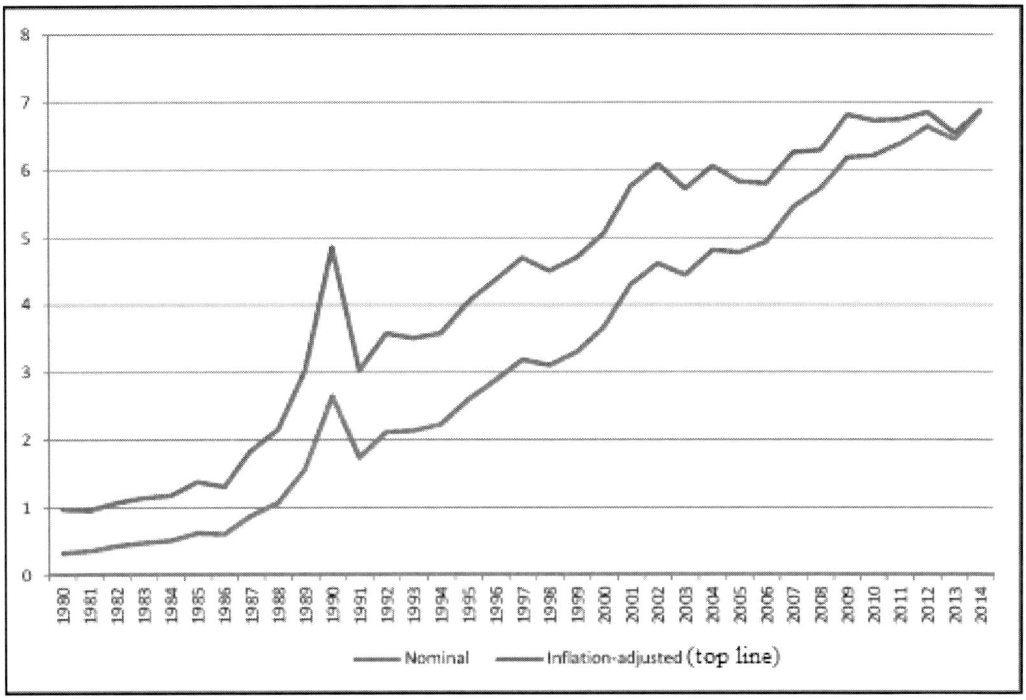

Source: U.S. Department of Justice, Bureau of Prisons.

Notes: Nominal appropriations were adjusted for inflation using data from the Consumer Price Index for All Urban Consumers (CPI-U). Inflation-adjusted amounts are presented in FY2014 dollars. The Consumer Price Index for FY2014 was based on the Congressional Budget Office's projected increase in inflation (taken from Table G-2 in The Budget and Economic Outlook: Fiscal Years 2014 to 2024). The spike in the BOP's funding for FY1990 was the result of Congress appropriating $1.512 billion for the B&F account (see Table 1). The FY2013 enacted amount includes the amount sequestered per the Budget Control Act of 2011(P.L. 112-25).

Figure 1. Nominal and Inflation-Adjusted Appropriations for the Bureau of Prisons, FY1980-FY2014. (Appropriations in billions of dollars)

BOP Operations

The BOP was established in 1930 to house federal inmates, professionalize the prison service, and ensure consistent and centralized administration of the federal prison system.[4] Congress has continued to modify the responsibilities of the BOP since its founding. Currently, the BOP has several congressionally mandated obligations, including

- managing and regulating all federal correctional institutions;
- providing suitable quarters and for the safekeeping, care, and subsistence of all persons charged with or convicted of federal crimes, or held as witnesses;

- providing for the protection, instruction, and discipline of all persons charged with or convicted of federal crimes; and
- preparing inmates for reentry after serving a term of incarceration.[5]

The sections below provide an overview of how the BOP operates the federal prison system in order to meet its responsibilities.

Managing Federal Correctional Facilities

All BOP correctional facilities are classified according to one of five different security levels: minimum, low, medium, high, or administrative. In general, high security facilities are referred to as U.S. Penitentiaries (USP),[6] medium and low security facilities are called Federal Correctional Institutions (FCIs), and minimum security facilities are known as Federal Prison Camps (FPC).[7] Federal Correctional Complexes (FCC) house more than one type of institution on the same grounds.[8] Administrative facilities are facilities with specialized missions (i.e., pretrial detention centers, which hold inmates who are on or awaiting trial; and medical referral centers, which hold inmates who need specialized medical care) and are capable of confining inmates at all security levels.[9] A facility's security level is based on the facility's features, which include the presence of external patrols, towers, security barriers, or detection devices; the type of housing within the institution; internal security features; and the staff-to-inmate ratio.[10]

After an offender is sentenced and remanded to the custody of the BOP by the U.S. courts to serve a period of incarceration, the BOP assigns the new inmate to one of its facilities. All assignments are conducted by the Designation and Sentence Computation Center (DSCC). All federal inmates are assigned both a security and medical classification and then assigned to an institution with a commensurate security level (i.e., minimum, low, medium, high, or administrative) and medical care level (i.e., Care Level I through IV, see below). An inmate's assignment to a particular institution is based primarily on

- the level of security and supervision the inmate requires;
- the level of security and staff supervision the institution is able to provide; and
- the inmate's program needs (i.e., sex offender, substance abuse treatment, educational/vocational training, individual counseling, group counseling, or medical/mental health treatment).[11]

Other factors that might influence the initial designation for an inmate include

- the inmate's release residence;[12]
- the level of overcrowding at an institution;
- any security, location, or program recommendations made by the sentencing court; and
- any additional security measures to ensure the protection of victims or witnesses and the public in general.[13]

Inmates can be reclassified and reassigned to a new facility based on a review by the DSCC at the request of the staff at the institution where the inmate is incarcerated. Inmates are also assigned custody levels (i.e., community, out, in, or maximum) in addition to their security classifications.[14] Each custody level dictates the amount of staff supervision the inmate requires.[15] An inmate's custody classification is based on the inmate's criminal history, current offense, and institutional adjustment.[16] An inmate's custody level is routinely reviewed and often changes during the period of incarceration.

The BOP considers proper management of the housing units in each facility to be one of the hallmarks of its inmate management philosophy.[17] Unit staff (e.g., the unit manager, case manager, and correctional counselor) have offices in inmate living units. This management structure facilitates regular contact between staff and inmates and allows BOP employees to identify inmate concerns and potential problems.[18] Unit staff are responsible for involving the inmates housed in their units in programs designed to meet their needs (see below). Unit staff meet with inmates on a regular basis to develop, review, and discuss their work assignments, program opportunities, and progress, as well as to address any other concerns the inmate might have.[19]

Providing for the Safekeeping, Care, and Subsistence of Inmates

All inmates undergo a comprehensive intake screening when they are admitted to a BOP facility. The intake screening includes

- conducting a social screening;
- administering a physical examination;
- screening for tuberculosis and other contagious diseases;
- assessing suicide risk and mental health;
- recording a history of current and prior medical conditions;
- performing a dental screening;
- dispensing appropriate and necessary medications;
- ordering appropriate tests;
- collecting DNA for inclusion in the National DNA database; and
- developing a medical treatment plan, if needed.[20]

After intake, newly admitted inmates complete an Admission and Orientation (A&O) program.[21] Each institution's A&O program provides inmates with information on

- the inmate's rights and responsibilities;
- the institution's programs; and
- the institution's disciplinary system.[22]

The program also provides institutional staff with an opportunity to identify and assist inmates who may be experiencing difficulty with adjusting to being incarcerated.[23]

Each inmate is assigned a "Care Level" based on the level of health care the inmate requires. Care Levels range from Care Level I, which is assigned to inmates with no health care needs or needs that are easily managed, to Care Level IV, which is assigned to inmates with complicated medical needs that may require hospitalization. BOP then ensures that inmates are assigned to a facility that is able to care for an inmate's specific health care needs or is in close proximity to a community hospital that may provide the appropriate health care.

All BOP facilities operate outpatient ambulatory care clinics.[24] In instances where inmates have an emergency medical situation that cannot be treated at the facility, they are transported to the nearest community hospital emergency department.[25] The BOP contracts with local hospitals to provide care to inmates who cannot be cared for in the facility's clinic. Each BOP facility solicits medical contracts that cover health care facility and physician services. Institutions may solicit comprehensive contracts in which costs are based on the prevailing Operating Federal Medicare rate for the applicable area for inpatient facility services, and the prevailing Medicare fee schedule amounts for the geographic area for outpatient and physician services.[26] In cases where comprehensive medical contracts are not available, institutions may use blanket purchase agreements for a negotiated rate, but the rate may not be benchmarked to prevailing Medicare rates.[27] The BOP operates six medical referral centers that provide care to inmates with a variety of chronic and sub-acute medical and psychiatric conditions.[28]

The BOP also provides a variety of mental health services through staff psychologists and psychiatrists, including formal counseling and treatment on an individual or group basis.[29] The BOP's policies dictate that all inmates receive an initial mental health screening (which consists of psychological interviews, social history reviews, and behavioral observation) upon admission to a BOP facility.[30] The purpose of the interview is to

- identify inmates who need referral for mental health, sex offender, or substance abuse treatment services;
- collect information that can be used in future crisis counseling situations;
- identify strengths as well as potential adjustment problems to incarceration; and
- discuss possible programmatic needs with inmates.[31]

Inmates with acute mental illness may receive psychiatric services within one of the BOP's medical referral centers, but most mental health treatment is provided in regular BOP facilities.[32]

Providing for the Protection, Instruction, and Discipline of Inmates

The BOP has an established inmate disciplinary system whereby sanctions are imposed on inmates for committing prohibited acts. Prohibited acts are divided into four categories based on severity: greatest, high, moderate, and low.[33] Penalties for committing a prohibited act include losing good time credit,[34] placement in disciplinary segregation, fines, or the loss of privileges.[35] The severity of the penalty is based on the severity of the offense the inmate committed.[36]

Incidents are resolved by either a Unit Disciplinary Committee (UDC) or a Disciplinary Hearing Officer (DHO). Allegations of misconduct are initially reviewed by a UDC. If the UDC determines that the inmate committed the prohibited act(s), the committee can impose any authorized sanction other than the loss of good time credit, disciplinary segregation, or fines. Inmates are allowed to appear before the UDC (unless it would jeopardize institutional security), where they can make a statement and present documentary evidence on their behalves.

The DHO is an independent officer who holds hearings and imposes sanctions for incidents of misconduct. The DHO can only hold hearings on cases referred by the UDC. All inmates charged with the two highest levels of prohibited acts (i.e., "greatest" or "high") or who are facing the loss of good time credit as a mandatory sanction have their cases forwarded to a DHO. In addition, the UDC, at its discretion, can forward a case to the DHO based on the seriousness of the charges. Accused inmates are allowed to appear at a DHO hearing (unless it would jeopardize institutional security) and they are permitted to have a staff representative to assist them at the hearing. Like a hearing before the UDC, inmates are allowed to make a statement and present documentary evidence on their behalves; however, the DHO can call and question witnesses, and inmates can request that witnesses appear at the hearing to testify on their behalves. If the DHO determines that the inmate committed the prohibited act(s), the DHO can impose any authorized sanction. Misconduct that rises to the level of criminal behavior is referred to the United States Attorneys for prosecution.

At times, inmates might be placed in the institution's Special Housing Unit (SHU) in order to ensure the safe, secure, and orderly operation of the facility.[37] Inmates placed in the SHU are separated from the general population. Inmates in the SHU are either on administrative detention status, which is non-punitive and includes inmates placed in segregation to protect them from other inmates, or disciplinary segregation status, which is punitive and is a sanction for violating regulations concerning inmate behavior. An inmate's status is reviewed regularly by BOP while he or she is housed in the SHU.

In some instances, inmates who demonstrate that they are unable or unwilling to comply with institutional rules and who engage in repeated acts of serious misconduct are transferred to Special Management Units (SMUs). Currently, five BOP facilities have SMUs.[38] Transfer to a SMU is non-punitive and is meant to help inmates habituate so that they can be returned to the general population without posing a threat to the safe, secure, and orderly operations of BOP correctional facilities and the public.[39] Candidates for transfer to a SMU are inmates who

- participated or had a leadership role in a disruptive group or gang;
- have a history of serious and/or disruptive disciplinary infractions;
- committed a serious institutional violation while a member of a disruptive group or gang;
- participated in, organized, or facilitated any group misconduct that adversely affected the operations of a correctional facility; or
- otherwise participated in or was associated with activity such that the inmate requires a higher level of supervision to ensure the safety, security, and orderly operation of BOP facilities, or protection of the public.[40]

Inmates are expected to complete the four-level SMU program in 18-24 months, though inmates who continue to demonstrate disruptive conduct can be held in a SMU beyond 24 months.[41] When inmates complete the program they are returned to the general population at another facility that is appropriate for their security and supervision level. Inmates housed in SMUs are separated from the general inmate population in the facility, and their movements and interaction with other inmates are more controlled and restricted than they would be if they were housed in the general population, but they are granted more freedom of movement as they progress through the levels of the program.[42] Inmates also have access to rehabilitative programming while in a SMU, albeit with some restrictions.[43]

In addition to SMUs, the BOP also operates Communications Management Units (CMUs) at two facilities.[44] Inmates housed in CMUs are subject to increased monitoring of their communications with persons in the community.[45] Like SMUs, inmates housed in CMUs are separated from the general inmate population, but inmates' movements are not as restricted and controlled as they would be in a SMU.[46] Examples of inmates who might be housed in a CMU include inmates who

- have a history of or a nexus to international or domestic terrorism;
- repeatedly attempt to contact their victims;
- attempt to coordinate illegal activities via approved communication methods (e.g., mail, telephone calls, or meetings with visitors) while incarcerated; or
- have received disciplinary actions due to their continued abuse of approved communication methods.[47]

An inmate is allowed to request a review of his or her conditions of confinement through the BOP's Administrative Remedy Program. Before an inmate can submit a formal request for an administrative remedy, the inmate is ordinarily required to present the issue informally to staff, and staff must attempt to remedy the issue.[48] Formal requests for administrative remedies are first reviewed and investigated at the institutional level. Wardens can also waive the requirement for inmates to first attempt to resolve the issue informally if the warden determines that the sensitivity of the issue makes informal resolution inappropriate.[49] If an inmate is not satisfied with the warden's response, he or she can appeal the claim to the regional office; and if the inmate is not satisfied with the regional office's response, he or she can appeal to the central office.[50] Inmates can appeal rejections of claims through the same process. Inmates may file appeals of *disciplinary actions* (e.g., confinement in a SHU) directly with the regional office. Inmates can submit a formal request for an administrative remedy directly to the regional office if the inmate reasonably believes the issue is sensitive and his or her safety would be in jeopardy if someone in the institution was aware that the inmate was pursuing a claim.[51]

Preparing Inmates for Reentry

The BOP offers a variety of rehabilitative programs to federal inmates, including

- mental health, sex offender, and substance abuse treatment;
- educational programming;
- vocational education;

- work opportunities through prison work assignments and the Federal Prison Industries (FPI);[52]
- parenting programs;
- cognitive-behavioral interventions that focus on promoting pro-social behavior; and
- religious programs.[53]

The BOP has developed a coordinated prisoner reentry strategy. The strategy involves assessing each inmate's strengths and weaknesses as they relate to the inmate's readiness for release, using the assessment to develop a skill development plan, and linking inmates with certain deficiencies to programs to address those needs.[54] The BOP also collaborates with other agencies to ensure that inmates with certain needs are provided targeted services.[55]

In addition to the rehabilitative programming offered to federal inmates, the BOP has a release preparation program for inmates who are within 18 months of release. The program includes classes on résumé writing and job search and retention skills.[56] The BOP's Inmate Transition Branch (ITB) provides inmates with pre-release employment assistance. The ITB holds mock job fairs in BOP facilities to provide inmates with an opportunity to test their job interview skills and to put inmates in touch with potential post-release employers.[57] The ITB also helps inmates prepare release folders that contain a résumé, education certificates, diplomas, transcripts, and other documentation that might be required during a job interview.[58]

The BOP contracts for Residential Reentry Centers (RRCs, i.e., halfway houses) to provide assistance to inmates nearing release.[59] RRCs provide inmates with a structured and supervised environment along with employment counseling, job placement services, financial management assistance, and other community-based social services and programs.[60] RRCs facilitate inmates' efforts at reestablishing ties to the community while allowing staff at the RRC to supervise inmates' activities. Pre-release inmates placed in a RRC remain under the jurisdiction of BOP until their sentences are completed. Inmates are expected to be employed in a full-time job within 15 days of arriving at a RRC and 25% of their gross income (not to exceed the negotiated per diem rate under the contract the BOP signed with the RRC) goes to a subsistence fee paid directly to the RRC contractor to contribute toward the cost of their confinement.[61] RRC staff can assist inmates with obtaining employment or locating post-release housing.[62] While housed in RRCs, inmates are eligible to receive mental health, sex offender, and substance abuse treatment services. Inmates who completed a residential substance abuse treatment program while incarcerated are required to participate in a transitional drug abuse treatment program while placed at a RRC.[63]

BOP APPROPRIATIONS

Nearly all of the BOP's operations are funded through annual appropriations provided by Congress.[64] The BOP's annual budget is divided between two major accounts: Salaries and Expenses (S&E) and Buildings and Facilities (B&F). The S&E account (i.e., the operating budget) provides for the custody and care of federal inmates and for the daily maintenance and operations of correctional facilities, regional offices, and the BOP's central office in

Washington, DC. It also provides funding for the incarceration of federal inmates in state, local, and private facilities. The B&F account (i.e., the capital budget) provides funding for the construction of new facilities and the modernization, repair, and expansion of existing facilities.[65] Appropriations for both accounts are presented in *Table 1.*

Table 1. Appropriations for the Bureau of Prisons, FY1980-FY2014
Appropriations in thousands of dollars

Fiscal Year	Salaries and Expenses	Buildings and Facilities	Total
1980	$323,884	$5,960	$329,844
1981	351,759	10,020	361,779
1982	378,016	56,481	434,497
1983	412,133	66,667	478,800
1984	464,850	47,711	512,561
1985	536,932	86,043	622,975
1986	561,480	44,082	605,562
1987	656,941	219,249	876,190
1988	772,013	297,076	1,069,089
1989	962,016	612,914	1,574,930
1990	1,138,778	1,511,953	2,650,731
1991	1,363,645	374,358	1,738,003
1992	1,649,121	462,090	2,111,211
1993	1,793,470	339,225	2,132,695
1994	1,962,605	269,543	2,232,148
1995	2,319,722	276,301	2,596,023
1996	2,546,893[a]	334,728	2,881,621
1997	2,748,427[b]	435,200	3,183,627
1998	2,847,777[c]	255,133	3,102,910
1999	2,888,853[d]	410,997	3,299,850
2000	3,111,073[e]	556,780	3,667,853
2001	3,469,739	833,822	4,303,561
2002	3,805,118	807,808	4,612,926
2003	4,044,788	396,632	4,441,420
2004	4,414,313	393,515	4,807,828
2005	4,571,385	205,076	4,776,461
2006	4,830,160	99,961	4,930,121
2007	5,012,433	432,425	5,444,858
2008	5,346,740	372,720	5,719,460
2009	5,600,792	575,807	6,176,599
2010	6,106,231	99,155	6,205,386
2011	6,282,410	98,957	6,381,367
2012	6,551,281	90,000	6,641,281
2013[f]	6,349,248	95,356	6,444,604
2014	6,769,000	90,000	6,859,000

Source: U.S. Department of Justice, Bureau of Prisons.

Notes: Amounts in Table 1 include all supplemental appropriations and any rescissions of enacted budget authority, but they do not include rescissions of unobligated balances. From FY1980 to FY1995, funding for the National Institute of Corrections (NIC) was included in a separate account. Since FY1996, funding for the NIC has been included in the S&E account. In Table 1, funding for the NIC for FY1980-FY1995 was added to the S&E account to make funding for the S&E account comparable across fiscal years.

[a] Includes $13.5 million appropriated from the Violent Crime Reduction Trust Fund (VCRTF).

[b] Includes $25.2 million appropriated from the VCRTF.

[c] Includes $26.1 million appropriated from the VCRTF.

[d] Includes $26.5 million appropriated from the VCRTF.

[e] Includes $22.5 million appropriated from the VCRTF.

[f] The FY2013-enacted amount includes the amount sequestered per the Budget Control Act of 2011(P.L. 112-25).

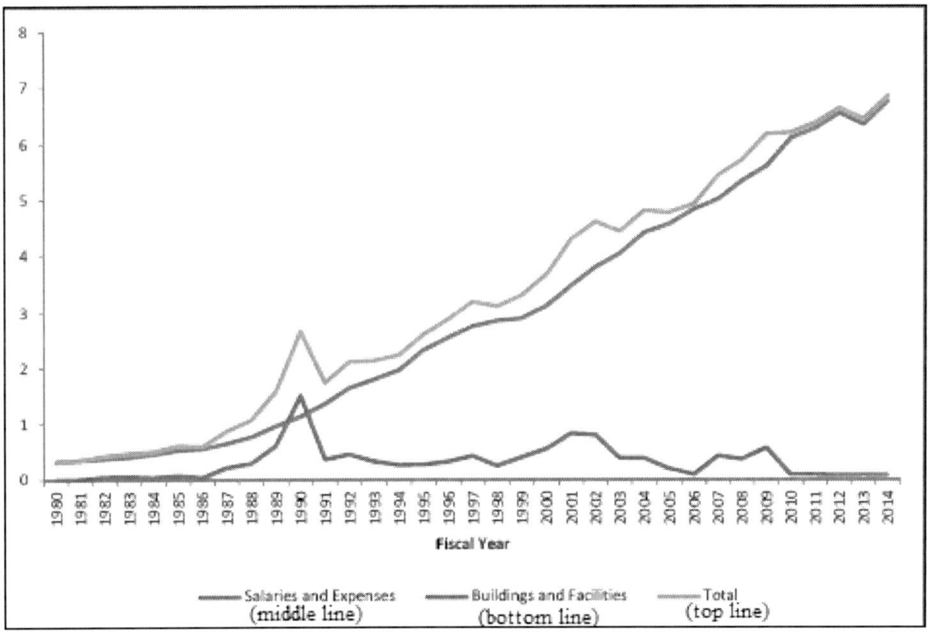

Source: U.S. Department of Justice, Bureau of Prisons.

Notes: Amounts in Figure 2 include all supplemental appropriations and any rescissions of enacted budget authority, but they do not include rescissions of unobligated balances. From FY1980 to FY1995, funding for the National Institute of Corrections (NIC) was included in a separate account. Since FY1996, funding for the NIC has been included in the S&E account. In Figure 2, funding for the NIC for FY1980-FY1995 was added to the S&E account to make funding for the S&E account comparable across fiscal years. The FY2013-enacted amount includes the amount sequestered per the Budget Control Act of 2011(P.L. 112-25).

Figure 2. Appropriations for the BOP, FY1980-FY2014. (Appropriations in billions of nominal dollars)

A review of the appropriations presented in *Table 1* shows two trends in the BOP's appropriations. First, while there has been a nearly continuous increase in the overall appropriations for the BOP, it is in large part driven by an unbroken year-by-year increase in appropriations for the BOP's Salaries and Expenses (S&E) account since FY1980 (see *Figure 2*). The one exception to this trend is the appropriation for FY2013, which is lower than the FY2012 appropriation for the S&E account due to the sequestration ordered pursuant to the Budget Control Act of 2011 (P.L. 112-25). It is not surprising that Congress would appropriate increasing amounts for the S&E account in light of the steadily growing federal prison population. Appropriations for the S&E account pay the salaries and benefits of both correctional officers and other institutional employees. The BOP has had to hire more officers and other employees as it opens more prisons and supervises more inmates. In addition, not only has the cost of operating the federal prison system increased because the BOP is responsible for confining more inmates, but the per capita cost of incarceration has also increased over the years. In FY2000, the nominal per capita cost for all inmates was $21,603; by FY2013, the nominal per capita cost of incarceration had increased to $29,291.[66] The increasing per capita cost of confinement is largely due to inflationary pressures, such as the increasing cost of health care, food, clothing, and utilities and the cost of hiring additional personnel to properly manage the inmate population.

Second, funding for the Buildings and Facilities (B&F) account is more irregular, with Congress appropriating more in some fiscal years and less in others. Congress appropriated more funding in fiscal years where the BOP expanded its prison capacity in an effort to relieve overcrowding. Also, there is a lag between when Congress appropriates funding for construction of a new prison and when the prison is operational because the BOP must first plan the prison's construction, acquire the land, and then contract for the construction of the facility. It can take several years after construction begins before a prison is ready to accept inmates. For example, there was a noticeable spike in appropriations for the B&F account in FY1990, followed by three fiscal years of above-average funding for the account.[67] Between FY1990 and FY1997, the BOP opened 27 new prisons. There was another increase in funding for the B&F account between FY1999 and FY2004. Appropriations for the B&F account during this time period averaged approximately $567.0 million per fiscal year. Between FY1999 and FY2005, the BOP opened 22 new prisons.

Each of the BOP's two appropriations accounts are divided into specific decision units, each of which fund more specific BOP operations. An examination of funding for the decision units under the S&E and B&F accounts provides more insight into how the BOP allocates its annual appropriation in light of the challenges it faces as it becomes responsible for confining more inmates. The S&E account is divided into four decision units, which are as follows:

- *Inmate Care and Programs:* This decision unit covers the cost of inmate food, medical supplies, institutional and release clothing, welfare services, transportation, gratuities, staff salaries, and operational costs of functions directly related to providing inmate care. It provides funding for inmate programs, including education and vocational training, psychological services, religious programs, and drug treatment. All of the drug treatment programs discussed above are funded from this decision unit. This decision unit also covers costs associated with regional and central office administration and support related to providing inmate care.
- *Institution Security and Administration:* This decision unit covers costs associated with the maintenance of facilities and institution security. It funds institution maintenance, motor pool operations, powerhouse operations, institution security, and other administrative functions. This decision unit also covers costs associated with regional and central office administrative and management support functions such as research and evaluation, systems support, financial management, budget functions, safety, and legal counsel.

- *Contract Confinement:* This decision unit provides for the costs associated with the confinement of federal inmates in contract facilities, which include private prisons, Residential Reentry Centers, state and local facilities, and home confinement. It provides funding for the management and oversight of contractconfinement functions. This decision unit also provides funding for the National Institute of Corrections (NIC).
- *Management and Administration*: This decision unit provides funding for costs associated with general administration and provides funding for the central office, regional offices, and staff training centers.

The B&F account is divided into two decision units:

- *New Construction:* This decision unit covers lease payments for the Oklahoma Transfer Center, the salaries and administrative costs of staff involved in new prison construction, construction of inmate work program areas and expansion and conversion projects (i.e., additional special housing unit space).
- *Modernization and Repair*: This decision unit provides resources to undertake essential rehabilitation, modernization, and renovation of correctional facilities and their grounds. This includes modifications to facilities to accommodate correctional programs, repair or replace utilities systems and other critical infrastructure, repair projects at existing institutions, and maintain all systems and structures in a good state of repair.

As shown in *Table 2*, since FY1999 approximately 80% of the BOP's S&E funding has gone to combined appropriations for the Inmate Care and Programs and the Institution Security and Administration decision units. Funding for the Inmate Care and Programs and the Institution Security and Administration decision units have increased at about the same rate as funding for the S&E account overall. Between FY1999 and FY2014, funding for the Inmate Care and Programs decision unit increased 128.6% and funding for the Institution Security and Administration decision unit increased 110.6%. In comparison, funding for the S&E account increased 134.3% over the same time period. Funding for the Contract Confinement decision unit increased 337.0% between FY1999 and FY2014. The steeper increase in funding for the Contract Confinement decision unit comes as the BOP has relied on confining more inmates in contract facilities. For example, in FY1990 about 6,900 inmates under the BOP's jurisdiction were held in contract facilities; by FY2013, approximately 42,400 inmates were placed in contract facilities. Funding from the Contract Confinement decision unit covers the cost of contracts that the BOP signs with RRCs, and since the growing prison population also means that there will be more inmates released from federal prison each year, there has been a growing demand for RRC bedspace. While funding for the Contract Confinement decision unit outpaced the growth of funding for the S&E account overall, funding for the Management and Administration decision unit grew at a rate below that of the S&E account. Between FY1999 and FY2014, funding for the Management and Administration decision unit increased 48.3%.

Table 2. Appropriations for the BOP, by Decision Unit, FY1999-FY2014
Appropriations in thousands of dollars

	Salaries and Expenses				Buildings and Facilities	
Fiscal Year	Inmate Care and Programs	Institution Security and Administration	Contract Confinement	Management and Administration	New Construction	Modernization and Repair
1999	$1,090,148	$1,401,349	$255,062	$142,249	$322,963	$88,034
2000	1,123,856	1,494,809	344,773	147,635	441,003	115,777
2001	1,208,480	1,601,518	511,579	148,162	710,816	123,006
2002	1,311,335	1,722,567	620,145	151,071	675,040	132,768
2003	1,454,481	1,868,538	567,365	154,404	262,956	133,676
2004	1,624,308	2,050,417	574,473	165,115	177,620	164,000
2005	1,682,656	2,094,917	627,135	166,677	25,372	179,704
2006	1,740,011	2,227,223	683,031	179,895	48,115	51,846
2007	1,774,048	2,297,055	757,851	183,479	368,875	63,550
2008	1,942,077	2,409,112	814,529	181,022	302,720	70,000
2009	2,070,002	2,495,196	840,933	194,661	465,180	110,627
2010	2,215,992	2,708,651	981,112	200,476	25,386	73,769
2011	2,294,174	2,783,664	996,772	207,800	25,335	73,622
2012	2,421,272	2,880,290	1,040,213	209,506	23,035	66,695
2013[a]	2,424,620	2,717,938	1,017,297	189,393	23,649	71,707
2014	2,525,039	2,966,364	1,074,808	202,789	22,852	67,148

Source: U.S. Department of Justice, Bureau of Prisons.

Notes: Amounts in Table 2 include all supplemental appropriations and any rescissions of enacted budget authority, but they do not include rescissions of unobligated balances.

[a] The FY2013-enacted amount includes the amount sequestered per the Budget Control Act of 2011(P.L. 112-25).

The data presented in *Table 2* also show that in most fiscal years since FY1999 a majority of the funding for the B&F account has been dedicated for new prison construction, which is probably not surprising given the BOP's need to expand prison capacity to handle an ever growing prison population. The BOP has, and continues to, face problems with prison overcrowding. Between FY1999 and FY2013, the BOP increased its capacity by more than 40,100 beds.[68] Even though the BOP has expanded prison capacity, crowding in the federal prison system increased from 31% over rated capacity to 36% over rated capacity between FY1999 and FY2013,[69] and even with the planned addition of nearly 7,000 beds by FY2018, the BOP expects prison crowding to increase one percentage point to 41% over rated capacity.[70]

As shown in *Table 2*, in most fiscal years between FY1999 and FY2014, a majority of the appropriation for the B&F account was for new prison construction rather than maintenance of existing facilities. Over this time period, the average appropriation for the New Construction decision unit was $248.3 million while the average appropriation for the Modernization and Repair decision unit was $99.1 million. However, funding for the Modernization and Repair decision unit has exceeded that of the New Construction decision unit in the five most recent fiscal years, but this was not the result of increased funding for modernization and repair projects. Rather, it was the result of Congress appropriating less funding for the B&F account overall. The total appropriation for the B&F account was less than $100.0 million between FY2010 and FY2014, which is approximately 75% less than the average appropriation for the B&F account between FY1999 and FY2009. The lack of funding for maintenance projects could place as much strain on the BOP's future budget as prison overcrowding. The BOP reports that about one-third of its current facilities are over 50 years old.[71] Moreover, failure to perform adequate maintenance on existing facilities could result in larger capital investment in future years as prisons and utility systems deteriorate and, according to the BOP, could cause direct and/or indirect security problems.[72] It is possible that the demand for maintenance funding would increase in the future as greater demands are placed on an aging infrastructure by prison overcrowding, unless Congress provides funding for a large-scale expansion of new prisons, which could potentially allow the BOP to close some older facilities.

Congress could choose to mitigate some of the issues related to federal prison population growth by appropriating more funding so the BOP could expand prison capacity to alleviate overcrowding, but this would only continue the upward climb in the BOP's appropriations. There is a concern that the rate of growth in the BOP's appropriations is not sustainable in light of efforts to reduce discretionary spending in order to reduce the federal budget deficit.[73]

Congress could also consider ways to reduce the number of inmates held in federal prison through methods such as increasing good time credit for inmates who participate in certain rehabilitative programs, placing more low-level offenders on community supervision in lieu of incarceration, or reducing mandatory minimum penalties for some offenses. Reducing the federal prison population could help bring down the cost of the federal prison system since the BOP would be housing and caring for fewer inmates. A smaller prison population would help alleviate prison crowding and it could improve staff-to-inmate ratios. Shrinking the size of the federal prison population could possibly help the BOP deal with its aging infrastructure, assuming that the prison population decreased enough to allow the BOP to close some of its older facilities. If nothing else, fewer inmates would allow the BOP to shift funding from building prisons to properly maintaining the bureau's current facilities.

End Notes

[1] E. Ann Carson and Daniela Golinelli, Prisoners in 2012: Trends in Admissions and Releases, 1991-2012, U.S. Department of Justice, Office of Justice Programs, Bureau of Justice Statistics, NCJ 243920, Washington, DC, December 2013, p. 39.

[2] Based on a CRS analysis of the BOP's annual appropriation for FY1980-FY2014 (see Table 1). Annual appropriations were adjusted using the Consumer Price Index for All Urban Consumers (CPI-U).

[3] Data provided by the U.S. Department of Justice, Bureau of Prisons.

[4] U.S. Department of Justice, Bureau of Prisons, About the Bureau of Prisons, p. 1; hereinafter, About the Bureau of Prisons.

[5] 18 U.S.C. §4042(a).

[6] In some cases, USPs can be designated to house medium security inmates. For example, USP Marion, USP Leavenworth, and USP Atlanta house medium security inmates.

[7] U.S. Department of Justice, Bureau of Prisons, About Our Facilities, Federal Prisons, http://www.bop.gov/about/facilities/federal_prisons.jsp.

[8] Ibid.

[9] Ibid.

[10] Ibid.

[11] U.S. Department of Justice, Bureau of Prisons, Inmate Security Designation and Custody Classification, Program Statement 5100.08, p. 1, http://www.bop.gov/policy/progstat/5100_008.pdf; hereinafter, Security Designation.

[12] It is the BOP's policy to try to incarcerate an inmate in a facility that is within 500 miles of the inmate's release residence. U.S. Department of Justice, Bureau of Prisons, Custody & Care, Designations, http://www.bop.gov/ inmates/ custody_and_care/designations.jsp.

[13] Security Designation, pp. 1-2.

[14] An inmate's custody level (i.e., community, out, in, or maximum) refers to the level of staff supervision the inmate requires. For example, an inmate with a "community" custody level may be eligible for the least secure housing, including any that is outside the institution's perimeter; may work on outside details with minimal supervision; and may participate in community-based program activities if other eligibility requirements are satisfied. However, an inmate with an "in" custody level is assigned to regular quarters and is eligible for all regular work assignments and activities under a normal level of supervision, but these inmates are not eligible for work details or programs outside the institution's secure perimeter.

[15] Security Designation, p. 2.

[16] Ibid.

[17] Traditionally, each BOP facility is divided into multiple housing units to which inmates are assigned. About the Federal Bureau of Prisons, p. 4.

[18] Ibid.

[19] Ibid.

[20] U.S. Department of Justice, Bureau of Prisons, FY2014 Performance Budget, Congressional Submission, Salaries and Expenses, p. 20; hereinafter, BOP's FY2014 S&E Budget Justification.

[21] Pretrial and holdover (e.g., inmates who are temporarily held in the institution while awaiting transfer to another institution) inmates are not required to complete the Admission and Orientation program. U.S. Department of Justice, Bureau of Prisons, Admission and Orientation Program, Program Statement 5290.14, p. 1, http://www.bop.gov/policy/ progstat/5290_014.pdf.

[22] Ibid.

[23] Ibid.

[24] BOP's FY2014 S&E Budget Justification, p. 20.

[25] Ibid.

[26] Ibid., p.21.

[27] Ibid.

[28] Ibid.

[29] U.S. Department of Justice, Bureau of Prisons, Custody & Care, Mental Health, http://www.bop.gov/inmates/ custody_and_care/mental_health.jsp.

[30] BOP's FY2014 S&E Budget Justification, p. 28.

[31] Ibid.

[32] Ibid.

[33] U.S. Department of Justice, Bureau of Prisons, Inmate Discipline Program, Program Statement 5270.09, p. 9, http://www.bop.gov/policy/progstat/5270_009.pdf; hereinafter, "Inmate Discipline Program."

[34] Each prisoner serving a term of imprisonment of more than one year, but not prisoners serving a life sentence, can receive a good time credit of up to 54 days per year to count toward serving the sentence. The amount of the credit is subject to the determination of BOP. 18 U.S.C. §3624(b).

[35] Inmate Discipline Program, pp. 44-54.

[36] Inmates sentenced for a federal offense after September 13, 1994, but before April 26, 1996, and who committed a crime of violence (as defined by the Violent Crime Control and Law Enforcement Act of 1994, P.L. 103-322), inmates who were sentenced for a federal offense after April 26, 1996, and inmates who were sentenced for a District of Columbia Code offense after August 5, 2000, all lose some amount of good time credit as a mandatory sanction for committing a prohibited act. Ibid., p. 11.

[37] U.S. Department of Justice, Bureau of Prisons, Special Housing Units, Program Statement 5270.10, http://www.bop.gov/policy/progstat/5270_010.pdf.

[38] Facilities with SMUs are USP Allenwood, USP Lewisburg, FCI Talladega, FCC Florence, and FCC Oakdale.

[39] U.S. Department of Justice, Bureau of Prisons, Special Management Units, Program Statement 5217.01, pp. 1-2, http://www.bop.gov/policy/progstat/5217_001.pdf.

[40] Ibid., p. 2.

[41] Ibid.

[42] Ibid., p. 5.

[43] Ibid., pp. 7-10.

[44] Facilities with CMUs are FCC Terre Haute and USP Marion.

[45] U.S. Department of Justice, Bureau of Prisons, State of the Bureau 2009, p. 37, http://www.bop.gov/ resources/ pdfs/ sob09.pdf.
[46] Ibid.
[47] Ibid.
[48] U.S. Department of Justice, Bureau of Prisons, Administrative Remedy Program, Program Statement 1330.13, p. 4, http://www.bop.gov/policy/progstat/1330_013.pdf.
[49] Ibid.
[50] Ibid., p. 7.
[51] Ibid.
[52] The FPI is a government-owned corporation that employs federal inmates. For more information on the FPI, see CRS Report RL32380, Federal Prison Industries: Overview and Legislative History, by Nathan James.
[53] U.S. Department of Justice, Bureau of Prisons, State of the Bureau 2008, pp. 2-3, http://www.bop.gov/resources/ pdfs/sob08.pdf.
[54] BOP's FY2014 S&E Budget Submission, pp. 35-36.
[55] Ibid.
[56] U.S. Department of Justice, Bureau of Prisons, Custody & Care, Reentry Programs, http://www.bop.gov /in mates/custody_and_care/reentry.jsp.
[57] Ibid.
[58] Ibid.
[59] U.S. Department of Justice, Bureau of Prisons, About Our Facilities, Reentry Centers, http://www.bop. gov/about/ facilities/residential_reentry_management_centers.jsp.
[60] Ibid.
[61] Ibid.
[62] Ibid.
[63] Ibid.
[64] The operations of the Federal Prison Industries (FPI) are supported by revenue generated through the sale of prisoner-made goods to federal agencies. In addition, some programs, goods, and services (such as compensation for inmates participating in non-FPI jobs) are paid for by funds generated through the sale of goods to inmates through the prison commissary.
[65] In addition to appropriations for the S&E and B&F accounts, Congress usually places a cap on the amount of revenue generated by the FPI that can be used for administrative expenses in the annual Commerce, Justice, Science, and Related Agencies appropriations act. Although Congress does not appropriate funding for the administrative expenses of FPI, the administrative expenses cap is scored as enacted budget authority.
[66] Data provided by the U.S. Department of Justice, Bureau of Prisons.
[67] Between FY1980 and FY2012, the average appropriation for the B&F account was approximately $299.0 million per fiscal year. This average excludes FY1990 funding for the B&F account because it was an outlier and including it would skew the average upwards (if FY1990 funding for the B&F account is included, the average appropriation for the account was approximately $336.0 million per fiscal year).
[68] Data provided by the U.S. Department of Justice, Bureau of Prisons.
[69] Data provided by the U.S. Department of Justice, Bureau of Prisons.
[70] BOP's FY2014 S&E Budget Submission, p. 3.
[71] U.S. Department of Justice, Bureau of Prisons, FY2014 Performance Budget, Congressional Submission, Buildings and Facilities, p. 13.
[72] Ibid.
[73] In the conference report for the Consolidated and Further Continuing Appropriations Act, 2012 (i.e., the "minibus," P.L. 112-55), the conferees expressed concern that "the current upward trend in the prison inmate population is unsustainable and, if left unchecked, will eventually engulf the [Department of Justice's] budgetary resources." U.S. Congress, House of Representatives, Agriculture, Rural Development, Food and Drug Administration, and the Related Agencies Programs for the Fiscal Year Ending September 30, 2012, and for Other Purposes, Conference Report to Accompany H.R. 2112, 112th Cong., 1st sess., November 14, 2011, H.Rept. 112-284 (Washington, DC: GPO, 2011), p. 241.

INDEX

D

H

I

J

L

R

S

T

U

V

W